THE HANDBOOK OF
Structured
Life Review

BY
Barbara K. Haight, Dr.P.H.
AND
Barrett S. Haight, J.D.

HEALTH PROFESSIONS PRESS

Baltimore • London • Sydney

Health Professions Press, Inc.
Post Office Box 10624
Baltimore, Maryland 21285-0624

www.healthpropress.com

Designed and Produced by Columbia Publishing Services, Baltimore, Maryland.
Typeset by Circle Graphics, Columbia, Maryland.
Manufactured in the United States of America by
Victor Graphics, Baltimore, Maryland.

The cases in this book are based on the authors' actual experiences. In all instances, identifying details have been removed to protect confidentiality.

Library of Congress Cataloging-in-Publication Data

Haight, Barbara K.
    The handbook of structured life review / by Barbara K. Haight and Barrett S. Haight.
        p. cm.
    Includes bibliographical references and index.
    ISBN-13: 978-1-932529-27-2 (alk. paper)
    1.   Autobiographical memory—Handbooks, manuals, etc.   2.   Reminiscing—Handbooks, manuals, etc.
    3.   Self-perception—Handbooks, manuals, etc.   4.   Self-evaluation—Handbooks, manuals, etc.
    5.   Reminiscing in old age—Handbooks, manuals, etc.   6.   Gerontology—Biographical methods—
Handbooks, manuals, etc. I. Haight, Barrett S. II. Title.
    BF378.A87H35 2001
    158'.3—dc22
                                                            2007031566

*This book is dedicated to the many people who so
willingly shared the stories of their lives and to the untiring group of
Therapeutic Listeners who listened to those stories.*

CONTENTS

FOREWORD

In their invaluable practice manual, Barbara and Barrett Haight introduce us to a useful tool for assisting people to come to terms with life and accept its past, present, and future challenges. They link this tool, the Structured Life Review, to Erikson's well-known theoretical framework. This framework suggests that there are developmental tasks that we need to accomplish, at least in some measure, at various ages and stages of life if we are to achieve peace and self-acceptance or, as Erikson would put it, integrity rather than despair.

The Handbook clearly and succinctly lays out an ordered approach to helping a variety of individuals carry out a Life Review, and it has wide relevance to many and varied health and human service professionals and their helpers. Here is distilled the practical wisdom, reflective thoughts, empirical research evidence, and implications for clinical practice, drawn from vast experience undertaking many Structured Life Reviews over a long period of time.

Barbara began this work as a graduate student and has continued it over many years. Along the way she persuaded many other local and international colleagues from various professional backgrounds to join her in this fascinating field of work. Many local staff and graduate students from the College of Nursing in the Medical University of South Carolina and international researchers in North America, Japan, and the United Kingdom who have shared in this work may have begun as colleagues but soon became firm friends. Now in so-called retirement, Barbara, in collaboration with her husband, has reflected on the implications for direct practice of a very substantial body of empirical research.

Written in straightforward language, this Handbook describes both the working tools and interview methods used in the Structured Life Review process. It provides clear guidance for assisting individuals to review and appreciate the long journeys they have traveled from the past to the present and, by so doing, gain courage to face whatever lies ahead. It details how to use, in flexible fashion, a structured approach to encouraging people, particularly older people, to look back, review, and reflect upon their life experience and, by learning from it, to arrive at some acceptance of the memories recalled—the life lived.

Each stage of the Life Review process is enriched by quotations from recorded Life Review interviews. Vivid practice examples permeate the entire book and illuminate all the stages of a life review and the linked developmental tasks. The entire process, from preparation through first to last interviews and from pretest to posttest stages of evaluation, is all carefully surveyed.

Do not be deceived by the seeming simplicity of the approach and the uncomplicated guidelines in this practical "how to do it" book. A wide range of professionals and laypersons alike will appreciate this comprehensive guide to an evidence-based, effective, and rewarding tool for engaging people in talking about and evaluating their lives. The Reviewers benefit from this process, but so too do the Listeners of the stories.

The Structured Life Review is a proven person-centered, life-enhancing, economical, and accessible tool that enhances self-esteem, improves mood, and enriches quality of life. In a word, it is therapeutic. It is especially relevant to people who are no longer able to live independently or are facing major changes in life. It also offers much to all people, older and younger, regardless of their health and living arrangements, as they seek to confront the inevitable, universal challenge of life, namely death itself.

Faith Gibson
Emeritus Professor of Social Work
University of Ulster
Northern Ireland

INTRODUCTION

*Life Review [is] a naturally occurring universal
mental process characterized by the progressive
return to consciousness of past experiences
and unresolved conflicts.*

—Robert N. Butler

Research has demonstrated that a structured review of one's
life is helpful, even therapeutic, especially for older people.
This Handbook shows you how an effective Therapeutic Listener can conduct the "Structured Life Review process." This
process will help a variety of people (Life Reviewers) to review
and reconcile their lives.

This Handbook is a comprehensive guide for conducting
a Structured Life Review and for training you to be a Therapeutic Listener. The Life Review is a form of reminiscing—
a natural human activity. We all do it; we tell "stories" we
have lived, both good and bad, long and short. Experts say
this is good for us. The potential therapeutic benefits from a
Structured Life Review are many: reconciling one's past life,
finding forgiveness, reducing depression, reconnecting with
friends or family, increasing life satisfaction, and increasing
self-esteem, among others.

Although these results particularly help older people, other
people affected by traumatic or significant events (family
deaths, prolonged hospitalization, hospice, divorce, entrance
to a nursing home, being fired, planning retirement, etc.) can
realize those benefits as well. This all-inclusive Handbook
teaches the professional as well as the layperson how to conduct a Structured Life Review. Use it as a guide.

Overview of the Handbook

This Handbook begins with the background of the Life Review process and then is divided into three parts, followed by an annotated bibliography, references, appendixes, and index. The three parts focus on: preparation, application, and uses of the Structured Life Review process.

Part I, Fundamentals of Structured Life Review, prepares you for conducting the Life Review. Part I includes:

1. The background for the Structured Life Review process
2. The foundation of a Structured Life Review
3. The use of specific counseling skills and interviewing techniques
4. The use of questions from the Life Review Form (LRF) in Appendix B
5. The relative roles of the Therapeutic Listener and the Life Reviewer

Part II, Conducting the Structured Life Review, applies what is presented in Part I to actual sessions of the Life Review, an 8-week process. Each of the chapters in Part II discusses each of the visits of the Structured Life Review process. Abbreviated guidelines for the Therapeutic Listener appear in a box at the beginning of each chapter. Each chapter:

- Applies helpful interviewing techniques and necessary counseling skills
- Relates to one or more stages of Erikson's developmental model (Eight Stages of Man)
- Focuses on key questions from the LRF
- Provides detailed information on the various types of Reviewers whom you will encounter

One hour per week is the recommended time per visit. Depending on circumstances, you may vary the length and the number of visits each week. Part II also contains helpful examples and excerpts from actual Life Reviews to guide you. Italic type is used for Reviewer comments in these excerpts to indicate that they are actual quotes, whereas bold italic type is used for actual Therapeutic Listener responses and remarks from past Life Reviews. Each chapter also contains recommended questions from the LRF to ensure that you get the Reviewers reminiscing about all the key stages of their lives.

Part III, Uses and Outcomes of the Structured Life Review, completes the Handbook by presenting many applications and purposes of the Life Review with diverse populations. An annotated bibliography is also provided as background material for understanding this Structured Life Review process and for future research.

The Therapeutic Listener

Who can be a good Therapeutic Listener? Anyone! Anyone can guide a Life Review who has a reasonable education, the diligence and intelligence to read and practice the instructions in this Handbook, and the ability to learn the skills and techniques required of a caring, attentive Listener. Conceptually, Life Review is simple. Practically, however, it is complex. You, as the Therapeutic Listener, must learn and practice good listening habits, good counseling skills and techniques, and good Life Review practices. You must identify and deal with a variety of "Life Reviewers" to guide each one through a successful Structured Life Review process. There is a lot to learn and apply. This Handbook will teach you. We suggest you study this whole Handbook in advance and then review the particular chapter related to each particular session as you go through an actual Life Review. Note that in front of each application chapter, we have provided a summary of that chapter in the form of "Listener Guidelines." This overview of the chapter can guide you in preparing for that particular session and ensuring you cover everything during that visit.

Almost everyone can benefit from the Structured Life Review process. Prospects are everywhere. We discuss specific potential reviewers and the benefits they gain in the last chapter. The process is pleasant for both participants. This is important work and you can bring therapeutic benefits to many people. We wish you success!

BACKGROUND

The elderly are continually talking of the past because they enjoy remembering.

—ARISTOTLE*

The Structured Life Review process is a type of reminiscing that originated in a nursing practice and has been refined by research. Since the 1970s, over a thousand older people have played a part in refining the Structured Life Review. Additional older groups have received the benefits of Life Review from students practicing the process while learning how to communicate with older adults. Over time, the Structured Life Review process has produced numerous favorable outcomes for most participants, prompting us to share the process in this Handbook. To do that, we start at the beginning with a true story.

The Beginning: Marjory's Story

The Life Review process began in 1977 with a woman named Marjory. A home health nurse knocked on the door of Apartment 302D to visit Marjory, a client who recently had lost her husband. In response to the knock, a weak voice called, "Come in." As the nurse entered the unlocked apartment, a dirty and disheveled woman walked out of the bedroom, leaning on a walker for support. Even though it was three o'clock in the afternoon, her nightgown was soiled and her hair was uncombed. Both arms and legs were bent from contractures, causing her to shuffle when she walked. Her nails had grown so long they were turning under back into her flesh. She wore no shoes and seemed oddly disconnected from her environment, functioning as if in a fog. As the nurse entered, Marjory sat down and lit a cigarette.

The nurse took a seat, introduced herself, and cautioned the woman about opening the door to strangers and not locking up when she napped. It soon became apparent that Marjory was confused and disoriented, unable to answer questions coherently. As the nurse assessed the situation, Marjory asked for a drink. The nurse went to the refrigerator and found it bare except for soda and cigarettes. While Marjory drank her soda, the nurse looked around but found no other food. Marjory said that she hadn't left her apartment in 6 years and now could only remember to order soda and cigarettes when she phoned the grocery store.

In view of Marjory's obvious lack of proper nutrition, the nurse arranged for meals to be delivered to Marjory starting the next day. She borrowed eggs and bread from next door and made supper for Marjory that night. Marjory ate hungrily and agreed to see the nurse again the next day. From that day on, the nurse visited twice a week. Marjory started becoming less confused but more argumentative, belligerent, and less likeable. Despite these difficult conditions, the nurse struggled to obtain a standard health history from her. Marjory, however, had her own agenda and wanted to tell her story in her own way—from the beginning—so the nurse listened.

> *She had her own agenda and wanted to tell her story in her own way.*

Born in the 1920s, Marjory grew up in poverty but enjoyed a close and loving family. She was the third child of five and recalled happy times playing with her sisters. She learned to be independent, to invent games, and to have fun without material things. She liked school but had to leave to go to work to bring money home for her family. She earned $3.75 a week as a waitress. When Marjory was 18, she met Jeff and married him despite her parents' objections. Jeff was a discontented person. He changed jobs often until he was drafted to fight in World War II. He was away for 5 years and returned a changed man, still discontent but also abusive and drunk most of the time.

Jeff and Marjory resumed their marriage until one morning Marjory woke up in the hospital with broken ribs, pelvis, arms, and legs. She was the victim of spousal abuse. She vowed never to see Jeff again and was discharged to her parents' home. As Marjory told this, she cried and said she was so ashamed to be in that condition. Before this day she had never talked about her feeling of shame about the abuse. But, as she cried over her memories, her behavior began to change. She became interested in her surroundings. She seemed to get clearer in her mind and younger in her actions each day. Now she could follow conversation and interact with the nurse.

By this time, the nurse was aware that something different was going on with Marjory. In consultation with her graduate school professor, the nurse learned about the concept of Life Review and found one fascinating article in the library by Dr. Robert Butler (1963). The article spoke of the natural occurrence and tendency of older people to review their lives. She realized that Marjory was beginning this Life Review process. The process continued during subsequent visits while she listened and Marjory began to talk about her second marriage.

Marjory healed from the abuse of her first husband while recuperating in her parents' home. Soon she met Terry, a friend of the family. She married him when her divorce from Jeff was final. This marriage was a good one, although they were poor. Marjory was happy until one evening she became ill. Marjory told of her arduous experience with a painful illness and subsequent addiction to medicine, resulting in her present deformed body. She was hospitalized 200 miles away from home. To visit her, Terry rode the bus 200 miles, slept in the bus station, visited the next day, and then rode the bus 200 miles back home. He did this trip on a weekly basis, every weekend. Her memories of her illness were cloudy and her story of the illness relied on whatever Terry had told her. But she did remember his weekly visits and devotion.

She was finally discharged from the hospital but remained disabled. She went home to Terry who became her caregiver as well as her sole contact with the outside world. Although she was homebound and dependent on Terry for all her needs, she was happy. They enjoyed listening to ball games on the radio together. They also cooked together, with her giving directions from her wheelchair. Because they didn't have a car or know how to drive, she was never able to leave the apartment. Terry would walk to the grocery store or take buses for their shopping needs. The love story continued for several years until Terry's death in 1976.

During the nurse's next visit, Marjory retold the story of Terry's illness and death. Terry was diagnosed with lung cancer, but he never told Marjory. He was angry at being a victim of a terminal illness and demonstrated that anger by rejecting the love and care offered by Marjory. One night he fell in the bathroom and was coughing up blood. He yelled out to her to call an ambulance and was taken to the Veterans Administration hospital. As the ambulance workers carried him out on a stretcher he yelled, "Why did you do this to me?" Marjory never saw him or heard his voice again. On Christmas Eve, the hospital called her to tell her that Terry had died. She lost the love of her life and her only connection to the outside world. For the next month she was isolated with only her memories and her questions. Then the nurse came to her door.

As Marjory talked, the nurse listened closely and responded to the story. Marjory couldn't understand why Terry blamed her for his illness. She loved him but his words hurt her; now he was gone. Marjory repeated his last phrase time and again, allowing the nurse to help her reframe the incident by giving the phrase a different meaning and offering Marjory a different viewpoint. The nurse suggested, "He was probably angry at being ill, and may have been calling out his anger in general. He was not necessarily blaming you for his illness." Later, during the conversation, the nurse introduced Marjory to Elisabeth Kübler Ross's stages of dying (1972). Together, Marjory and the nurse read about the angry stage of dying. Marjory began to understand Terry's anger and to accept the nurse's interpretation of his cry, "Why did you do this to me?" Marjory talked about his illness and his last days again and again, crying every time. The repetition of his death story and her tears seemed to alleviate the pain she was feeling. The repetition acted as a catharsis for Marjory.

Marjory slowly worked through the grief surrounding Terry's death and, as she did, her thoughts became clearer and she began to make plans. The nurse suggested that she take a taxi to the grocery store. When she did go, convenience foods and TV dinners amazed her. Since going out in a taxi worked, she went to the hairdresser next, then to the podiatrist. As Marjory's healing progressed, she socialized with other residents in the high-rise apartment building. A job came open at the main desk for a part-time reception-ist and Marjory got the job. Then, her days were full of people. She began to be concerned about the lives of other residents and did what she could to help them. Marjory overcame her despair and was reaching out for a new life.

> *Marjory's ability to put her past behind her and to move on in her life may be fully attributed to the power of the Life Review.*

Marjory's long story, told from my view as the nurse, illustrates the benefits of the Life Review for an isolated individual with mild cognitive impairment. In Marjory's case, her cognitive impairment may have resulted from a combination of poor nutri-tion, grief, depression, and lack of human contact. Each of these issues was addressed during my visits. However, Marjory's abil-ity to put her past behind her and to move on in her life may be fully attributed to the power of the Life Review.

Using the information gleaned from Marjory's experience, I put the pieces together and tried to develop a structured process similar to what she had experienced naturally. Because her memories had taken her from birth to the present, it made sense to use a developmen-tal format based on the stages that humans experience throughout life. There were many similarities between Erik Erikson's model of the Eight Stages of Man (1950) and Marjory's natural experience. From these similarities, the structure of the Life Review Form (LRF, see Appendix B) was developed with questions to implement the structured interviewing process. Some of these questions appeared in the appendixes of two dissertations dealing with adult development. I selected certain questions, added new ones, and devised a for-mat that would take each individual through the same stages of life. The reason behind this structure was to make the Life Review experience very similar, even for a variety of peo-ple, so that I could measure the outcomes from different people who had participated in the same process. The interview procedures and LRF questions were tested and revised through a series of research projects conducted with many different people. With very sig-nificant outcomes, these studies have validated the Structured Life Review process and the LRF and have shown therapeutic benefits, such as decreased depression, increased life sat-isfaction, increased self-esteem, and multiple other psychosocial benefits.

After establishing this successful, evidence-based therapeutic intervention, it seemed important to write down the process for others to use. Thus we developed this Handbook to share our knowledge with you so that you too can conduct a successful Structured Life Review.

Erikson's Model

Marjory's process matched Professor Erik Erikson's model of the Eight Stages of Man. Essentially, Erikson described the stages of human development as he saw them, including the eighth and last stage of man, which he described as Integrity vs. Despair. He stated that man must accept his life as it was lived in order to gain integrity, wisdom, and happiness. He went on to say that if man cannot accept his life as it was lived, he would end up in despair and hopelessness. Erikson defined integrity as: *"The acceptance of one's one and only life cycle as something that had to be and that by necessity permitted no substitutions."*

> *Man must accept his life as it was lived in order to gain integrity, wisdom, and happiness.*

Erikson is notable because he created the first psychosocial model of development that went beyond childhood to include adulthood (1950). Prior to Erikson, developmental psychologists only described the developmental stages of childhood, presuming that development stopped when people left adolescence. Erikson, however, described eight stages of man's development from childhood to old age in a chronological (epigenetic) developmental ladder to depict man's growth. Erikson's "stages" focus on psychological outcomes rather than strict chronological ages or stages, as described in detail in the following pages.

Erikson asserted that such an epigenetic system creates stages dependent on one another for growth. He claimed that an individual needs to traverse the first stage successfully in order to reach the second stage, and so on. The premise behind the Life Review process is that it can help people later in life resolve the past and overcome any unsuccessful earlier stages. With Erikson's epigenetic guidelines in mind, a different stage of life is addressed each week during the Life Review process.

The following is a short explanation of each life stage as described by Erikson. He believed that failing at certain stages in one's life contributes to pathology (dysfunction) in adulthood, making it even more essential to successfully complete each stage of life in order to be healthy in adulthood. The research with the Structured Life Review has demonstrated that a person can review his or her prior unsuccessful stages during a Life Review and still reach Integrity by successfully reconciling those failed stages during the structured review of his or her life.

The Eight Stages of Man

The first four stages of Erikson's model address childhood; the remaining four stages cover adulthood. Each Life Review session applies the Life Review process to one or more of Erikson's stages. Thus, each "application" chapter of this Handbook (Part II) discusses—and instructs you—how to evaluate and apply one or two of Erikson's stages during a particular visit or session corresponding to that chapter.

Trust vs. Mistrust (Early Childhood). The first stage, Trust, starts in infancy. Infants learn to trust when their needs are met: when they cry out of hunger, they receive food; when they cry from discomfort, their diapers are changed. Trust is learned and generally developed from good parental care. The antithesis of trust is mistrust: When needs go unmet, children feel unable to depend on anyone. Consequently, they become wary, develop mistrust, and cannot easily put their faith in others. These feelings of mistrust may persist throughout life unless outside persons or events intervene or unless the mistrusting persons change themselves.

Autonomy vs. Shame and Doubt (Childhood). The second developmental stage, Autonomy, also occurs in early childhood. During this stage, children are confronted with choices. If aided and supported in the choices made, the child develops self-esteem and autonomy. Denied free choice, the child begins to doubt himself or herself, feeling shame and lacking in confidence. People who never develop autonomy often feel unsure of themselves and doubt their capabilities and actions throughout their lives. According to Erikson, a sense of autonomy fostered in a child and enhanced as life progresses instills a sense of order and a willingness to follow rules as the child grows.

Initiative vs. Guilt (Childhood). Initiative is the third stage of life when the child is faced with developing appropriate objectives for himself or herself and then planning and undertaking various tasks to achieve those objectives. The child is growing, eager to cooperate and learn from others while becoming competitive. The child knows enough to make a plan, initiate the plan, and follow through on the plan. Occasionally, the plan is not executed properly and the child experiences failure. With failure, children can develop a sense of guilt; thus they must be helped to understand effort versus setbacks as normal growth. Children often develop initiative through play and "make-believe."

Industry vs. Inferiority (Young Adolescence). School-age children should develop a work ethic and competency during this stage. The child becomes a part of productive situations. For most children, the learning environment may be school; for others, their situation may include learning to adjust to chores and a job. These school-age children can experience achievements as well as disappointments. If children during this stage often do poorly and experience repeated failures, the danger lies in them developing low self-esteem and lack of self-responsibility with a sense of inadequacy and inferiority unless encouraged and guided by a parent, relative, or mentor.

Identity vs. Role Confusion (Adolescence). The child becomes an adolescent as childhood proper comes to an end. As developing youths, there is great concern by adolescents about how others view them. It is important to be like everyone else and to belong to the cliques that are common during this stage. Belonging helps develop one's identity and tests fidelity to the group. Not actually belonging, or believing that one does not belong, tends to cause role confusion and thwarts the quest for one's own identity.

Intimacy vs. Isolation (Young Adulthood). The sixth stage coincides with young adulthood. The young adult emerging from a search for identity generally wishes to fuse that identity through relationships with others. These persons may be ready to commit to a concrete affil-iation and to abide by the demands of that commitment, although the commitment itself may call for serious compromises. The fulfillment of sexual drives takes place during this stage and love may happen. Failure or inability to commit to another individual—or to love—results in a tendency to isolate one's self for long periods. Isolation-prone people tend throughout life to avoid contacts with others that might lead them to intimacy, hence increasing their isolation.

Generativity vs. Stagnation (Older Adulthood). Generativity is an aspect of maturity. It concerns establishing and guiding the next generation. The mature adult becomes the parent/teacher/mentor during this stage and gives back much that has been learned by passing the knowledge forward. Those who do not invest in the next generation become self-absorbed and stagnated, failing to grow fully as adults, with an adult sense of respon-sibility toward others.

Integrity vs. Despair (Maturity). Achieving integrity (an accepted life) is the ultimate task and optimum goal of maturity. Integrity is the acceptance of the way one's life was lived, as something that seemed like it had to be—believing that it probably permitted no substi-tutions. In other words, the Reviewers who reach Integrity accept and like the summation of their life from birth to the present. If a life cannot be accepted at this stage, there often develops a profound despair because it may be too late to make alterations, or at least the Reviewer believes it is too late. Those who despair may fear death because they have such unfinished business and they believe that they can no longer complete those tasks properly in the time they have left.

Applying Erikson's Model to the Life Review

The Therapeutic Listener, the person who helps the Life Reviewer through the process, uses each visit of the 6- to 8-week Life Review process to ask probing questions about each particular developmental stage. The reason for reviewing and looking back at each stage specifically is so the Reviewer—guided by a Therapeutic Listener—can reframe and reconcile the memory of a stage that was not successfully completed at the proper time in the past. Through reframing, the Reviewer can make the required adaptation in the present, using both the Life Review process and the Listener as aids. As a con-sequence of reframing, and in retrospect, the Reviewer may be able to complete or rec-oncile the stage now under discussion and move closer to Integrity. Questions in the LRF that are related specifically to Erikson's stages are highlighted in Appendix B. The LRF and Erikson provide the structure around which the Life Review is built.

> *The Reviewer—guided by a Therapeutic Listener—can reframe and reconcile the memory of a stage that was not successfully completed at the proper time in the past.*

Butler's Observations About Reminiscence and Life Review

No discussion of the Life Review process is complete without some mention of the work of a pioneer in this field, Dr. Robert Butler. He wrote his observations of older people's reminiscences in a seminal article called, "The Life Review: An Interpretation of Reminiscence in the Aged" (1963). Butler's article has precipitated numerous discussions since it was published. Some of his assertions have been challenged, and others misinterpreted, but his work still stands as the most important paper on Life Review.

When Butler published his now well-known paper in the 1960s, reminiscing was thought to be a phenomenon engaged in only by elderly people. Reminiscence was said to represent an aimless wandering of the mind. In his paper, Butler debunked the myth of aimless wandering of the mind and noted that older people naturally recalled the past. He defined the recall as both Reminiscence and Life Review and developed the following definition that is used as the basis for a Structured Life Review: *"A naturally occurring universal process, characterized by the progressive return to consciousness of past experiences and unresolved conflicts which are surveyed and reintegrated"* (1963).

By reintegration, Butler meant "to process again." He described the Life Review that he had observed in older people as potentially contributing to changing and reorganizing their personalities. He stated that the more intense the conflicts have been in peoples' lives, the more work is necessary for them to reintegrate life's events into an acceptable whole.

Butler added that when the process of Life Review proceeds internally, in isolation, without benefit of a listener, the more negative affective and behavioral consequences tend to occur, such as despair. *"The existence of the Life Review occurring irrespective of the psychotherapeutic situation suggests that the aged particularly need a participant-observer, professional or otherwise."* In another article, Butler (1974) said it would be better to have even a high school student volunteer to hear a Life Review than to have an older person review alone because the Reviewer needs feedback while reviewing. Any Listener acting as a sounding board can provide helpful feedback for the Reviewer. Butler worked with older adults and noted that the recalling of one's past life was often prompted by a crisis, such as illness or anticipated death. Because the initial work was done with older people, the Life Review became associated mainly with them, but today it includes many other groups of people.

The Growth of Life Review

Since 1960, there have been more than 200 publications addressing either Life Review or Reminiscence. Clinicians who have come in contact with Life Review in their practice and have observed the way people responded to Life Review interventions have reported unexpected favorable results. But, the reported research was very hard to sort out because of a confusion of terms and the interchangeable use of the words "Reminiscence" and "Life Review." Presently, the research is much more specific and sophisticated, covering a wider spectrum of ages and subjects. Scholars from many disciplines are not only looking at the process, but they also are analyzing one important outcome product: the "life story." Many manifestations of Reminiscence and uses for Reminiscence have developed over time: theater and the arts produce plays to express collective life stories in a dramatic format, health professionals use the process to gain therapeutic outcomes, and psychologists study and examine the variables that make up Reminiscence and Life Review. Research is ongoing; clearer definitions and goal-directed interventions will continue to differentiate and clarify specific reports using Reminiscence as their basis.

The Structured Life Review Process

The discussion and instruction in this book are designed to give the reader a better understanding of a specific Reminiscence approach: the Structured Life Review process. This process, as presented here, is based on Erikson's model, Butler's seminal article, and many research projects. The goal of a Structured Life Review for the Life Reviewer is to achieve "Integrity" (an accepted life). Butler's definition of "Life Review" provides a direction for reaching Erikson's definition of "Integrity." The Structured Life Review process is the road map. The person conducting the Life Review (the Therapeutic Listener) is the guide who directs the process and helps the Reviewers to reach their optimum, ultimate goal of Integrity. As people review their lives, accept them, and reintegrate their past into an acceptable whole, they are on the way to attaining Integrity. The Therapeutic Listener uses the key questions on the LRF to guide and structure the Life Review process.

This Handbook will teach you what you need to know to become a Therapeutic Listener. Like any new skill, it takes study, diligence, and time to become a very good Listener and guide. Even as a beginner, however, you can bring added peace, satisfaction, and joy to those who agree to have you conduct and listen to the review of their lives.

Barbara K. Haight, Dr.P.H.

PART I

FUNDAMENTALS OF STRUCTURED LIFE REVIEW

THE STRUCTURED LIFE
REVIEW PROCESS

To listen closely and reply well is the highest perfection
we are able to attain in the art of conversation.

—FRANCOIS DE LA ROCHEFOUCAULD

The Structured Life Review process is a method of recall based on Erik Erikson's life stages model and put into practice through corresponding questions from the Life Review Form (LRF; see Appendix B). The structured process consists of a series of usually six to eight 1-hour visits that use the LRF to guide older people through the memories of their lives. A Therapeutic Listener—an individual trained in the process—facilitates the Life Reviewer's journey through the past by attentive listening and by the use of the LRF.

This chapter provides an overview of the entire structured process. You must understand the essential characteristics that differentiate the Life Review from other types of reminiscing as well as from formal therapy. The chapter covers:

- The goals of Life Review
- The use of the questions on the LRF
- How and when to be flexible during the Life Review
- The four unique characteristics of the process: Structure, Duration, Individuality, and Evaluation

The chapter also includes some considerations to keep in mind when conducting the Life Review process: work, self, repetition, power and control, supervision, confidentiality, audiotaping, and life review with relatives.

Goals of the Life Review

The main goal of the Life Review is to help the Reviewer reach Integrity. Erikson defines Integrity as accepting one's life as it was lived; Integrity is the last successful stage of life. Erikson teaches that success during the early stages of life influences each subsequent stage. We believe, however, that Reviewers can reconcile less successful stages by working through old issues during a Life Review. Accordingly, the Therapeutic Listener tries to guide the Reviewers through their entire lives one visit at a time until Life Reviewers accept their lives as they were lived with minimal reservation.

In addition to guiding the Reviewers toward reconciling their lives and reaching Integrity, the Life Review often yields other important therapeutic results, including:

- Reduced depression
- Greater life satisfaction
- Reconnection to others, such as family and old friends
- Self-acceptance
- Bonding
- Catharsis
- Enhancing other relationships
- Peace, and others

Although reaching Integrity is the optimum goal, some Reviewers never achieve it. Too many variables can affect a person's personality formation throughout a lifetime for a simple intervention like Life Review to be effective in every situation. While Life Review can help people approach Integrity by allowing them to reconcile the way they lived their lives, it can't treat pathologies or change personalities. Even people who do not fully attain the goal of Integrity, however, usually enjoy the process of recalling the past, and therefore benefit from this reviewing. The few who don't enjoy the process may drop out, may accept the need for more in-depth help, or may choose to stay as they are.

The Life Review Form (LRF)

The Life Review Form in Appendix B serves as a guideline for the Life Review visits. The format of the LRF is based on Erikson's Stages of Man, and guides the Reviewer from early childhood to the present. Although the Life Review is developmental, it is not rigidly chronological, allowing Reviewers to move back and forth from one stage of development to another as they talk about their lives. The LRF should be used to guide Reviewers through all the developmental stages of their lives. The questions themselves, originally adapted from two unpublished dissertations, have been changed and added to over time, depending on the needs of specific groups of Reviewers (Falk, 1969; Gorney, 1968). The present LRF consists of probing questions that have been validated and developed over the years through applied research. Past Life Reviewers contributed to the revision and retesting of this LRF. For example, one old man living in a high-rise was very disappointed when his Life Review ended and he told us that we had neglected to ask him some important questions about his life. He told the following story:

> *He was homosexual but never had the opportunity to discuss the issues of a homosexual identity with anyone else. He lived with his mother until she died and then lived alone as he grew older. At age 82, he moved to a high-rise apartment where he continued a reclusive life. In his own words, he said he had never come out of the closet because in his day people who were different didn't talk about it. Now in the twilight of his life, he wanted to talk about how difficult it had been when, as a child, he realized he was different, and how that realization had directed his whole life. He wanted to learn about others who had encountered similar dilemmas, and he wanted to learn about being homosexual.*

A few more visits were added to his Life Review until he exhausted the topic to his satisfaction. He then felt that he was not so different and his critique taught us to stay alert to innuendos from other Reviewers about topics we might be missing. The LRF now contains additional questions that open the topic of sexuality to discussion early in the childhood visits, such as, *"Did you enjoy being a girl (or boy)?"*

LRF Questions

The questions in the LRF give structure to the Life Review. The Therapeutic Listener should use the form as a guide, not as a literal interrogation, as some new students use it. Students often enter a room with the LRF clutched in one hand for security and ask the questions as if the visit were a test. They are often so nervous about asking all the questions or the "right" ones that they don't really hear the answers or respond appropriately to the emotional levels of the conversation. Quite the contrary, the person conducting the Life Review is supposed to be an active Therapeutic Listener. The Listener must continuously keep this identity in mind. The questions that make up the LRF are only there to help explore a life and need not be covered and answered in their entirety. Note, however, that the LRF questions do provide structure for the process, so we recommend using most of them in most cases.

Questions and Reviewers

Different people review their lives differently. Because of these differences, Therapeutic Listeners will find it helpful to know which techniques and questions are good for drawing out each type of Reviewer. A brief example here of the "storyteller" type of Reviewer demonstrates that all questions are not necessary; in fact, the Listener might not get to ask many questions at all, like this new Listener who was just learning the Life Review process. She came to a supervision meeting very upset after conducting the first visit of Life Review. She said she was only able to ask one question during the entire hour, so we asked her to tell us about her visit.

She was visiting a homebound woman who apparently loved to tell stories. The young Listener asked the woman to tell her about her first memory. The Listener said it was like opening a floodgate. The Reviewer talked about the first Christmas she could remember, the tree with the beautiful lights, the people who were there to celebrate the event, the meal and all its trimmings, the doll she received as a gift, and the beautiful clothes the doll had to wear. As she talked, she smiled and laughed, her eyes sparkled, she became animated, and she had the time of her life reliving each part of that memory. She was a storyteller and would respond each week with another story to tell.

Our Listener was smart enough to let the woman control the conversation. The Listener only complained to us that she had been limited to one question and that the Reviewer spent the whole hour on her first memory. We explained that one question can be enough and during the next visit the Listener would have opportunity to ask another. This storytelling Life Reviewer continued as she had begun—in her own style, sharing lengthy anecdotes—and she completed a successful Life Review. The task of the Listener in this instance was to adapt and to ensure mainly that the Reviewer covered each developmental phase of her life. The LRF's questions are just prompts used to stimulate memories, to help people recall the important events of their lives, and to provide often-needed structure to the Life Review. They are not critically important in themselves.

Questions and Structure for the Life Review

The main importance of the questions is that they structure the Life Review process. For example, the Reviewer who talked about her first memory of Christmas for the entire first hour should be asked in the second visit if there were any major problems in her childhood or adolescence that she wished to talk about during this second visit. This opening gives the Life Reviewer opportunity to mention any troubling events during those years while allowing the Therapeutic Listener to move the Life Review process along. If the Reviewer says no, the Listener can proceed (perhaps after summarizing the first visit) to questions about school that should make the transitional link to adolescence. With only a few questions, the Listener can structure the Review to move the Reviewer through all the developmental stages of life.

Questions and Erikson's Life Stages

The questions in the LRF follow the structure of Erikson's model, which forms the developmental foundation of the Life Review. The Therapeutic Listener needs to focus on each of those stages through appropriate queries during the sequence of visits of the Life Review. For example, Reviewers who were treated with affection as children usually reflect this care by showing "trust" in their lives, thus meeting the first of Erikson's stages: Trust vs. Mistrust. In subsequent chapters, we suggest additional questions for addressing each of the other stages and we discuss their relevance to Erikson's framework. The table on page 21 shows the connection between Erikson and the Structured Life Review process.

Adaptation of Erikson's Life Stages Model to the Life Review Process		
Stage	Age	Visit
1. Trust vs. Mistrust	Early Childhood	2
2. Autonomy vs. Shame and Doubt	Childhood	2
3. Initiative vs. Guilt	Childhood	3
4. Industry vs. Inferiority	Young Adolescence	3
5. Identity vs. Role Confusion	Adolescence	4
6. Intimacy vs. Isolation	Young Adulthood	4
7. Generativity vs. Stagnation	Older Adulthood	5
8. Integrity vs. Despair	Oldest Adulthood	6 & 7

Schedule

The schedule for the Life Review is flexible but, optimally, consists of eight 1-hour visits, using only six of the visits for the actual process. The first visit is for getting acquainted with the Reviewer and assessing the entire situation: the location and the Reviewer's physical and mental status. The last visit is for closure to that Review. The visits in between—Visits 2 through 7 in Part II—are devoted to conducting the actual Life Review process, following the developmental structure of Erikson's model and the LRF. Listeners are not restricted to only six or eight visits; however, that number has proved optimal in the past. Nonetheless, this number of visits is not rigid and there are always exceptional cases. Some Reviewers do not have a lot to say and complete the process sooner than six visits. If this is the case, they will tend to let you know when the review gets repetitious for them and it is okay to make the entire process a little shorter. Still others may need more than eight 1-hour visits, or may not be able to tolerate visits that are longer than ½ hour. The schedule should be adjusted accordingly for individual differences.

Flexibility

Therapeutic Listeners should schedule 8 weeks for each Life Review, but Listeners must remain flexible. If people are old and frail, they will tire easily if they talk for a whole hour. If that is the case, each Life Review visit can be delivered in two ½-hour visits each week or some other schedule that works. For example, shorter visits over a longer time span worked well for one study with cancer patients who were receiving bone marrow transplants in a hospital. They were very ill and became tired even after talking for ½ hour. Consequently, the regular schedule was adjusted. Although tailoring the schedule is important, the format should remain within the context of eight visits—six for the actual

Life Review. Therapeutic Listeners need to be alert for individual differences among their Reviewers.

Weekly Visits

One visit per week usually works best. However, Life Review can also be flexible in this area as long as enough time is given for the Reviewers to process their thoughts between visits. Many people continue to think about the Life Review on their own, in private, after the Listener has left the 1-hour visit. This private processing is important to the success of the Life Review and often consists of the Life Reviewers "editing and evaluating" their memories by themselves. Reviewers also need time to think about what the visit meant to them. This is part of the process of self-evaluation. People are often surprised at what they remember and what those memories mean when participating in a Life Review. A surprising memory can be like a new memory that needs to be considered and worked through by Reviewers. The more time spent thinking about the visits, the more the memories are relived and reconciled or revised, and hence valuable to the Reviewer. Weekly 1-hour visits seem to work best to allow this time for processing.

> *People are often surprised at what they remember and what those memories mean when participating in a Life Review.*

The Process

The Life Review process, described in detail in Part II, is the complete procedure for conducting the Life Review in 6 to 8 weeks guided by the Therapeutic Listener using the LRF as the guide. Overall, the eight visits cover: assessment, application, outcomes measurement, and closure.

The first visit is very important. Mainly, you must be prepared and organized. Be ready to meet and greet your Life Reviewer and to make a good first impression. The first visit is also the time for you to make a baseline assessment of the Reviewer using the checklist in Appendix A. Before every subsequent visit, you should review the appropriate chapter in this Handbook that relates to that particular visit, and bring a copy of the Handbook or at least that chapter's "Listener Guidelines" as a reminder for yourself. You must be friendly, open, observant, and ready to practice good (therapeutic!) listening techniques. You must start at the beginning to build a bond of trust with your Life Reviewer.

Visits 2 through 7 focus on applying the format for the Life Review outlined in the LRF, guided by Erikson's model, starting with Childhood. The process continues through all of life's developmental stages for the next five visits. Note that the fourth visit is often a turning point for Reviewers. They can either really get into the process or perhaps feel regret at having shared so many previously undisclosed facts. Knowing that Visit 4 is a turning point prepares the Therapeutic Listener for dealing with the issues that may arise at that time: a real bonding or a possible withdrawal because of regret.

Finally, use Visit 8 of the process for closing the relationship, measuring the outcomes, and leaving good thoughts behind. In the past, some Listeners have been afraid that Reviewers will become dependent on them and that it will be difficult to conclude the process. In fact, the contrary generally proves true. The end of the process is generally well received because the Reviewers realize they have accomplished an agreeable task and are eager to move on with their lives. Visit 8 also provides time for assessment, either subjectively or objectively, by posttesting with a paper-and-pencil test similar to that used as the pretest (see Appendixes E and F). It has been our experience that scores on these paper-and-pencil tests improve more over time than right at the end of the Life Review. Therefore, improvement shown by testing scores will be greater at 6 months after the process than directly after it (Haight, Michel, & Hendrix, 1998). With a grateful and happy closure of each Life Review, good thoughts of the 8-week visits should remain behind with Reviewers.

Unique Characteristics of the Life Review Process

Research shows that the Structured Life Review process is different from other forms of reminiscing. Four unique characteristics of Life Review have been found critical to the process and set it apart from other forms of reminiscing (Haight & Dias, 1992):

1. Structure
2. Duration
3. Individuality
4. Evaluation

These characteristics contribute to the unique therapeutic benefits of a Structured Life Review. They are briefly presented in the box on this page, and a full explanation of each characteristic follows.

Structure

The Life Review process is uniquely structured to guide Reviewers through the memories and developmental stages of their lives. Structure is a key characteristic of this Life Review because it systematically causes Reviewers to consider all the developmental stages of their lives, even when they might want to disregard one or more. A complete "Structured" Life Review requires an

> **Unique Characteristics of the Life Review Process**
>
> **Structure:** Covering all of life's stages using the LRF questions
>
> **Duration:** A span of six to eight 1-hour sessions over 8 weeks
>
> **Individuality:** Conducting the Life Review process on a one-to-one basis, not in a group
>
> **Evaluation:** The process of introspectively weighing and valuing life events

examination of all stages from birth to the present. Erikson's model provides the underlying basis for this structure and the questions in the LRF actually apply this structure. The Therapeutic Listener, using the questions and good interviewing and counseling skills, also provides structure by keeping the Reviewer on track to ensure that all the life stages are covered in a systematic, intelligent manner.

> *Unstructured spontaneity is fun but can lead to irrelevance and lack of focus.*

These elements of structure in the Life Review set it apart from other types of reminiscing. Most other reminiscing is unstructured, with a strong element of spontaneity and freedom. This unstructured spontaneity is fun but can lead to irrelevance and lack of focus. With a Structured Life Review, however, each developmental stage of a Reviewer's life is systematically considered and addressed and the focus is ongoing.

The Structured Life Review has been challenged for its strict organization. Bender et al. (1999) state that "*using a time-limited checklist runs the risk of losing light and shade and of reducing a life to a march that agrees with a galloping series of questions.*" The possibility of taking the energy and essence out of memories does exist with structure that is too rigid. This should not be a concern if the Therapeutic Listener fully understands the purpose of the structure and uses the questions sensitively and intelligently, while allowing for spontaneity, flexibility, and individual differences.

The Listener needs to remember that although the LRF serves to reinforce structure, these questions are only prompts to begin the process of recalled memories. Any similar questions that are responsive to the Reviewer's recall will work equally well. As is shown in the application chapters in Part II, Listeners can and should use intuitive, unprompted questions and replies that have not been scripted but are appropriate or responsive to the situation of a particular Life Reviewer. Listeners who are experienced do this easily, but new Listeners may have to make a conscious effort to respond easily and appropriately. Regardless of skill level, the Listener's important task is to protect the structure of the entire process by attempting full coverage of each developmental stage, hence of the Reviewer's entire life.

Although the Life Review process is structured, it also allows elements of flexibility and naturalness in using the questions to recall memories. Erikson's model and the questions in the LRF are in chronological order, but memories do not need to be recalled in that order. They just need to be recalled in their totality. Remembering life events out of sequence can occur for many different reasons. Traumatic events in the Reviewer's childhood, for example, can lead to memories that have been lifetime secrets that Reviewers will not readily share in the early Life Review process that covers childhood. A coping mechanism that Reviewers often use is to continually push troublesome memories back from conscious thought, creating a barely bearable burden for themselves. Listeners need to be aware of this possibility and adjust and adapt the questions as needed, while at the same time relating uniquely to each Reviewer in a way that allows bonding and trust to develop. This bonded relationship between Reviewer and Listener encourages a feeling of safety and security, allowing the Reviewer freedom to reveal his or her secrets, if any.

Another example of remembering life events out of sequence might occur when Reviewers recall an event from their own childhoods only to have that event trigger another memory relating to their own children. In a matter of seconds, Reviewers can move from thoughts of childhood to thoughts of adulthood. Since it is important to keep the Life Review as spontaneous as possible, Listeners should not remind Reviewers that they were talking about childhood, but should follow the Reviewer's thoughts closely until the Listener can turn the discussion back to childhood. If a Reviewer is unable to move back in time during one particular visit, the Listener can begin the next visit by summarizing the high points from the week before and asking the Reviewer what else he or she remembers about childhood, prompting the Reviewer with gentle questions such as, *"Who did you admire the most as a child?"* or *"Do you remember being sick?"* Reviewers may jump from one age to another in the 1 hour allotted for that review visit, as long as they address all stages of the person's life at some time during the entire Life Review process.

Even though the structure provides an adequate amount of time to talk about each developmental stage, Reviewers may be ready to proceed with the discussion of the memories of their life without spending the suggested amount of time in each area. The allotted time for each life phase is only a guideline, just as the questions are only prompts to begin a review. For example, if a Reviewer is not responsive to additional probes about adolescence, and seems eager to move on to adulthood, this response would be acceptable. If, however, an incident occurs during a Life Review visit that raises questions about whether the Reviewer is truly ready to move forward or is instead denying the existence of a problem, then the Listener should consider this possibility at the beginning of the next visit and ask appropriate questions at that time.

Duration

The optimum amount of time recommended for the Life Review process—six to eight 1-hour visits—is of particular concern to both participants. Clearly, Reviewer and Listener need enough time to discuss the details of a lifetime. Research shows that 6 weeks of intervention provides an opportunity to forge trust, establish a relationship, and recall a life. The recommended length of this structured process partially accounts for the good outcomes achieved through a Structured Life Review, especially when compared with the outcomes achieved with some shorter reminiscing interventions. It actually is remarkable that all the benefits gained from the Life Review can occur in 6 weeks!

Reviewers are generally not really open to talking about troubling issues until about the fourth visit (3rd week of the actual Life Review). Therapeutic Listeners also agree that, in about the 4th week, Reviewers are either really invested in the process or choose to drop out, mainly because they feel they have revealed too much or are otherwise uncomfortable. The 4th-week experience happens almost universally and is definitely a product of time and the structured process. Therefore, new Listeners should expect a similar experience with their Life Reviewers.

Listeners using other reminiscence techniques do not often consider time (duration of intervention; number of visits) as a critical factor. Frequently, reports of reminiscing in groups indicate better outcomes than one-to-one interventions, but such groups are also usually of a longer duration. Typically, people attribute the good outcomes to the group process, when in fact the good outcomes may be due to the time duration factor, that is, the length of the group intervention. In contrast, one-to-one reminiscing interventions of one or two visits may not have good outcomes. Thus we have the following dilemma: "What influences the outcomes most: time or mode?" We believe that time may be the key element. The duration of an intervention makes a measurable difference in achieving good outcomes and should be considered when planning interventions.

Individuality

Individuality means that the Structured Life Review is conducted solely between a Therapeutic Listener and a Life Reviewer. In the Life Review process, one-to-one interaction achieves better results than group reminiscing, mere storytelling, or other forms of informal reminiscing. In a Structured Life Review, there is an assurance of privacy and confidentiality, which provides a sense of safety for Reviewers that is so essential to honest, trusting disclosure and self-evaluation of their lives, leading to therapeutic outcomes. Even with individual private visits, it takes time for Reviewers to develop enough trust to share their innermost thoughts with another human being, but it is a lot easier to establish trust in that confidential setting. Note that the Listener is obligated to ensure this confidentiality and safety for the Reviewer.

People who benefit the most from Life Review often have carried a lifelong burden, sometimes unknowingly, that surfaces in an individually private Life Review. Butler (1963) defines Life Review as "*the progressive return of unresolved conflicts that are surveyed and reintegrated.*" Individuals in a group are not likely to share unresolved conflicts that are the secrets of a lifetime. They surely are not going to share if they live in a communal setting. With almost all privacy lost in communal settings—such as assisted living sites—painful and personal experiences are generally kept private; they are not topics for group discussion. With a trusted Therapeutic Listener, however, Reviewers with burdensome secrets can benefit from private sharing on a one-to-one basis.

One woman we visited told about being sexually abused by her uncle when she was a child. She said she thought about that incident often but had never told her husband, her children, or anyone else because she felt ashamed. Now, she was caring for her husband who had Alzheimer's disease and he would never understand what she was talking about if she told him. The Listener encouraged her to tell her children, but the Life Reviewer was left to make her own choices in regard to the telling of this dark event. When she told her secret to the Therapeutic Listener, one-to-one, she experienced and showed great relief. That sharing with another person may have been enough to relieve her burden.

Another advantage of the one-to-one process is the development of a special intimacy and bonding that occurs between the two people sharing the interaction of Life Review. Some people have never had a close trusted friend nor have they experienced the feeling of intimacy and relatedness with another such person. Sadly, some people find it difficult to forge relationships and to bond with others. They are lonely; as one woman put it poignantly, "I was just born lonely." Another spoke of her Life Review as the first time she ever had a real friend. She was 82. Often Listeners and Reviewers evolve to share a special bond and the one-to-one relationship is a critical and unique component of the Life Review process.

Evaluation

Evaluation is the most important and unique characteristic of a Life Review. Evaluation is the process whereby the Reviewer assesses, weighs, and values life's events as they are recalled. Socrates said, *"The unexamined life is not worth living."* He meant that we must look back and assess the events of the past to truly understand the impact of those events on the present and the future. The process of reconciling difficult events, making meaning of others, and accepting all of them contributes to understanding. Understanding why the past life was lived the way it was is the key to acceptance. Understanding generates new meaning and contributes to the goal of the Life Review: Integrity, that is, accepting one's life as it was lived.

> *Understanding why the past life was lived the way it was is the key to acceptance.*

Many people practice evaluation naturally and assess their actions on their own, some on a daily basis. They continuously organize the past themselves to maintain a coherent account of their lives, just as Reviewers examine and evaluate their lives in a Life Review encouraged by the questions of the Therapeutic Listener. Evaluation is a subjective experience and is the internal work of the Reviewer, only guided by the Listener. Occasionally, the Listener's direction and guidance are not needed if the Reviewer automatically begins to evaluate an event while talking about it.

For some people, evaluation does not come naturally or automatically. Many Reviewers have not been accustomed to looking closely at the past and understanding its influence on the present. The Listener can recognize the nonevaluator over time by the way this type of person talks about the past, often without that person adding personal opinions, feelings, or judgments. When Reviewers lack the skill of evaluation, the Listener needs to teach them how to evaluate in a Life Review by interjecting appropriate focusing questions and prompts, such as *"How did that make you feel?"* or *"Tell me more about what that means to you."* Over time, automatic exploration and evaluation can become second nature and Reviewers may unconsciously adopt this technique and make it their own without ever realizing the change. Becoming adept at bringing the process of evaluation to a Life Review is exceedingly important and is the responsibility of the Therapeutic Listener. The following supervision meeting for a Listener demonstrates the importance of evaluation by illustrating a Life Review visit that required evaluative questions, but did not receive them:

> *We were listening to our own tapes and those of students in our supervision group. One student was visiting a well-adjusted, fun-loving lady who seemed to be happily married and had lived a normal and uneventful life. The Reviewer told the Listener that an old boyfriend from high school had called and invited her to lunch. The Reviewer was very excited to hear from him after 50 years and accepted the lunch date with the full approval and blessings of her husband. As the Reviewer told about meeting this old boyfriend, the Listener interrupted to ask her what she was wearing. After reporting on her clothes, the student asked what they had for lunch, what restaurant they went to, and then what the man was wearing. Because the Listener asked numerous unimportant questions, the hour was over and an opportunity was lost.*

The scenario should have been played out as follows. The Therapeutic Listener would have asked: "*How did you feel when you saw him?*" More than likely the Reviewer would have gone on to describe her feelings, to reflect on choices made comparing her husband to the old boyfriend, and being happy with the choice she made. Any unresolved issues or sadness would be discussed and the lady would have closed an old chapter in her life, or as Butler said, "surveyed and reintegrated an unresolved conflict."

Surveying an unresolved conflict causes the Reviewer to look at that past conflict introspectively in order to evaluate the conflict, to develop insight, and then to gain resolution. With insight, the Reviewer is able to accept and reintegrate the conflict in order to move on to other things in life. Reintegration is accepting what you now see in the present and making it a part of your history. Remember, evaluation is the most critical unique characteristic of Life Review and is essential to surveying the past. Evaluation includes several parts:

1. Listening to what is being said and picking up on the nuances of the statement and the accompanying emotions.
2. Responding appropriately and asking for clarification, which directs the Reviewer to appraise the situation.
3. Inquiring about the Reviewer's thoughts and feelings, which initiates evaluation.
4. Giving the Reviewer time to do all that work and then to use you, the Listener, as a sounding board to get feedback.
5. Integrating the reappraised thinking into the Reviewer's own life story.

Additional Considerations About Life Review

In addition to the four unique characteristics that define the Structured Life Review process, there are certain other considerations inherent in a Structured Life Review that distinguish the Life Review from other ways of reminiscing. Each of these factors is addressed and explained in the following paragraphs.

Hard Work

The first consideration is that Life Review is "work," because it requires Life Reviewers to perform an in-depth evaluation of their entire life span. The inclusive survey of a Life Review can remind Reviewers of unpleasant events that they might prefer not to remember or to share. When remembered, Reviewers often have to work through and integrate what may have been an unsavory event. To integrate, Reviewers must examine the recalled event, evaluate it, and then decide if they wish to share the memory with the Therapeutic Listener. Then, if they share it, they relive the unpleasant memory over again. For example, recalling the deaths of loved ones is difficult. One Life Reviewer, Mr. J, talked about his experiences with death and grief in his family as a part of his Life Review:

> *I still miss my sister. I remember when we were children and played together. I still feel the guilt I felt when I talked her out of her new funny book. I remember being angry when she wouldn't let me play with her and her friend. I was lonely when she and her friend went off to the first grade, leaving me behind because I was too young. Every time I think of her I miss her again and grieve.*

Mr. J worked to understand his feelings about his sister, who had died. He was not enjoying the process but needed to resolve his grief and the loneliness he still felt for her. It is hard work to face such difficult memories again and to reconcile them. In the long term, however, reconciliation makes the rest of life easier to remember and to live.

In contrast to Life Review, reminiscing can be mostly fun—remembering school, comrades, games that were played, and so forth. Although reminiscers also remember sad events, they can often choose not to. On the whole, when they reminisce, they do it for fun. They often laugh about good times, such as recalling the Saturday afternoon matinee and eating a box of Jujubes while watching Roy Rogers capture the bad guy and get the girl. Obviously, this is an easier process than discussing grief or other difficult memories. But the Life Review questions do provide structure for the Life Review process, and their

---

Additional Characteristics of Life Review

- Hard Work
- Self
- Repetition
- Power and Control
- Supervision
- Confidentiality
- Audiotaping
- Life Review with Relatives

> *Life Review is "work"
> because it requires Life
> Reviewers to perform an
> in-depth evaluation of
> their entire life span.*

careful use is recommended in most cases even though they cause the Reviewer to work harder.

Self

For reminiscing to be a true Life Review, the main character of the story must be the Self. The Self is one's identity as a person. It is internalization. "I did this and I thought that" shows involvement. Without the real Self as the main character, the Reviewer is just retelling an event from the past. When Reviewers talk *about* an event rather than what they *thought* or *did* in the event, there is little deep emotion involved and Reviewers can remain somewhat detached from their own story. Life Reviewing without the Self as the main character is almost like talking about a television program, something the Reviewer observed instead of a story in which the Reviewer probably played an active part.

On the other hand, reminiscers can talk about events all day without looking at the personal impact on themselves. Take, for example, a discussion of an important event such as World War II. These topics can be discussed on an impersonal level by just talking about the most noted events. Self enters into the equation when the effect of the war on that individual is told. Even civilians have felt the effect of war. The following is an account of World War II with the Self as part of the story:

> *As a little girl I remember shortages of butter and bubblegum. I don't think I had any bubblegum for four years and I really missed it. I remember bringing the grease from cooking to the butcher shop, but I don't know why. We also flattened all the tins from food and brought them back to the grocery store for the war effort. And we couldn't get shoes or gasoline without ration stamps. My mother used to complain about not having stockings.*

> *We often endured blackouts so that we would be ready in the event we were bombed. I remember we stayed in the bathroom during blackouts in order to keep a small light on because the bathroom had only a little window and we could block the bathroom light from the outside. We would line the tub with pillows and my sister and I would fall asleep in the tub. Before we fell asleep, my mother dragged in a rocking chair and read stories by the dim light. My father was a volunteer warden, so besides the fun and coziness of the stories in the bathroom, we waited and worried about him until he joined us. Despite the fact that it was wartime, I had some good memories.*

This woman's story is a good example of a personal reaction and peripheral involvement in a historical event. She told the story with pride in her family's war efforts and shared some warm memories about her family doing things together during wartime. Telling the story allowed her to feel good about herself.

Conversely, Mr. R spoke of the same event as if he never experienced the war personally.

> *World War II happened around 1940. The newspapers always had stories and the President was on the radio. Grownups used to talk about it all the time. The invasion of Normandy was a pretty big thing and some guys married German war brides after the war was over. Life went on pretty much the same.*

Mr. R had a gift for ignoring himself. People like Mr. R need to be constantly reminded that the Life Review is about their personal life and cannot just be about an event without reporting what the event meant personally. Such people can be helped to include themselves with pointed questions: *"What were you doing when the President spoke on the radio?"; "Did you understand him?"; "Were you worried about your family having to serve?"* Over time, with practice, Reviewers will include themselves, their feelings, and the impact on Self in the story that they are telling. This leads to evaluation—an important part of the Life Review.

Repetition

Repetition, as used here, is the act of reiterating the same memory over and over. Many older people seem to engage in the act of repetition, especially when reminiscing. Often, relatives complain of this activity in their loved ones because they view the act of repetition as boring and meaningless. Relatives get tired of hearing the same story over and over and usually stop listening. They occasionally attribute repetition to a failing or wandering mind and handle the issue by reminding the Reviewer that they have heard that story before.

In fact, repetition often has a point. Repetition can serve to help Reviewers work through problem areas in their lives. The encouragement of repetition is unique to Life Review. Therapeutic Listeners need to encourage reasonable repetition as a way of ridding Reviewers of troublesome events that Reviewers may have raised intentionally or even casually. Often with repetition, it seems that Reviewers are discussing bothersome events until they are not bothersome anymore. It is not always possible to purge the event with one telling, but after a few recitations, the enormity of the event may become lessened and the event can be accepted more easily. Actually, repetition is partially responsible for the cleansing that happens in a Life Review, a catharsis and a release of the anxiety that accompanied the specific story. The following Review illustrates the work of repetition.

> *Mr. K grew up in the rural areas of Japan. He was very poor and as a child had to go out and forage for food for his family. During World War II, there was very little food available, so he mostly stole what he could find. He was always hungry and his memories were of hunger and then of disgrace when he was caught stealing food. Now in his nineties, he was experiencing the beginnings of Alzheimer's disease and*

those old memories of hunger became stronger. He now lived with his daughter and
repeatedly castigated her for growing flowers instead of food. Recently he began
hoarding food from the dinner table and hiding it in his room. He was becoming
a problem to his family because of his obsession with hunger and food.

For three visits, Mr. K talked about his never-ending hunger as a child. During the fourth visit, he started to laugh and said he finally had enough to eat and was through worrying about food. He would enjoy the flowers. For the rest of the Life Review, he became more upbeat and reminisced about both the good and the bad in his life. He could now see other things because he had freed himself from those bad memories of hunger and could move on. He was finally grateful for his current existence.

Repetition often encourages exploration and eventual resolution of troubling past events. Once a problem is solved in the mind of the Reviewer, acceptance begins. Meaningful repetition can only occur in a one-to-one setting where the Therapeutic Listener appears willing and eager to explore a troubling thought with the Reviewer. When people reminisce, especially in groups, they do not get the opportunity to work through their troubles by repetition. A topic may be raised and discussed, but often the group is finished with the topic after everyone has had a turn. To the troubled person, this is like opening a wound without giving the wound a chance to heal. The Structured Life Review allows Reviewers to work through problems until the healing has taken place. Note, however, that it is possible that the repeated stories do not have such deep meaning. Rather, the Reviewer may simply like the story and repeats it without sensing that it is boring.

Power and Control

Power and control are significant components of a therapeutic relationship. In a traditional therapeutic relationship, the power and decision making regarding that relationship generally are in the hands of the therapist. Once the relationship has been initiated, the therapist often decides the topic to be addressed and asks intimate questions, prodding clients until they begin to reveal and understand themselves. In the Life Review, on the other hand, the power primarily belongs with the Reviewer. The Therapeutic Listener does try to cover the whole life and probes occasionally, but then only by invitation, as when the Reviewer mentions a new topic first, thus opening the subject for discussion and questioning.

> *Relying on Reviewers to raise issues is not good therapy, but it is good Life Reviewing.*

The placement of power is an important aspect that differentiates Life Review from formalized therapy. At the very beginning of the Life Review, Listeners tell Reviewers that they are interested in the Reviewer's history but will not discuss anything that Reviewers wish to keep to themselves. Listeners will introduce the topics on the LRF but not press further questions. Except for the prompting questions on the LRF, Listeners must let Reviewers raise sensitive topics first before these topics become part of the discussion. Admittedly, relying on Reviewers to raise issues is not good therapy, but it is good Life Reviewing. This simple difference that separates Life Review from therapy contributes to a very safe environment for Reviewers. Reviewers rely on Listeners to maintain this environment.

The Life Review requires Reviewers to work at exposing past events while covering their important life stages, but the Therapeutic Listener does not ask Reviewers to change their lives. All the Listener asks is to hear a Reviewer's life story. Notably, change does occur, but it happens internally and sometimes by chance. Whatever change occurs is brought about by the Reviewers themselves as they participate in the Life Review process and then evaluate their lives. Katie's story demonstrates the ability of a Reviewer to keep control of the process:

> *Katie lived in an assisted living facility where we taught our gerontology students. She participated in four Life Reviews to help us train students and then she volunteered for more. We could tell that Katie had something important to reveal but just couldn't make herself do it. When she talked of childhood, she always talked of a mean father who manhandled her mother and grandmother. Her father drank a lot and spent a lot of time carousing in the community. She never mentioned herself as being one of her father's victims, but Katie was afraid of her father. Her fear of her father was apparent when she talked of other incidents. She talked disparagingly of males and told how she had shied away from boys as she grew up. She said she always felt dirty and often wasn't able to bathe or have nice clean clothes like the other kids.*
>
> *At the end of each Life Review she was asked how she liked the process. Though she said it was horrible and she needed to forget those things again, she continued to volunteer to talk about her past with new students.*

There obviously was a great deal of trauma in Katie's childhood, but every time she got close to talking about it, she would change the subject. Katie definitely kept control of her Life Review; the power was hers and she retained it. No one prodded her further or more deeply. She rejected a referral to talk to someone else—a therapist—and Katie probably continues to carry her burden today.

Listeners must remember that Reviewers are in control of the Life Review. If the Reviewer does not raise a topic, or respond to one that is raised, then it is the responsibility of the Listener to further ignore the topic. Preserving the trust that the Reviewer gets to keep control is the promise of Life Review. Reviewers always control the content. You may be saying to yourselves: "*How does the Reviewer control the content if the Listener uses the questions in the LRF?*" The Listener uses the questions only as prompts and to guide the process through the developmental stages in 6 weeks. It is the Reviewer, however, who ultimately controls the final content and conversation (Dunn, Haight, & Hendrix, 2002).

There is really no middle ground for this rule. Most Reviewers decide to share their personal secrets before the Life Review is finished because they see the opportunity that the Life Review offers. But if they wish to keep their secrets or be evasive, the Therapeutic Listener must respect those choices.

Supervision

Supervision, as used here, occurs when practitioners who work in mental health fields request a more experienced practitioner to oversee their work. Most practitioners seek supervision to get feedback regarding their interactions with clients. Many professions require a number of hours of supervision before allowing practitioners to sit for licensing exams. Supervision is important because most mental health practitioners spend their days isolated from their peers while talking and listening to clients. Supervision provides them with feedback, critique, praise, and collegiality. The same applies to Listeners of Life Reviews. Supervision can take place on a one-to-one basis or in groups with peers and/or with more experienced supervisors.

When doing Life Reviews, supervision can be a social event as well as a time for feedback. It is an opportunity to visit with other Listeners to hear about their techniques and their problems. If Listeners question the way they may have handled a certain type of Reviewer or Reviewer response, they may ask about their technique and get feedback from others. If a Listener does not have peers or supervisors, the Listener may try to find other interested Listeners for feedback through the Internet or with other health care organizations or groups. It is always beneficial to talk about the situations that arise in the Life Review and to learn from the experience and input of others. Whenever discussing Reviewers, however, remember to protect their identities and confidences.

Ideally, supervision should be a weekly event. If the Listener's schedule is too full, then meeting every other week will suffice. If a Listener needs feedback when the group has no scheduled meeting, the Listener can always ask a peer to listen to him or her on actual tapes. The tapes should be identified only with a number and visit to protect the identity of the Reviewers. Only the Listener conducting the Life Review should know the identities of the Reviewers. Therefore, Reviewer names in the tapes should be disguised to preserve confidentiality. The opportunity to ask a peer to review a tape when there is no planned "supervision" meeting helps to supplement the weekly meeting and provides Listeners with timely feedback.

Confidentiality

Confidentiality is important to Reviewers for many good reasons. It strengthens the relationship between the Reviewer and the Listener that is developed in this one-to-one process. If Reviewers feel assured of confidentiality, they will have a more effective

Life Review because they will speak from the heart with fewer reservations of the mind. They may explore some of their life decisions for the first time with a person they have come to trust who is, or was, actually a stranger. A stranger may be perceived as a safe confidante because when the Life Review is complete, the stranger will walk out of the Reviewer's life and the Reviewer will never be reminded of the secrets that were shared. In any case, assuring Reviewers of confidentiality creates a safe environment for them.

> *If Reviewers feel assured of confidentiality, they will have a more effective Life Review because they will speak from the heart with fewer reservations of the mind.*

Confidentiality exists forever even after the person has died. Everlasting confidentiality needs to be stressed because of the nature of the Life Review. Families are usually aware that Dad or Mom has talked to a Listener about his or her life story. Because our practice is with older people, many of them die within a close enough time frame for family members to remember that we recorded the life story of their loved one. Often members of the family will ask for the tapes as a memoir of their parent. Listeners should refuse this request and destroy the tapes. Confidentiality remains with the Listener.

One instance of a Listener being pressured to produce a tape for a family demonstrates the folly of doing so.

Amelia was the director of an agency that helped aging people. As part of the Aging Services Community, she was aware of the ongoing Life Review Project. Amelia asked if we would do a Life Review with her father, who lived alone and seemed depressed and very lonely. She thought a weekly visitor would cheer him up. We responded that we would include him in our project if he qualified. Amelia's father did qualify and spent eight rewarding weeks talking about his life with one of our Therapeutic Listeners. The Life Review lifted his depressed feelings and he reached out to socialize more. He enjoyed two more happy years before he died.

Because we all worked in Aging Services, Amelia and I and the Listener often crossed paths. Amelia remained grateful that we helped her father. After he died, she asked us if she could have his tapes; they would be a comfort to his wife and the family who missed him. We refused, but the requests continued repeatedly. Finally, the Listener was worn down and told Amelia she could listen to the tapes but couldn't have them. On the tapes, the most therapeutic part of her dad's story was his adulthood when he spoke of his regrets over marrying his father's choice instead of the girl he loved. Then he talked about how having children so early in the marriage prevented him from pursuing more education in his profession. He said in effect that he had wasted his potential because of a poor marriage and early parenting. As he proceeded with the

> *A stranger may be perceived as a safe confidante because when the Life Review is complete the stranger will walk out of the Reviewer's life.*

Life Review, he began to reframe and accept his choices, and to find the good parts. But for his daughter Amelia, the damage had been done. She was devastated by his unhappiness with his family.

The experience with Amelia reinforced our rule: Never share tapes or the identities of the life stories with anyone!

Audiotaping

Audiotaping serves many purposes, including being a good way to record and track what is happening in a Life Review. Tapes also serve as a good source for supervision because the project director can listen to anonymous tapes at any time to see how Listeners are doing and to oversee the work of a project. The tapes are actually an oral history. If they are transcribed without identifiers, and with the permission of Reviewers, they serve as important research materials for the future. Transcribed, they serve as a source for qualitative research. Also, they can be helpful in teaching others how to do a Life Review. Despite the issues surrounding tapes, they contribute a great deal to the Life Review process.

One issue that must be addressed when taping is ownership: Who owns the tapes, Reviewers or Listeners? Here we must side with Listeners or, if part of a project, with the project director, not the Reviewer. Even though it is the Reviewer's story on the tapes, the tapes themselves should be kept from the Reviewer. Sometimes Reviewers want the tapes themselves because they intend to listen to them, give them to others, or write an autobiography. Refusing them possession is very difficult but again necessary. Sometimes Reviewers don't remember how open they have been and are surprised at the content when they listen to the tapes again.

There were problems when tapes were once given to a Reviewer. This Reviewer lived in a nursing home. She kept the tapes hidden in a bureau drawer. Every morning when she woke up, she checked to see if the tapes had been disturbed, and she did the same thing every night. After a while, she began to develop dementia and paranoia; the tapes became a great source of anxiety for her, because she feared someone would listen to them. For years the tapes contributed to her paranoia and disturbed her peace of mind. Thus, Listeners should keep the tapes, resist giving even a copy to Reviewers, and should safeguard or destroy the tapes when finished with them.

The last issue involved in taping is anonymity. As mentioned under confidentiality, the tapes themselves should have no identifiers, just the participant's number and the number of the tape; for example, visit 3, #447. Listeners can keep notebooks or a master list on their computers, where they identify Mr. Jones as #447, but that should be the only identifier. Although taping is very helpful to Listeners, it is the responsibility of the Listener to guard the identity of the person on the tape.

Life Review with Relatives

Many people who are learning about Life Review want to conduct a Life Review with grandparents or parents. Doing a Life Review with a relative is not a good idea except for couples who are candid with each other. Most relatives do not have the extra layer of confidentiality that is available with a partner or the necessary emotional distance of a Therapeutic Listener who is a stranger. Relatives who are Reviewers will probably hold back hurtful information because they are concerned with the feelings of the Therapeutic Listener or with gossip, or for other good reasons. As a consequence, the process of Life Review will not be as therapeutic as it could be with a stranger.

Often the request to work with a relative is prompted by a desire to record the relative's life for a history, to learn about the life story, or to record the Reviewer's story to keep for the grandchildren. If any of those reasons is the motivation for Life Review, there are many good books in bookstores or greeting card stores that will serve this purpose. In those commercial books, the top of each page has a question for the Reviewer followed by a space for the Reviewer's answers, filling up the page with a story. If a family member wants a relative to participate in a Life Review because he or she thinks that relative needs one because of depression, social isolation, loneliness, or anxiety, then it is best to find a colleague who is a stranger to that relative, who will respect confidentiality, and who can be more therapeutic. Strangers make the best Therapeutic Listeners.

THE PARTICIPANTS

When people talk, listen completely.
Most people never listen.

—ERNEST HEMINGWAY

There are two active participants in the Life Review Process. The first is the Life Reviewer and the second is you, the Therapeutic Listener. Each has a defined role that contributes to the process. This chapter describes the specific roles that both Listener and Reviewer should play throughout the Life Review process. In addition, this chapter describes selected skills and techniques that will contribute to your expertise as a Therapeutic Listener.

Therapeutic Listener

The Therapeutic Listener structures the Life Review by guiding the developmental nature of the process. Anyone who learns the Life Review process through studying this Handbook can be an effective Therapeutic Listener. The main requirements of the Listener include asking probing questions from the LRF, then listening attentively and responding appropriately to the stories told by Reviewers. The word "therapeutic" indicates a conscious effort by the Listener to be responsive and helpful during the process, building a bond and sense of trust with the Reviewer, so that the Reviewer will benefit from the Life Review.

Although attentive listening is the key role of the Listener, additional skills and techniques are necessary to help people effectively review their lives. Such behavioral skills make

Interviewing Techniques for a Therapeutic Listener

Attentive Behavior: Demonstrating interest and paying attention

Repetition: Telling the same story over and over

Reframing: Giving thoughts another meaning by restatement

Responding: Saying or doing something helpful as a reaction

Reflecting Feelings: Perceiving and giving back the Reviewer's emotions

Sharing Behavior: Contributing to the conversation

Paraphrasing: Restating the words of the Reviewer

Self-Disclosure: Telling a pertinent story about yourself

Encouragement to Talk: Using short remarks to indicate continuing interest

Summarizing: Restating the main points of the Life Review

Integrating: Making a composite of separate parts

Adapted from Ivy (1971)

listening more than a passive exercise; they enable Listeners to lead the Life Review process. This chapter explains selected counseling skills (Rogers, 1961) and interviewing techniques (Ivy, 1971) that will help you become an excellent Therapeutic Listener. Although many prospective Listeners use these skills and techniques intuitively in their work or conversations, others need to learn them. Each of the following interviewing techniques contributes to the mastery of being an effective Listener.

Therapeutic Listeners need to display genuine interest in all that Reviewers say, while helping them explore their thoughts and feelings surrounding specific past events and stages of development. Listeners can facilitate Life Reviews wherever they can find privacy and find people who want to be Reviewers. Often, potential Listeners are already working in the helping professions and, once they learn how to do Life Reviews, can add that process to their repertoire of helpful interventions, particularly for needy, older persons.

Interviewing Techniques

There are several interviewing techniques to learn that are easy to master and apply to your role as a Therapeutic Listener. These techniques make you a more effective communicator and are particularly appropriate for conducting a Life Review. Although these methods are a basic part of good conversation, they are described here so that you will recall them and remember to use them. Fortunately, these interviewing techniques are easy to understand and to learn, and many people already use them naturally. A Listener can make these techniques second nature by practicing them in normal conversation with friends, family, and colleagues.

Attentive Behavior. Attentive behavior requires you to pay close attention to your Reviewers and to what memories they are recalling at that time. This technique is used throughout the Life Review. It is essential to show your undivided interest in the Reviewer and in the Reviewer's current story. You must concentrate on the Reviewer and show interest in him or her through body language, eye contact, and appropriate responses to the Reviewer's words.

Attentive behavior consists of three actions practiced simultaneously:

1. **Demonstrate a relaxed demeanor by sitting with a natural posture that will put the Reviewer at ease.** Leaning forward, nodding when it is appropriate, and creating a sense of intimacy encourages the telling of the life story. A sense of involved comfortableness will enable you to listen more closely to the Reviewer and will enhance the Reviewer's sense of well-being and self-importance.

2. **Make and maintain eye contact.** Eye contact with the Life Reviewers creates an atmosphere of interest and involvement that encourages memories to unfold. Listeners who often glance at the clock or, worse, at their watches, or who check their schedules while a story is being told appear disinterested, which is distracting to the Reviewer. If exact time is important, pre-position your watch or a clock where you can occasionally glance at it. Avid interest by the Listener is key to an ongoing Review. Eye contact, however, can be variable depending on the comfort level of the Life Reviewer. Some cultures think direct eye contact is rude. Certain people, regardless of their culture, become uncomfortable with continued, direct eye contact. Thus, a skilled Therapeutic Listener will assess the situation, including the Reviewer, before engaging in continuous eye contact. Listeners need to observe the use of eye contact by Reviewers and perhaps mirror their behavior while increasing the amount of eye contact each week. As Listeners establish comfort and trust, continued eye contact by both parties will probably increase.

3. **Use appropriate comments and questions to encourage the Reviewer.** Comments should be responsive to both the content and the emotional level of the Reviewer's story. If Reviewers demonstrate grief when talking about the death of a loved one, for example, Listeners need to empathize and respond to the Reviewer's feelings of sadness while verbally acknowledging the Reviewer's continuing grief. Facial expressions as well as words can show the Listener's attentiveness.

Repetition. Repetition is the act of encouraging or allowing Life Reviewers again and again to repeat the details of a traumatic event that caused them great unrest in the past and prevented them from looking ahead to the future. Events that would benefit from repetition are those that cause a Reviewer to get stuck in a certain stage of Life Review and lead to despair. When you are listening to their stories, it is usually easy to identify those particularly troubling events, first because of the Reviewer's reluctance to discuss them fully, and second because of the despairing emotions that often accompany these particular stories.

When you hear these stories and identify them as despairing, you can use probing questions to get the rest of the story. When you meet the following week, you can raise the issue again. For example, *"Mr. H, I've been thinking of what you told me last week about your mother's death and your adoption; tell me more about the circumstances that caused your Mother's death";* and *"How did it feel to be put up for adoption?";* and *"Did you miss the rest of your family?"* When the Reviewer has exhausted the topic, you can move on to other parts of the Life Review for the current and subsequent weeks. In this example, when you come back the next week, start with, *"Today we are going to talk about your young adulthood, but before we start on that topic, is there anything else you'd like to share about your Mother's death?"* The Reviewer may need to repeat the issues again, but by the third time there is usually some reframing and acceptance going on, allowing the Reviewer to relinquish that trouble and move beyond it in the Life Review and in the Reviewer's own life.

Reframing. Reframing is a technique that the Listener uses to provide a different slant on events, a new view of the past, by restating past events in a different context or encouraging the Reviewer to take another look from a new viewpoint. Reframing is used when there are many sides to a story to show the Reviewer that past events can be interpreted differently than the Reviewer has interpreted the story so far. Reframing usually can change a negative tone to a more positive tone. Reframing is a way to encourage Reviewers to evaluate and judge events differently than they have done previously because of new ideas, new interpretations, or new insights gained from reexamined evidence or a different perspective. For example, Mrs. U accepted her Listener's reframed suggestions during her Life Review:

> Mrs. U was a working mother who was feeling guilty about being away from home so much while her children were growing up. She constantly brought up her guilty feelings as she talked about the adult part of her life. She bemoaned the fact that she had missed some of her children's concerts and games, and that guilt became a large part of the story of her adult life. Mixed in with the guilt were stories of the children's successes in life—all were college graduates, hard workers, and attentive children.
>
> As the Listener heard these stories and put them together, the Listener's picture was different. The Listener saw a hard-working woman who had made many sacrifices to assure her children's success in life, and she shared that viewpoint with Mrs. U: **"You were always home to greet your children after school and help them with their homework. Every night they had a hot dinner and, when they were little, a bedtime story. The additional work made a college education possible for your children. I think you did everything you could for them and you should feel proud, not guilty."**
>
> The reframed interpretation was a new view for Mrs. U. She began to consider the Listener's viewpoint and slowly accepted that this new version was true as well. With this version, she began to think differently of herself as a working mother and appreciated that she had in fact given her children a great deal more than she could have ever imagined. As a result, she had a more accepting view of her adult life and her job as a mother.

Responding. This technique involves a suitable reaction from the Listener in response to the telling of a notable event that the Reviewer shares during the Life Review. For example, the Reviewer may be talking about a promotion that was very important to him, requiring the Listener to share the Reviewer's pride and joy when retelling the event. Or conversely, the Reviewer may talk about a shameful childhood event, which should be heard without shock but with acceptance. Thus, the tone and timing of the response are extremely important and can influence the future sharing of events. The reaction must be right on target toward the content and context of the story and appropriate for that Reviewer. The tenor of a response should send the following message to the Reviewer: *"Continue to talk, I'm interested, I understand."* With an insightful reaction and response, Reviewers will be made to feel safe and able to share other and perhaps more disturbing facts as the Life Review proceeds.

Responding must also convey a strong conviction of acceptance; or a feeling that it is alright, it is not your fault, it could happen to anyone. Often Reviewers will relate, perhaps for the first time, traumatic events that they have never shared before, expecting to see alarm and rejection on the Listener's face that reaffirms their own distasteful picture of the events or of themselves. When the response is instead empathy, understanding, and acceptance, Reviewers can begin to change their personal view of themselves to: *"I guess I (or it) wasn't really so bad after all."* Many people harbor secrets that they have never told to another human being, and it is the giving up of these secrets and being accepted regardless of them that is part of the therapy that results from the Life Review process. Responding effectively contributes to an effective Listener and a therapeutic Life Review. So, Listeners must be attuned to their own behavior as well as to the Reviewer's behavior.

> *Many people harbor secrets that they have never told to another human being.*

Reflecting Feelings. As an interviewing technique, reflecting feelings means to perceive and return the emotions shown by Reviewers as they recall their memories. Reflection of feelings is helpful for unveiling emotions that are a part of the Reviewer's story but may not be fully recognized by either the Reviewer or the Listener. By reflecting the feelings, the Listener brings the apparent emotions out in the open for examination by both Reviewer and Listener. Reflection of feelings validates the emotions that seem to be underlying the Reviewer's story. Reflection of feelings is similar to paraphrasing, with the primary difference being one of emphasis. In reflection, the Listener concentrates on the emotional aspects of the Reviewer's story so that the Listener can validate and return the Reviewer's feelings back to him or her. In paraphrasing, the Listener focuses on the words and the meaning, and in turn clarifies the meaning of the words. An experienced Listener uses both techniques together for the most effective responses to the Reviewer, but you should understand their individual uses as well.

A large part of the therapy resulting from the Life Review comes with a new under-standing of blurred or repressed past events. If the Listener can listen for and paraphrase the Reviewer's words while responding to the feelings of the Reviewer, the Listener can facilitate the Reviewer's own self-awareness and self-understanding of the past. For example, a Reviewer who is talking about loneliness as a child may be experiencing cur-rent sadness when he recalls past incidents of loneliness. He may not realize that he is still sad. As the Reviewer talks about being lonely as a child, the Listener notices the prevailing sadness and comments about it to the Reviewer. The Reviewer may be sur-prised at the observation but gains insight regarding the impact of his past on his pres-ent emotions.

To practice the reflection of feelings technique, you must listen for expressions of feel-ing, such as, "It really made me **mad** when my mother did that to my brother." Listeners must also look for behaviors such as blushing, or faster, louder speech, or angry speech, which may reveal feelings about the topic that the Reviewer has not yet recognized. In response to this display of feelings, Therapeutic Listeners need to acknowledge and state their observation of the emotions surrounding the Reviewer's experience. For example, a response to the angry tone might be, *"Do you still feel angry toward your mother for dis-ciplining your brother unfairly?"* Such a response will evoke self-examination in Review-ers, who will look at their present feelings more closely and discover that they may still be angry, or they may deny that the anger still exists. With this eye-opening technique, Lis-teners facilitate Reviewers' self-awareness, self-reflection, and self-understanding. To do this well, Listeners must try to understand what feelings Reviewers are experiencing at the moment and communicate understanding and empathy to the Reviewers.

During the Life Review, Reviewers are encouraged to talk about their own feelings and emotional responses to particular events and to examine them closely; this is evalu-ation and it leads to integration. If the emotions are not readily visible to the Listener, a well-used phrase such as *"How did you feel about that?"* will cause Reviewers to exam-ine events themselves. As the Life Review progresses, Reviewers may automatically examine their feelings associated with important life events. By the time the Life Review is finished, Reviewers may have learned the skill of examining their own emotions sur-rounding an event. They may automatically evaluate and integrate and continue to prac-tice this skill privately on their own, thus reconciling their past and reaching personal peace long after the actual Life Review is finished.

Sharing Behavior. Sharing means participating in and contributing appropriately to the dialogue. The Listener can talk about a topic, event, or emotion that relates to the Life Reviewer's life stage being discussed at that time. Sharing behavior can be used when a Life Review is stalling and the Reviewer seems at a loss for something to say. In such a case, Listeners can tell a short story that might interest the Reviewers and remind Review-ers of similar memories in their past. Sharing behavior is especially useful when work-ing with Reviewers who say they have nothing to talk about and are therefore considered to be Reluctant Reviewers. Listeners using sharing behavior often can prime the pump of the Reviewer's memory, or of the inclination to talk, by telling a story relevant to the stage of life that the Reviewer is trying to recall. For example, one Listener related that in a town similar to the Reviewer's town everyone remembered when there was no bridge to a nearby island and they all had to take a ferryboat to go back and forth to town. When that Listener talked about the ferryboat, several of her subsequent Life Reviewers recalled similar stories in their own lives that were set on a ferryboat, such as going to the beach on the weekend, or selling farm produce in the market after getting it to the market on the ferryboats. These same Reviewers also recalled the demise of the ferryboat when a bridge was built that finally connected the island to the mainland. Thus, Reviewers living in this locale were familiar with both the ferryboat and the bridge, and the commonality of the events prompted such Reviewers to recall comparable memories.

New Listeners often may find it difficult to use sharing behavior because they may have had few experiences or have heard from fewer Reviewers. In this case, the use of a prepared historical timeline or a relevant history book covering the Reviewer's lifetime can be helpful. A timeline listing major events from the 1960s to the 1990s could include the death of John F. Kennedy, the walk on the moon, and the explosion of the Challenger space shuttle. Most people remember those events. Then, Listeners can ask Reviewers what they were doing when they heard of the assassination or moon walk or the explosion and how they felt when they heard about it. Responding to questions about these historical events may jog the Reviewers' memory for related and personal events. For example, a Reviewer response to the Kennedy question such as, *"I was in grammar school when I watched the funeral for President Kennedy on television,"* can introduce whole new worlds of personal memories about school and the people whom the Reviewer knew in childhood. When Reviewers finish their memory about the assassination, they can be asked: *"What else do you remember about grammar school?";* or *"Did you watch the TV at home or in school?";* or *"Who watched the funeral with you?";* or *"What other things did you do with your family?"* Even beginning Listeners can find relevant stories from timelines and historical events that relate to a Reviewer's lifetime.

When employing sharing behavior, Listeners must be enthusiastic about the subject they are going to share as well as make that subject relevant to Reviewers. Listeners need to remain in a relaxed posture and continue to maintain eye contact with Reviewers while they search their own minds for their own recall. Often, Listeners must look inward for an appropriate vignette while still being attentive to the Reluctant Reviewer. When telling their story, Listeners should not allow their thoughts to wander, but should remain focused both on the topic and on the Reviewer. Finally, Listeners should know when to stop talking and allow Reviewers to again take the lead. Enthusiasm and relevance make such stories interesting to others, but Listeners must keep them short.

Paraphrasing. Another interviewing technique is paraphrasing, which is restating the Reviewers' words back to them with the meaning that is heard and understood by the Listener. Paraphrasing is used mostly to clarify details that are confusing or complex for the Listener. Often when the Listener restates what was said, however, the Reviewer's thoughts become clearer as well. Paraphrasing has three purposes:

1. To convey to Reviewers that the Listener is listening to them and trying to understand the point they are making.
2. To crystallize the Reviewer's thoughts by repeating the Reviewer's comments in a more precise and clear manner. The rephrasing helps Reviewers understand what they seem to be trying to say and conveys the message that the Listener also understands or is at least trying to understand.
3. To allow Listeners to check their own perceptions to ascertain that they really do understand what the Reviewer is saying. Paraphrasing, used selectively, is extremely functional for clarifying confusing content or intent.

An example of paraphrasing follows:

REVIEWER: *My son is really a problem. He's had very little training, lacks the proper education, and can't follow instructions.*

LISTENER: **So you don't think he is competent.**

REVIEWER: *Oh no, I don't mean he is not competent; he just hasn't had the right training.*

Or

REVIEWER: *I guess he is not competent; I never really thought about that before.*

Self-Disclosure. Self-disclosure is an interviewing technique similar to sharing behavior that allows the Listener to tell a personal and pertinent story about oneself that is related to the memories the Reviewer is recalling. Self-disclosure differs from sharing behavior in that sharing behavior is the reference to a relevant historical-type event, whereas self-disclosure is the telling of a related event personal to the Listener. Self-disclosure is especially helpful for getting Reluctant Reviewers involved in the Life Review. A story that the Listener shares through self-disclosure may interest Reluctant Reviewers and inspire them to recall and discuss a similar event in their own lives. However, the Therapeutic Listener must use self-disclosure carefully. There is always the danger of the Listener sharing too much or taking the initiative away from the Reviewer. A self-disclosure is a short story-prompt in this context and it is important to use self-disclosure sparingly.

Self-disclosure contributes to the interpersonal bonding process between Listener and Reviewer, minimizing the newness in their relationship. This type of sharing also encourages conversation by shy Reviewers. Listeners, however, must be in tune with Reviewers and aware of the direction of the conversation. The self-disclosure must be congruent with where the Reviewer is at the time and not just an opportunity for the Listener to talk. Therapeutic Listeners need a great deal of sensitivity and awareness when talking about themselves. Listeners must not dominate the dialogue with their own stories. An example of a short self-disclosure and question is, *"I liked third grade the best. What grade did you like?"*

Self-disclosure allows Reviewers to know their Listeners a little better personally. Remember, in the beginning sessions, the Life Review process is an association of two strangers, one of whom is getting ready to disclose the details of his or her life to another. Self-disclosure by the Listener takes away some of the initial awkwardness, and the two parties in the Life Review feel they know each other a little better as they go along.

Encouragement to Talk. Encouragement to talk is another interviewing technique for the Therapeutic Listener to use to show interest in what the Reviewer is saying and to keep the conversation actively moving along. The Listener can use encouragement by employing concise, responsive comments that show continued interest in the Reviewer's stories. Once Listeners help Reviewers begin talking about their lives, the task is to keep them talking. Some Reviewers need little encouragement to talk; others need more. If needed, a well-placed word or two after the Reviewer pauses can elicit more information and feelings about that phase of life. This technique of minimally encouraging more conversation shows Reviewers that the Therapeutic Listener is tuned into the story and causes Reviewers to elaborate and take a more in-depth view of the life story being told.

Minimal encouragement means that Life Reviewers themselves should continue to control the story and the flow of the exchange. Therefore, words of encouragement should consist of short phrases. Repeating a key phrase that the Reviewer just said usually will achieve the desired result. Also, responsive phrases such as *"You took the train alone!"* or *"Then what happened?"* or *"Give me an example"* will keep the dialogue flowing. *"Umm-hmm"* is also useful to show that the Listener is paying attention, but too many "Umm-hmms" may make the Listener appear bored. Encouraging words keep Reviewers involved without taking the initiative away from them. It is important not to interrupt the Reviewer's recollections but rather to encourage the telling of the life story.

Summarizing. Summarizing is another useful interviewing technique. It is used often in most Life Reviews by restating the main points of what has been recalled by the Reviewer. Summarizing offers clarification to Reviewer and to Listener by stating what the Listener has heard so far. Summarizing is used particularly at the end of a session to clarify where the Review has been to date and where it should go next. Listeners may also summarize repeatedly during one session to clarify events as they are recalled, or Listeners may wait until the end of a visit and then summarize the entire session. As Listeners summarize, Reviewers can correct misperceptions or accept the summary as is, again providing both Listener and Reviewer with clarity. Listener summarizing also gives Reviewers an opportunity to rework a past event that may still be bothering them.

As Listeners summarize each session for Reviewers by clarifying what they have heard and restating it for the Reviewers' approval, Reviewers will learn the skill of summarizing themselves. Summarizing contributes to the ability to evaluate and to integrate and is used by both Reviewer and Listener in the last two sessions of the Structured Life Review process. A successful Life Review follows the process of summarizing a life, evaluating that life, and then accepting the life as it was lived. Reviewers who experience summarizing throughout the Review acquire the most skills to summarize and evaluate on their own.

Integrating. Integrating is an interviewing technique that consists of putting things together, reconciling, and making an acceptable whole of separate parts. This technique is most useful when a life story consists of disparate events that seem to have no clear point but yet are told with great energy and emotion by the Reviewer, showing that the story, difficult as it is to understand, means something important to the Reviewer. In the following example, watch the Listener weave various threads together, helping the Reviewer integrate his thoughts until both Reviewer and Listener understand the event.

> LISTENER: *"So you moved to another town as a teenager and didn't feel like you belonged there."*
>
> REVIEWER: *"Yes, yes, and all my brothers were football players."*
>
> LISTENER: *"You said you were bookish."*
>
> REVIEWER: *"I was bookish, and skinny, and didn't fit in."*
>
> LISTENER: *"Are you saying that you would have fit in better if you played football?"*
>
> REVIEWER: *"It was a football town; everyone went to the games except me."*
>
> LISTENER: *"At the time you missed not belonging as a football player, but I remember you talking about the Chess Club and about friends you made through the Drama Club. Did you feel like you belonged then?"*
>
> REVIEWER: *"I guess so."*
>
> LISTENER: *"So you belonged, but to a different group in a different way."*
>
> REVIEWER: *"I guess I did belong. I never thought about it that way."*

A fitting analogy to integrating events is to picture a tapestry. When one looks at the back, the tapestry is a tangle of threads with no visible picture. But when the tapestry is turned to the correct side, an obvious picture is present. The mass of tangled threads on the back is the life prior to the Review. The Life Review process, with the Therapeutic Listener as the tool, helps a lucid picture emerge. The Listener in the above example helped the Reviewer make a comprehensible and acceptable picture of what had previously been a group of incongruent, unhappy thoughts.

The Listener needs to help the Reviewer integrate when the Reviewer is telling a disconnected story filled with emotion but lacking apparent meaning. Follow the example of the Listener in the above vignette, repeating and connecting the Reviewer's sentences until a full picture emerges that the Reviewer recognizes and you both understand. Many skills are needed to help a Reviewer integrate, including summarizing, clarifying, and some reframing, before finally reaching an understanding of the story being told for both Listener and Reviewer.

> *The Listener needs to help the Reviewer integrate when the Reviewer is telling a disconnected story filled with emotion but lacking apparent meaning.*

Summary of Interviewing Techniques. The interviewing techniques we have presented will help make you a better Therapeutic Listener. Effective listening is the essence of a helpful partner in the Life Review process. These interviewing techniques are designed to assist the Reviewers to tell their life stories, to evaluate the past events, and finally to integrate them to reach Integrity. Practice these techniques daily, use them selectively in your Life Review sessions, and strive to be a true Therapeutic Listener. Note that even though your Life Reviewers may not be good Listeners themselves, do not let that become an issue for you. Concentrate on being the best Listener you can be.

Counseling Skills

This section presents five counseling skills important to the ongoing effectiveness of the Therapeutic Listener during the Life Review process and to the eventual overall success of the Life Review. Both the interviewing techniques described above and these counseling skills add to the Listener's proficiency when using the LRF and asking and answering questions. The following skills are more like behaviors that may be a natural part of a good Listener's repertoire, but if they are not instinctive, Listeners need to learn them to become effectual and efficient. Effective counselors incorporate these skills into their own practices as formal methods of counseling. It is worthwhile for Therapeutic Listeners to do so as well.

Counseling skills are behaviors that project caring and compassion to another person (the Reviewer) in a variety of ways. They are unconsciously a part of the behaviors used by most helping persons, especially those with experience. New Listeners can develop or sharpen these skills by putting personal values aside, even if Listeners are not in agreement with what the Reviewers are saying. These skills portray understanding and acceptance for the Reviewer and the Reviewer's recollections. They are best learned by example, perhaps through listening to more experienced Listeners use them in their practice and noting how they convey their compassion to the speaker—the Reviewer. By combining these skills with the preceding information on interviewing techniques, the Therapeutic Listener can develop the basic traits and behaviors needed to become an effective Listener. Each skill is described separately in the following text, so that the Listener will be able to understand all of the skills and then to use them together over the course of the Life Review process. These five skills, also defined in the box on page 50, are: Acceptance, Caring, Unconditional Positive Regard, Empathy, and Congruence.

Acceptance. Acceptance means to welcome and embrace the Reviewer while enjoying the opportunity to conduct a Life Review. Acceptance should be present and felt by the Reviewer during the entire Life Review. When you accept someone, you adjust to their deficiencies and reconcile yourself to their differences—like in long marriages and friendships. Acceptance may embody acquiescence if there are inherent differences between you and the Reviewer. As a Listener, it is your job to adjust to the Reviewer and put differences aside so the Life Review can be conducted therapeutically.

To be accepting, Listeners must be aware of their own prejudices. For example, if a Listener grew up in an alcoholic home, the Listener may have some difficulty listening to the Life Review of an alcoholic man who deserted his family and lost his job, but is now sober and proud of being sober, although he remains unremorseful despite the numerous losses he and his family experienced. If there is some known history in a Life Reviewer that is unacceptable to the Therapeutic Listener, the Listener should find someone else to conduct the Life Review who can be truly accepting and not bothered by the Reviewer's past. Therapeutic Listeners need to know themselves first, before trying to help others.

Caring. As a counseling skill, caring is characterized by feelings of concern, interest, and affection that one person manifests for another. Caring should be practiced during the entire Life Review process and should be a consistent part of the Therapeutic Listener's persona. Caring by the Listener embodies warmth, openness, giving, and an active interest and concern for the Life Reviewer. In a caring relationship, the Listener's interest and concern for the Reviewer must be readily apparent and genuine. The Listener should demonstrate a caring perceptiveness and responsiveness to the Reviewer's stories that builds trust and reinforces the mutual relationship between Listener and Reviewer. The Therapeutic Listener must genuinely care about the Life Reviewer as to what the Reviewer is saying, feeling, and doing; how comfortable the Reviewer is; and how the life story is progressing. The caring should be obvious from the Listener's words and actions toward the Reviewer. This skill really embodies all the other techniques and skills discussed in this chapter.

Unconditional Positive Regard. Unconditional positive regard is a warm, uplifting emotion projected toward the Life Reviewers and their stories, holding them in high esteem without reservation. The aura of acceptance inherent in unconditional positive regard should be present for all Reviewers all the time during the Structured Life Review process. Listeners must truly accept Reviewers and must manifest openness to the Reviewer's story. This attitude resembles one's unconditional love for a child. Unconditional positive regard shows positive feelings without judgment, limits, or valuation.

A separate examination of each word may contribute to understanding this counseling skill. "Unconditional" means no boundaries, limits, or restrictions; "positive" means hopeful, optimistic, and encouraging; "regard" means consideration, respect, and esteem. Therefore, if the Listener projects unconditional positive regard, there are no limitations on the Listener's positive respect for the Reviewer. The Reviewer must be made to feel free to say whatever comes to mind; the Listener will always respond in a receptive, encouraging manner.

> *Therapeutic Listeners need to know themselves first, before trying to help others.*

As with the other counseling skills, unconditional positive regard needs to be a continual part of the Listener's persona during a Life Review. The Listener needs to practice this skill when conversing with friends until it becomes second nature. If the Listener cannot feel open respect for the Reviewer, the Listener should not conduct the Life Review. Effective Therapeutic Listeners may have to submerge their own personal values and judgmental thinking if their values, in fact, are actually not the same as those of the Reviewer.

Empathy. Empathy is comprehending and sharing the feelings, thoughts, or experiences of another. Empathy requires a certain perception of another to be able to feel *with* the person instead of *for* that person. The Listener must feel and project the same feelings as the Reviewer during the ebb and flow of the Life Review. Often empathy is a natural reaction for a seasoned Listener or counselor and emerges in response to an emotional event in the speaker's life.

Many people confuse empathy with sympathy; perhaps, the concept of empathy is clearer when compared to sympathy. Sympathy is feeling pity or sorrow for another's losses without a true understanding of how those losses actually feel. Empathy is understanding *and* internalizing the losses from the Reviewer's viewpoint—not the Listener's viewpoint—and conveying this understanding to the Reviewer. Sympathy is more objective, whereas empathy is more subjective. In the Life Review, empathy requires appropriate listening and timely responses to reflect the Listener's feelings while sharing the Reviewer's emotions. Therefore, sympathy implies *"I am so sorry,"* and empathy implies *"I understand and I feel your pain."*

Examine your own feelings after a Review to see if you can identify what you were feeling when Reviewers told their stories: empathy or sympathy. Repeated self-examination regarding these skills and then continued practice in other settings with friends will help you develop empathy until it becomes second nature and you are a more effective Listener.

Congruence. Congruence is an agreement that is readily apparent to the Reviewer. By "agreement," we mean that the Listener matches and reflects back the Reviewer's mood, feelings, and intent.

Congruence implies real harmony and compatibility. To be congruent, you must be genuine and without façade, openly experiencing and responding to the feelings of the Reviewer when the life story is told. Your feelings must be accurate yet honest. When Therapeutic Listeners project congruence, Reviewers feel more harmonious with the Life Review situation. In other words, Listeners must be "one" with Reviewers. They match, they fit, and they are compatible in their thoughts.

> *Congruence occurs when Reviewers and Listeners are emotionally and intellectually engaged at many levels during the Life Review.*

Congruence also means listening to the story of the past while feeling the same emotions that Reviewers are projecting, or at least accepting those emotions. If the story is a sad one, feeling sadness with the Life Reviewer is appropriate for Listeners. The same is true for happiness, which is always enjoyed more when shared with another person. Congruence occurs when Reviewers and Listeners are emotionally and intellectually engaged at many levels during the Life Review.

The burden of generating congruence belongs to the Listener, who must try to understand the story from the Reviewer's viewpoint. It is a hard thing to do if this agreement is not naturally felt, but it is necessary for being therapeutic. Therapeutic Listeners cannot be congruent if they cannot understand the particular story of the Reviewer, from the Reviewer's viewpoint.

Sometimes, Listeners have to put their own value systems aside in order to be congruent. Consider a graduate nursing student who was an Army Officer guiding the story of an aging Lutheran minister's Live Review:

> *During World War II, I was the pastor for a German-speaking Lutheran Church in the Midwest. It was a rural community and the residents did not understand my parishioners, even though some of my parishioners had been citizens longer than their neighbors. My parishioners were devastated by their treatment at the hands of the community, so to cheer them up we held a drive for the War Effort, but we sent the money to the German Red Cross and played a trick on everyone.*

The student was very patriotic and to her the minister had committed an act like treason 60 years ago. But in telling the story, he thought it was funny and was proud that he had provided his parishioners with a diversion from the prejudice they were experiencing. The student, in the role of Listener, needed to put her patriotic thoughts aside and accept the minister's joy over his success. She needed to be congruent, to understand from the Reviewer's viewpoint, and to reflect his joy over his past cleverness. She was able to respond appropriately—congruently—leaving the minister with his pride. But she had to work through the incident many times for herself to believe she had done the right thing.

Summary of Counseling Skills. The purpose for emphasizing skills used by counselors is to enhance the Listeners' interactions and rapport with their Reviewers. These skills will help Listeners to relate to the variety of people with whom they will be working and to draw out those individuals' Life Review stories. Listeners must internalize these skill behaviors, practice them, and use them with Reviewers on a daily basis. They must continually evaluate their own behavior. Listeners will bond faster with Reviewers and earn their trust while seeking the therapeutic benefits of the Life Review process. Therefore, Listeners must be congruent with Reviewers, hold them in unconditional positive regard, accept them and their stories, show sincere empathy, and, most of all, be selflessly caring toward them.

Life Reviewers

The most important person in the Life Review is the Reviewer. The Reviewer is the focus of attention for the 8 weeks of the process. Normally, the process itself makes Reviewers feel special because someone is actually interested in what they have to say. But they can be made to feel even more special and important by an effective Therapeutic Listener using the skills and techniques described at the beginning of this chapter.

> *The process itself makes Reviewers feel special because someone is actually interested in what they have to say.*

In the past, Life Review has been an intervention primarily for older people, although presently that is no longer solely true. Younger groups now report enjoying reminiscence as well, though the Structured Life Review process is most applicable when the younger individuals have experienced a traumatic event or significant loss. Because most of our reviewers have been at least 50 years old, our examples and stories have been from that older age group. Older people usually enjoy telling their stories, particularly after they are retired and have more time to meet and reflect on the past. Most older people consider the Life Review a welcomed opportunity and believe they have something to say or teach to younger people because of their years of life and accumulated wisdom. They do not consider Life Review as therapy, and it is not meant to be therapy; however, in most instances, recalling a life is, in fact, therapeutic.

Because Life Review is a natural storytelling process, it engages older people who may be depressed but who refuse mental health services. Also, the relocations that older adults often experience—to nursing homes or smaller homes, or to live closer to adult children—can cause short-term situational depression. Consequently, Life Review can be very helpful for coping with change, such as being newly admitted to institutionalized settings. If new residents had an opportunity to talk about their lives as soon as they moved to more sheltered living, they would know one staff member intimately and the staff member would know about them and their needs. Reviewers would feel they had a friend, not to mention the therapeutic benefits gained by talking about and evaluating the past.

On the other hand, some Reviewers may be suspicious of the process when asked to talk about themselves, particularly if newly relocated. Some may refuse to participate because they really guard their privacy. Our most effective recruitment efforts have been through describing the Life Review to senior groups as a whole, anywhere groups gather—senior centers, churches, retirement homes—and then asking for voluntary participation.

If you work or volunteer in an assisted living facility or a nursing home, you have a ready population waiting to talk and to reap the benefits of Life Review. The process can be easily added to your repertoire. After you learn how to do a Life Review, you can modify the process so that it becomes a natural part of your work. For example, when working in a resident's room, instead of talking with a colleague about your last night's date, talk directly to the resident, asking about his or her life.

There are many potential reviewers out there who can benefit from this process and enjoy it. Reviewers come in all forms, are of all ages, and live in all settings. The main criterion is that they could benefit from reconciling parts or all of their past lives. Reviewers can be people who are depressed, lonely, sickly, or grieving. They can be individuals who recently experienced a trauma or a loss or a difficult change in their life, such as being fired, a death, a move, or a hospitalization. Any of these people can find therapeutic help from being guided through their lives by a caring, experienced Therapeutic Listener.

> *Reviewers come in all forms, are of all ages, and live in all settings.*

Types of Reviewers

There are as many types of Life Reviewers as there are types of people. Everyone tells their personal life stories in their own personalized way. The following description of Life Reviewers is not meant to label people's reminiscing abilities, but to make Listeners aware of the relevant differences among the people they will meet as Life Reviewers. Different sets of listening, counseling, and interviewing skills may be required for different types of Reviewers. The key is to strike a balance between allowing the Life Reviewer to be "in control" and having the Listener guide the Life Review in a structured way. For example, "Storyteller Reviewers" need only occasional encouragement to talk because they are in their element with a good captive Listener to talk to. The opposite is probably true for "Reluctant Reviewers," who may need to hear other people's anonymous stories to recall their own stories. The good Therapeutic Listener should be able to recognize the many types of Life Reviewers (see box on next page) so as to know what skills and techniques would be most helpful in conducting a particular Life Review. A complete description of each type of Reviewer follows.

The Storyteller. The storyteller is a Reviewer who enjoys talking about life and who uses many examples to illustrate important events. Some might call the storyteller long-winded, and such a Reviewer could become a problem in a group where time for talking needs to be shared. Storyteller types make it easy for a Therapeutic Listener to conduct a Life Review. It is almost as if the storyteller has been lying in wait for the opportunity to talk. When opportunity knocks, the storyteller makes the most of it. The true storyteller can expound on any topic, usually in an entertaining way.

The challenge presented by storytellers is to keep them talking along the developmental structure of the Life Review. Storytellers can easily divert the Therapeutic Listener to the point where the Listener may no longer be structuring the Life Review

Types of Reviewers

Storyteller: Reviewer who enjoys talking about life and who uses many examples to illustrate events

Reluctant Reviewer: Reviewer who communicates with terse comments and replies; not used to socializing or talking about the past

External Reviewer: Reviewer who talks freely of past events but not about personal past events

Creative Reviewer: Reviewer whose identity and memory have been influenced by what he or she wished was true; often not aware of creating discrepant stories

Denying Reviewer: Reviewer who wishes to block out a traumatic past event by refusing to acknowledge its existence

Bleeding Reviewer: Reviewer who believes that his or her life has been exceedingly difficult and continues to feel self-pity

and the process becomes a mere one-sided conversation. Storytellers can also omit or evade the personal and evaluative part of the Life Review while they are entertaining their audience. Although the Listener may be enjoying both the Review and Reviewer immensely, there is a time when interruption may be necessary. The Therapeutic Listener should insert various probes into the story such as, *"How did that make you feel"* or *"Tell me more about the effect that had on you,"* to focus on the evaluative part of the Life Review rather than just continuing the entertaining story.

The second challenge for a Therapeutic Listener with a storyteller is to get the storyteller through the entire Life Review—and each developmental stage of life—in 6 to 8 weeks. The developmental stages are the important parts of the structure, facilitated by the questions on the LRF. Addressing each developmental stage assures an attempted recall of the entire life span up until the present. No stages are avoided and left out, which people tend to do when a particular stage is painful or embarrassing, or otherwise difficult to share.

If it looks like answers to every question will be long, drawn-out responses, the Listener needs to preselect one question each week and start the visit with that one question. For example, the following technique might work best with storytellers: Week 1: *"What is your earliest memory?"* Week 2: *"Tell me about your family."* Week 3: *"Was your marriage a good one?"* Week 4: *"Tell me about your work."* Week 5: *"What was your biggest disappointment?"* Week 6: *"Tell me about your proudest moment."* These particular preselected questions will address every developmental phase and should cover life's important events and decisions, but keep the LRF by your side in case you need backup questions.

Other techniques, such as moving on to another subject by interrupting the story, can also guide Reviewers through their entire life. But interruption is a less favorable technique because it might project a lack of interest in the present ongoing story. The key issue for the Therapeutic Listener with a storyteller is to assure that the Reviewer achieves ongoing insight and evaluation, while moving the review along its developmental stages within 6 weeks. Listeners who keep this issue in the forefront of their minds—while listening—will conduct a successful Life Review.

The Reluctant Reviewer. The Reluctant Reviewer is one who communicates mainly with terse comments and replies, if at all. This type of Reviewer often does not naturally socialize, nor does this Reviewer generally talk easily about the past. The Reluctant Reviewer is somewhat the opposite of the storyteller. This Reviewer may agree to do a Life Review but then find it hard to give more than one-word answers to questions. This Life Reviewer does not elaborate easily and both the Reviewer and the Listener find it hard work to process the Life Review.

A possible stereotypical composite of the Reluctant Reviewer may be a man who lives alone, has no family, and is not used to social conversation. Everyone has met these kinds of individuals, often living in single-room hotels or high-rise apartments where they do not interact with others and are never called upon to socialize. Therapeutic Listeners need to be aware of these hidden, potential Reviewers, so that they find them and draw them out. Listeners offer socialization through this reminiscence process and, perhaps, the Reluctant Reviewer's socialization can continue with others when the Life Review is complete. Therapeutic Listeners must keep in mind that Reluctant Reviewers, although appearing reticent, will gain as much from the Life Review as Storyteller Reviewers do, and may gain even more than others as they are drawn out into a more sociable existence.

If the Life Reviewer appears reluctant, it is helpful to have some prior history with which to work. A brief personal history (including place of birth, work life, and so forth) can be obtained in one short conversation. If the Listener is working in or with an assisted living facility, this information can be obtained from the admission paperwork. Even a short oral history provides useable material when trying to start a conversation. For example, an older person brought up in New York City will have different life experiences than one who was brought up in the rural South. Therefore, to the city person, conversation about the subway will be natural, whereas to a person from the rural South, responding to stories about the subway will have no reminiscent effect because he or she will not know or care what the Listener is saying or asking about riding the subways.

It also is helpful to use memorabilia from the past that might strike a responsive chord in a Reluctant Reviewer. Old postcards, photos, and pictures are particularly effective. Those about the local areas where the reviewer has lived often initiate memories. Those of well-known sites, such as the Empire State Building in New York City, can be useful in recalling vacations or stories about the sites. Old, famous pictures from the Reviewer's young adulthood can cause memories to surface. As the memories rise to the top, the Reluctant Reviewer will tend to become more open and participate in more dialogue. Because it is more difficult for the Therapeutic Listener to elicit a reluctant story, the Life Reviewer's enjoyment is not as immediately evident. However, it will happen with persistence and imagination.

The External Reviewer. The External Reviewer is one who talks freely of past events but not from a personal perspective. Thus, it may be difficult to get personalized insight about such a Reviewer's "Self." If the Life Review is not about a personal life, it will not be therapeutic. Because of the absence of Self, the External Reviewer is reciting history but not participating in a personalized Life Review. One Reviewer said her Mother told her that it was rude to keep talking about herself. Others also may not draw themselves into the Life Review because their parents and teachers told them not to talk about themselves so much. Moreover, many Reviewers are surprised when Listeners ask them to talk about their lives because they believe their lives are inconsequential or boring. Thus, with an External Reviewer, the Therapeutic Listener may be dealing with long-term learned behavior and beliefs that inhibit conversation and insight about oneself. With continuous gentle reminders, Listeners must help such Reviewers to unlearn the hesitant behavior and teach them to talk about themselves throughout the Life Review.

Listeners must keep in mind that the Reviewer's personalized Self, together with the Reviewer's particular life events, are the focus of the Life Review. Accordingly, Listeners must be relentless in their pursuit of the Reviewer's involvement in the life story. Therapeutic Listeners can learn certain techniques to draw out life stories of Self in conjunction with the life's events. For example, the Listener can ask about notable historical events. Most Americans of a certain age remember the day the Challenger missile exploded on its designated mission, or the occasion of the man walking on the moon, or most recently 9/11. External Reviewers may recall these events objectively, as observers, but Therapeutic Listeners with appropriate rejoinders can help Life Reviewers become more subjective and more personalized when they talk about the events. You want to know what these events meant to them personally, so you need to ask where they were at the time, who they were with, if they were frightened, and so forth.

A historical time line of key events is helpful to give the Listener some ideas about new topics for discussion. Also, the well-used probe *"How did that make you feel?"* can be used more than once and tends to elicit a personal answer. Each time the External Reviewer comments on an event too objectively, the Listener should question the meaning for the Reviewer and cause the Reviewer to elaborate. Eventually, the External

Reviewer will automatically make himself or herself a part of the discussion. Finally, the use of self-disclosure on the Listener's part can set an example for the Life Reviewer.

The Creative Reviewer. Creative Reviewers embellish the truth more than is necessary, but they are probably not deliberately lying. They believe what they are saying is a true rendition of the facts, even though at times their Life Reviews are really works of fiction.

> *The life story is the Reviewer's story as the Reviewer apparently sees it and wishes to tell it.*

A Creative Reviewer is a Life Reviewer whose identity and memory have been influenced by what they wished was true. Creative Reviewers enjoy and benefit from the Life Reviews as much as other types of Reviewers, even with their fictionalized stories. Creative Reviewers may overstate their stories for different reasons—perhaps because the past is too difficult to share or perhaps because it is just more fun to present an exciting story. Regardless of the reasons for embellishing stories, the accuracy of the story is not important. The life story is the Reviewer's story as the reviewer apparently sees it and wishes to tell it.

Many people actually see past events differently when examining them from their present position than they did in the past. When such Reviewers complete the Life Review, the view from the present may change again, especially with reframing, which causes them to judge events differently than they did before. For example, recall the mother who felt guilty for working when she had school-age children. With her working reframed as an opportunity for her children to get a college education rather than as an incident of neglect, her belief in herself changed, and in the future that story of her working life probably will be felt and told differently.

The point in describing Creative Reviewers here is mainly to acknowledge their existence and to point out that truth is not essential to a successful Life Review; people sometimes make their own truth. By the time they are older, Creative Reviewers may have thought of and told their stories so many times (if only to themselves) that the fiction seems truer than the facts, and they themselves believe the revised version. Therapeutic Listeners should not waste time trying to discern the truth; they should instead encourage a Structured Evaluative Life Review to take place. This will best serve the Reviewer.

The Denying Reviewer. The Denying Reviewer is one who tries to block out traumatic past events by refusing to acknowledge their existence. Such denial is prevalent at the start of a Life Review when the participants are strangers. Occasionally, Reviewers will correct their stories around Week 4, after bonding has taken place and the Reviewer can trust and feel comfortable with the Therapeutic Listener. Contrary to general psychotherapy, Life Review believes it is okay for Reviewers to hide what they don't want to discuss. Granted, the Life Review might be more therapeutic if traumatic issues were addressed, but Reviewers should be able to control the content of the Life Review. Life Reviewers need to discuss only issues that they raise themselves. Listeners can ask about issues that Reviewers raise or seem to raise, but Listeners should not persist if Reviewers desist.

The Denying Reviewer is different from the Creative Reviewer in that the Denying Reviewer is deliberately hiding something and knows it. These Denying Reviewers will talk about wonderful parents and happy times when asked about their childhood, when, in fact, childhood was not that happy. Their stories may be an old defense mechanism that they have used to serve a personal purpose. Denial sometimes serves many people well. However, around the fourth visit during the discussion of adulthood, when trust has been established with the Listener, some Denying Reviewers may start referring to their childhood as not so ideal. In raising the possibility of an unhappy childhood, they open the door for the Therapeutic Listener to re-explore the Reviewer's childhood and its traumas more fully. Instead of proceeding on with adulthood questions, the Listener needs to refer back to childhood and ask Reviewers to elaborate on their latest disclosure. At such a point, Reviewers who finally feel trust may unload a lifetime of bad childhood memories, or even later-life situations, and Listeners need to encourage such discourse until Reviewers are finished, before moving on to the next phase of the Review.

On the other hand, what does the Therapeutic Listener do if there is no disclosure and the protective fences remain in place? The answer is nothing. Continue with the normal Life Review. Enjoy the story as the Denying Reviewer wants to tell it and help the Denying Reviewer to protect those defenses.

The Bleeding Reviewer. Bleeding Reviewers believe their lives were exceedingly difficult. They feel sorry for themselves and continue to talk about their difficulties, possibly looking for reinforcement, and certainly looking for sympathy. Research describes their use of memory as "bitterness revival," remaining obsessed about disturbing events in the past (Webster, 1993). Bleeding Reviewers would probably benefit from professional therapy but have never taken the opportunity to seek it. Often, the best outcome of a Life Review with Bleeding Reviewers is their personal recognition of their need for therapy. Effective Therapeutic Listeners can assist them in gaining such insight. At any rate, from talking about their lives for 6 weeks, they begin to see the number of despairing thoughts they have and begin to see their need for more intense work to change their thinking.

Because Bleeding Reviewers often have in fact lived difficult lives, there may be reasons for their negative attitudes, and they may need to be seen by someone more qualified than a Therapeutic Listener. Bleeding Reviewers report problems that range from being abused or neglected as a child or adult, to not being a favored child, or other unusual circumstances. The amount of pain that accompanies their disclosures is dependent on the individual, but often it is a pain they have been carrying for a long time. Many Bleeding Reviewers wait for someone to listen to them so as to give their burden away. They may literally meet you at the door on each arrival and immediately start talking about troublesome life events. Having the opportunity to talk about and examine their past in a

> *Keep listening; you may be the best thing that has happened for this Reviewer in a long time.*

Life Review is usually tremendously beneficial to Bleeding Reviewers. Nevertheless, they usually need more help than a Listener can give them. If they trust their Therapeutic Listener, they will follow the Listener's direction to seek more professional help.

What else should you do for this Reviewer? The answer is listen. Do not give up. Do not leave. Keep listening; you may be the best thing that has happened for this Reviewer in a long time and although you may not feel therapeutic, you are serving the Reviewer well. The problem here may be that the burdens are too great for you to listen to each week. In that event, be sure to seek supervision for yourself so that you can share this weight with someone else. But stay the course until the end of the 8-week session.

Conclusion

It is obvious that different people are, in fact, different. You must be ready for them and adapt the skills, techniques, and descriptions that have been presented in this chapter. If you are a prepared Therapeutic Listener, you can successfully implement the Life Review process and bring its positive results to all types of Life Reviewers. Try your skills using the guidelines presented in Part II.

PART II
CONDUCTING THE
STRUCTURED LIFE REVIEW

Visit 1

GETTING STARTED

*It is the province of knowledge to speak
and it is the privilege of wisdom to listen.*

—OLIVER W. HOLMES, SR.

This chapter discusses the important tasks to complete before beginning the actual Life Review process. Preparation is essential. The better you prepare before beginning, and before each weekly session, the more you can focus on what is most important: the Life Reviewer and the Reviewer's story.

Preparation includes:

- Meeting the prospective Life Reviewer
- Assessing the location for the sessions
- Assessing the Life Reviewer's physical, functional, and mental status
- Arranging subsequent sessions

Meeting the Prospective Life Reviewer

It is probable that you will be meeting the Life Reviewer in person for the first time. First impressions are important! You are laying the foundation for a significant relationship with the Reviewer. You want to start building a bond and trust. You must be prepared. It is recommended that you read this entire Handbook before beginning so that you can accurately describe what the Reviewer needs to know of the process and be prepared for any questions. You must be confident, gracious, and knowledgeable. In a word, you must be PREPARED!

Appendix A provides a checklist for the entire process, including this first visit. Before meeting the Reviewer, study and check off the list. Bring the necessary equipment and business/appointment cards. Be ready to assess the probable location site for the subsequent sessions and be ready to assess the prospective Reviewer's mental and functional condition. At the first meeting, you will need to give the prospect a full disclosure of the Life Review process so that the Reviewer can make an informed decision about agreeing to participate further.

Full Disclosure

Full disclosure is one of your first tasks because Reviewers may choose not to participate in the Life Review process after being fully informed. By taking care of this task first, Listeners may save everyone some time. Ideally, Reviewers need to know exactly what to expect in the coming weeks. The best way to fully inform Reviewers of the complete process is to share a copy of the Life Review Form (LRF) (see Appendix B) while talking to Reviewers about the overall process. The LRF also serves as a guideline for future meetings. The LRF includes the types of questions and topics that the Therapeutic Listener (you) will ask the Life Reviewer to discuss. As Reviewers read the LRF, they can decide if any of the questions are too invasive. If their assessment is that the questions or the answers are too private, they may choose not to participate. You should be prepared to negotiate a bit by taking a flexible approach with the prospective Reviewer. You may need to clarify the Reviewer's hesitation or objections and see if you and the Reviewer can work around them. If the candidate appears adamant or unsure, you should nicely put the ultimate question to that person: *"Do you wish to participate or not?"* Then, abide by the Reviewer's decision.

Various people respond to the LRF in a variety of ways. Some people do not bother to read it at all. They may just be looking for company and are glad to be considered for the activity of Life Review, or they may have other similar reasons. Other individuals are more particular and wary about sharing memories of their private lives, especially if they have been carrying "secrets" around for years. Still others respond to the LRF in their own personal way. For example, one Reviewer, a schoolteacher, took the LRF and later wrote out her answers on the form, presenting it to the Listener during the next visit as though it were a "homework assignment"! That was her way of doing things. The Listener handled this turn of events by accepting the form and then saying that she still would like to visit and spend time with the schoolteacher. The Life Review visits began and the process continued for 6 weeks with occasional reference to the answers already given on the form. Both Listener and Reviewer enjoyed the visits immensely, as do most people!

Written Agreement

Some form of written agreement between Listener and Reviewer regarding participation in the Life Review process would be helpful to both. When the Life Review is conducted as a research intervention, Reviewers must sign an informed consent sheet giving researchers permission to conduct the Life Review. Many therapists also have their clients sign an agreement to participate in therapy. For Life Review, such a signed sheet makes the ensuing process clear to both Listener and Reviewer and serves as an informal contract concerning the agreed upon process. This document will appear to protect both Listener and Reviewer. The agreement should state that Reviewers can drop out of the process at any time; however, once the process has begun, it is to the Reviewer's advantage to complete the process. The signed agreement will probably serve as a deterrent to dropping out before the Review is completed. A sample agreement form is provided in Appendix C.

Audiotaping

If you intend to tape the sessions, permission to tape must be obtained from Reviewers in writing and/or recorded on the tape by Reviewers themselves. One advantage to audiotaping is that the tapes provide a memory prompt for Listeners. Listeners can review the preceding visit before the next Life Review visit and recall important comments made by Reviewers. Sometimes just the tone of the tape provides additional insight to Listeners before making the next Life Review visit. Permission to tape should be obtained during this first visit before the Life Review begins. Therefore, if the Reviewer gives permission, turn on the recorder and confirm permission: "*Mr. ___, I understand that you consent to my taping our visits. Is that correct?*"

If Reviewers refuse to have their visits taped, then their wishes must be respected and the Life Review will take place without being recorded. There are many reasons for them not wanting to record a Life Review. For example, Reviewers may fear a permanent record of their conversation, so they must be assured of the anonymity of the tapes and the confidentiality of the entire process. Also, if they are uncomfortable with a tape recording but consent anyway, they may be unable to disclose freely and the presence of the tape recorder will affect the quality of the Life Review. You must decide which way to proceed. For some, being taped may seem like having another person listening in to the dialogue. Others may refuse, but don't know why—they just don't want it. If you sense that the Reviewer might reconsider the initial refusal to having the sessions taped, you can revisit this subject again to try for permission in a subsequent session during the actual Life Review.

Whether Reviewers consent or refuse to tape, Therapeutic Listeners should not take notes during the Life Review process, because note taking is distracting to Reviewers. They may feel that they do not have your full attention, and they are correct. However, Listeners should make notes immediately after each visit so they will remember the high points of the past visit to use as prompts for the next visit.

If Reviewers agree to the taping, Listeners should place a small recorder on a table or chair as close to the Reviewer as possible to clearly record the Reviewer's comments, including the consent to be taped. Listeners should also check for background noise, such as the playing of the television or radio, and make sure the environment is as quiet as possible. If there is a television playing, the Listener can ask to use another room or ask permission to turn off the TV. Turn the recorder on during this first session and check later to make sure you clearly hear both voices being taped. Experience has shown that once the recorder is put in place, both Listeners and Reviewers will generally forget about the recorder. An advantage to taping is that if the recorder beeps at the end of the hour, it serves as a timer, becoming a good reminder for both participants to end the 1-hour session.

Business Cards

You, as the Therapeutic Listener, should leave a business card with the now confirmed prospective Reviewer at the end of your first visit. The cards should include: the name of the Listener, your telephone number, place of business or sponsoring agency, and a blank line to write in the next appointment time and date. If Listeners do not have business cards, they can make appointment cards with the same information on 3 × 5–inch index cards to leave with Reviewers. Index cards may even be better because they are larger and easier to see and read. (Use large printing.) Each week you should leave a new card with the next appointment time.

There are many advantages to using these cards. If Reviewers are in a nursing home or assisted living facility, the card can inform them and others of the coming event; it is helpful to leave a copy with staff, or at least tell them of the next appointment. Staff who see the card usually make sure the Reviewer is ready and dressed for the next time the Listener visits. Families often call the number on the card to ask the Listener questions about the Life Review process. Finally, the card acts as a reminder to Reviewers who might otherwise easily forget an appointment with a Listener. Even Listeners who are employed as staff within an institution should use reminder cards to prompt Reviewers' memories and to help them look forward to the next Life Review session. Anticipation of an event is often the most enjoyable part of it. Finally, you need to make yourself a similar card or use an appointment book. Don't forget your appointment; they are commitments.

Tests and Measures

Researchers use some form of evaluation to show the therapeutic effects of their intervention. These are also helpful to practitioners, who can use them to measure their client's progress and change over time. Research tests that have shown positive therapeutic changes as a result of a Life Review intervention include tests for physical and cognitive function and mood, to name a few. Samples of these measures are presented in Appendixes E and F. These paper-and-pencil tests are easy to use and the results are readily apparent.

If Therapeutic Listeners choose to use paper-and-pencil tests as a way to assess Reviewers before starting the Life Review, then the first visit is the time to give one or more of them as pretests. Identical tests that are given again after the visits are completed are usually referred to as posttests. By subtracting the pretest score from the posttest score, Listeners will have a tangible piece of evidence attesting to the value of the Life Review. The difference in scores is the *change score,* which provides an objective measure of the Reviewer's progress in response to the process. Research has shown that change is often greater 6 months after the intervention than right after the completion of the Life Review, so consider revisiting the Reviewer to posttest again after 6 months.

Before using paper-and-pencil tests, talk to the Reviewer about the tests and explain their purpose. Then, give a copy to the Reviewer to study for a few minutes and to ask questions if there are any. Next, read the questions, with the Reviewer following along, and mark the Reviewer's answers on your copy of the test. If the Reviewer is not certain about the answer to give, discuss it and mark down the compromise. Do this for both the pretest and for the posttest. When you compare the pre- and posttests and get results, you should share the results with the Reviewer, either in person or through the mail. Reviewers generally are very interested in the outcomes and will be more eager to cooperate with the testing if they understand the reason for it and then are informed of the results.

Of course, the Life Review produces many changes—some are easily measured and others are not. Many Listeners find it helpful to make notes about the Reviewer right after their first visit, so that they can later note perceived changes in the Reviewer's general well-being over time. Appearance, grooming, activity levels, conversation, and improved appetite would all signify improvement of well-being in many elderly people. The change in Marjory, described in the Background chapter, is a good example of profound change that is not easily measured. In Marjory's case, the Listener subjectively noted great change from the first visit to the last and had notes to track these changes. Therefore, even though Marjory had no objective outcome measures, her improvement in well-being was notable and recorded in that Therapeutic Listener's notes. A quick checklist to ascertain a Reviewer's well-being at the initial visit is provided in Appendix D. This assessment may be used when beginning the Life Review and again when the Life Review is complete.

> *The Life Review produces many changes—some are easily measured and others are not.*

Assessing the Environment

The Listener should assess both the surroundings and the individual Reviewer before beginning the Life Review. Ideally, the visit site should be private and comfortable, conducive to an effective Life Review. However, Listeners may meet with Reviewers in a variety of places—assisted living sites, nursing homes, offices, Reviewers' homes, or the homes of their families—and these locations may not always be suitable. Because of such diversity in sites, Listeners must pay close attention to selecting and controlling the best possible environment for conducting the Life Review. If meeting with a Reviewer in an institutional living facility, you must first gain permission from that facility to conduct a Life Review on their premises before approaching the Reviewer for permission. Also, perhaps search out one or more possible sites in advance.

Reviewer capabilities and differences can influence the selection of a location as well. Changes in vision and hearing can cause problems for some Reviewers in certain locations. Environmental noise, even background noises made by an air conditioner, for instance, can make a huge difference in the ability of the compromised individual to hear conversation. Those with sensory hearing loss will have a greater problem blocking out environmental or ambient noises. Thus it is necessary for Listeners to assess both the environment and the Reviewer in light of the following criteria.

Privacy

Privacy is key to encouraging confidentiality and developing trust. The Life Review should be conducted as privately as possible, away from spouses or caregivers at home and away from other residents in congregate living sites. If the Listener presents the need for privacy to the family members sharing the same location at home, the family will usually comply with the Listener's request for privacy by leaving the Reviewer and Listener alone to talk in private. Or, a family member may leave the house for an hour to run errands or do some grocery shopping. In a congregate environment, finding privacy is even more difficult than finding privacy at home. However, in such a communal site, privacy is even more important. Privacy is such an important factor that it behooves Listeners to take their time in finding an appropriate site that will provide this privacy. The site should also add to feelings of warmth and trust that are sure to develop during the Review.

Light

Light is as important to ambience as it is to actual vision during the Life Review. Without an inviting light, a site can look cold and sterile and be very unappealing, inhibiting the Life Reviewer. The Life Review room should be comfortably lit with soft-white or daylight bulbs in table lamps. Table lamps generally make a setting warm, comfortable, and inviting, providing a sense of coziness and intimacy.

Conversely, fluorescent lighting is cold and uninviting and causes overhead glare. Glare is particularly important to consider when working with older people, because they can be blinded by glare. For Reviewers with cataracts, glare can actually cause so much temporary blindness that the Reviewer may not be able to see the face of the Listener. Always ask the Reviewers if they can see you clearly enough to make out your smile. In a Life Review, the Listener's facial expressions provide a great deal of feedback, so it is important for the Reviewer to be able to see the Listener's face. Additionally, Reviewers should always be seated with their backs to the windows to avoid blinding glare from the daylight. Managing light and glare is an important preliminary task for Listeners.

> *Always ask the Reviewers if they can see you clearly enough to make out your smile.*

Noise Level

We emphasize the importance of managing the noise level. Excessive noise is such an annoying and important environmental drawback that the Listener needs to anticipate it. Undue background noise is so common and widespread that we rarely notice it. For example, in stores, background music is usually playing continually, but we don't really hear it. When we hear a car alarm go off, we just ignore it and attribute the noise to malfunction. People keep the radio or television on for company and forget that it is playing. Background noise is everywhere, but for our purposes it should be eliminated if possible. When there is noise in the background, it is more difficult for Listeners and Reviewers to hear the spoken word unless voices are raised, which is not desirable. The sounds of speech and background noise blend together and both become indistinct. People who suffer sensorineural hearing loss are the most affected by extra background noise.

Noise is a not just a distracter to the Reviewer and Listener, but it is especially detrimental when taping the Life Review. With music or a game playing on the radio or television in the background, it is difficult to get clear tape recordings. Additionally, if the Life Review is going on with noise in the background, Reviewers may tend to pay attention to that noise, becoming distracted from telling their story. Once distracted, it is difficult to refocus on the topic or memory at hand. Interruptions of any kind are detrimental to the flow of the Life Review. So before the actual Life Review is begun, the Therapeutic Listener needs to clear the area of as much noise as possible by silencing the TV, radio, and background music or by moving to a quieter spot.

Unless you are visiting a person living at home alone, the problem of potential noise during the time of the visit will exist and you need to anticipate and be aware of it when choosing the best time and place to meet. In a communal facility, noise is much more prevalent and presents a more pervasive problem. For example, the institution's dining room appears to provide a big empty space, with moveable tables and chairs, and is deserted when it is not mealtime. In a densely populated facility, the empty dining room seems an ideal place for a private Life Review. Despite the emptiness, there is the noise and odors of meal preparation before mealtimes, and after mealtimes there is the cleanup noise and the noise of dishwashers in the background. These noises can be as distracting as other people talking. Listeners need to check their potential location choices at various times during the day, because seemingly quiet places may get noisy at other particular times, especially in communal living facilities. In such places, you may want to ask the staff if there is a more quiet or private room where you and the Reviewer can talk.

Temperature

The temperature of the chosen Life Review setting should be comfortable for the Reviewer. Older people feel changes in temperature more acutely than younger people. Often, what seems comfortable to the Listener may be too extreme for a Reviewer. For example, a comfortably air-conditioned seating area may seem too cold to an older person and will require adjustment to make the older person more comfortable. If Listeners have no way to adjust the temperature, then they should bring an extra blanket or sweater with them in case the Reviewer gets chilly. Similar adjustments must be made if it is too warm, and then a quiet portable fan may cool the air enough, providing it does not blow directly on the Reviewer or make too much noise. It is advisable to check the Reviewer's opinion of the temperature periodically to keep the Reviewer comfortable throughout.

Seating Arrangement

Seating arrangement is central to a smooth-flowing dialogue between Reviewer and Listener. Chairs should be comfortable and placed near one another to enhance hearing, especially for the Reviewer. Listeners should be sitting in front of Reviewers, face to face, so that Reviewers can see the Listeners' facial expressions as they talk. Good Therapeutic Listeners can demonstrate acceptance and interest through their facial expressions as well as through their body movements, showing attentiveness by leaning forward to hear Reviewers better. Because many effective counseling skills are partially demonstrated through body movements and facial expressions, these need to be clearly seen by the Reviewer. Consequently, the seating arrangement can enhance or detract from the dialogue and the effectiveness of a Life Review.

Often in nursing homes and hospital rooms there are not two comfortable chairs facing each other in the Reviewer's room. There may only be a bed and one chair. Since the bed belongs to the patient, but may not be comfortable for an hour of talk, Listeners need to make arrangements for meeting in an alternative location. If the Reviewer is unable to move, then the Listener needs to assure the Reviewer's comfort in the bed before beginning the Review each week or give the comfortable chair to the Reviewer and bring in a straight chair that will enable the Listener to face the Reviewer. With prior planning, Listeners can prepare the most comfortable spot possible within the confines of the environment.

It is also important to remember that wheelchairs are not comfortable for sitting for long periods. Although they may look comfortable and have the advantage of ease in arranging their placement, they are often not comfortable. Normally there is no back support and the seat is usually a leather strip that contours to the body without support or cushion. Many Reviewers sit in their wheelchairs for long periods of time, but they are usually traveling around and moving when on their own. It is a lot harder to sit still in a wheelchair for an hour. Therefore, when preparing for the Life Review, it will be best to help Reviewers transfer to a comfortable lounge chair with a pillow at their back and their feet raised on a stool.

Assessing the Life Reviewer

Assessing the Life Reviewer is as important as assessing the environment. As stated earlier, aging can interfere with a Reviewer's ability to concentrate and comprehend, which in turn affects intimate conversation. It is important to be familiar with the abilities of each Reviewer in order to individually adjust for lost capabilities. Keeping a record in a file or on a small index card for each Reviewer will serve as a reminder of a Reviewer's individual needs. (See also Appendix D.)

Patterns and Habits

Your respect for the Reviewer's daily habits and patterns can contribute to your success or failure as a Listener when conducting a Life Review. Before starting the Life Review, Listeners need to assess the Reviewer's living patterns. For instance, a Reviewer may be in the habit of taking an afternoon nap. Not wanting to give up the

> *Be familiar with the abilities of each Reviewer in order to individually adjust for lost capabilities.*

nap, the Reviewer may refuse to participate in an afternoon visit or become resentful if the Listener shows up in the afternoon for a Life Review session. Other considerations include television habits, scheduled phone calls, visits from family, and even sporting events. Listeners need to remain open to whatever is important to Reviewers and make adjustments in the subsequent visiting schedule that will accommodate the Reviewers' choices. This first week is a good time to inquire about the Reviewer's daily and preferred schedule. You can check about the schedule with your Reviewer and with the family or the facility's staff.

In addition to the individual's patterns, knowing the pattern and schedule of nursing homes and assisted living facilities is just as important. A successful Listener needs the support of the surrounding environment and of the people who work or live there. Many nursing homes have very busy mornings, and staff would not welcome a visitor on the premises as they struggle to complete the baths and feedings assigned to them. However, once the required chores are complete, staff will welcome a diversion for their residents and will be more willing to participate in readying the resident for a Life Review visit. The tactful

> *Respect for the Reviewer's daily habits and patterns can contribute to your success or failure as a Listener.*

Listener needs to ask in advance and work cooperatively with the nursing home personnel to conduct a successful Life Review visit. Consultation and cooperation with personnel on site means that you care about the staff's schedule as well as your own and respect staff needs to complete assignments.

Functional Abilities

A functional assessment examines the Reviewer's abilities to perform certain necessary daily tasks in multiple domains. Knowing the functional abilities of your Reviewer enables you to plan for the help needed, if any, to get ready for a visit. If your Reviewer is highly functional and can travel and drive a car or ride a bus or taxi, then little help is needed to prepare the person for a Life Review visit. You might even meet in your office. Function can be assessed with valid paper-and-pencil measures that test basic activities of daily living as well as instrumental activities of daily living. Selected measures for you to use are given in Appendixes D–F.

Physical Function. Physical function is not a measure of illness or health but instead measures an individual's ability to perform the necessary activities of daily living to function independently. For example, someone in a nursing home may be unable to walk or transfer from bed to chair. Therefore, that Reviewer will need assistance to prepare for a Life Review visit. The availability of staff to help the Reviewer get ready will influence the start time and duration of the visit. Those living at home probably can still care for their personal needs but may be unable to drive or cook. The physical functional assessment for these individuals should measure the Reviewers' ability to manage their own lives, which may also influence the future visits (see Appendix E).

Mental Function. Mental function includes both cognitive abilities and psychosocial status, which in turn can influence all other functions. Reviewers may conceal the status of these mental functions, and therefore they are difficult to assess without targeted paper-and-pencil tests. The most difficult functional loss to recognize through ordinary observation and conversation is the loss of cognitive mental function. Because of this difficulty in determining an individual's cognitive status, you should do a baseline assessment on all Reviewers, especially if they seem forgetful and unable to focus on your conversation. A baseline assessment tests people as they are when you meet them and provides you with a good picture of the Reviewer's present capabilities—information that helps you to know where to start and how to proceed in the Life Review. The tool to measure general functioning at baseline is provided in Appendix D.

Cognitive Function. Cognitive function is the part of mental functioning that includes the ability to think, to remember, and to process thoughts clearly. Routine testing for cognitive status allows Listeners to determine a Reviewer's cognitive losses that are not obviously apparent but can be measured with paper-and-pencil measures created to test mental status. The Mini-Mental State Exam (MMSE) is the standard for evaluation of cognitive status and can easily be given to everyone. The MMSE provides an objective measure of cognitive function during this first preparation visit (see Folstein et al., 1975).

Psychosocial Functions. Psychosocial functions include depression, mood, and general well-being, to name a few. Depression is the most common psychosocial problem for older people. Older people most often experience minor depression, which generally affects their response to life and interactions with others, possibly leading to isolation and further depression. In minor depression, there is a great deal of denial leading to refusal to recognize that there may be a problem. Many older people believe that depression is a weakness, so they try to conceal it. If your Reviewer appears depressed, a paper-and-pencil test is helpful to assess the presence and amount of depression the Reviewer may be feeling. The short-form Geriatric Depression Scale is helpful for assessment (see Appendix F).

Medications

Medication information is important because some medications can interfere with the process of Life Review. Some medications cause drowsiness requiring the Reviewer to nap after taking the medication. Other medications, such as diuretics, may cause Reviewers to interrupt the Life Review to use the bathroom. People who are experiencing great amounts of pain will not be attentive to reviewing their lives unless they are medicated. Thus, Listeners can plan better visits if they know about the Reviewer's needs and schedule for medications.

The easiest way to learn about Reviewer medication is to ask Reviewers directly. Ask them to get all their prescription drugs to show you the bottles and to tell you how and why they take them. If you or they do not know what the medications are, jot down the name of the medication and look it up in a *Physicians Desk Reference* (PDR) or go to the drugstore and ask a pharmacist. If Reviewers are living in a facility where their medications are given to them, there will be a chart where the medications and times given are listed. The nurse in charge of giving the medications should be able to share this information with you.

Speech

Of course, the ability to speak is the most important function in the Life Review. Unfortunately, some people lose their ability to speak through illness, such as stroke. Depending on the damage caused by the stroke, some are able to understand and formulate answers but have difficulty expressing themselves in words. Although speech might be diminished, it would behoove both Listener and Reviewer to explore other means of communication, perhaps a little speech mixed with writing. A thorough assessment of speech, with consultation from a speech therapist, will help you determine the remaining abilities of the Reviewer who has lost the apparent ability to speak. Do not give up on using the Life Review and its therapeutic benefits just because it is a little difficult to do so.

The ability to communicate is also lost when the Reviewer and Listener speak different languages. It might be possible to communicate through an interpreter, but then confidentially is lost and the Review is not as satisfying to the Reviewer. If you do not speak the Reviewer's language, you must at least be able to understand the story enough to respond appropriately and to lead the Life Review. Of course, some therapy will happen for the Reviewers just by telling their life stories.

Hearing

Reviewers with poor hearing present another challenge to Therapeutic Listeners. The hearing loss that most older people experience is a sensorineural hearing loss, making the speech they hear garbled and the words of the Listener difficult to interpret. Ambient noise directly affects this type of hearing loss, reinforcing the need for privacy and for decreased noise levels. Addressing this type of hearing loss in a Reviewer, Listeners must be sure to speak distinctly—rather than more loudly—and to enunciate consonants. Female Listeners especially should enunciate clearly because their high-pitched voices are harder to hear when there is a sensorineural loss.

Often people with hearing losses adapt to their losses by lip reading, reinforcing what they hear with what they see. To enhance lip reading by Reviewers, they need to sit with their backs to the window to avoid daytime glare and to be able to see the Listener's face and lips during the Review. Female Listeners, whose voices are harder to hear, may enhance Reviewer lip reading by outlining their own lips with a fresh application of bright lipstick.

Fortunately, there are many prostheses to help individuals who have hearing loss. Nurses have used their stethoscopes as microphones by putting the earpieces into the Reviewer's ears and speaking into the bell. Though effective, the stethoscope routine is only helpful for short periods because it gets uncomfortable for older people who are not used to wearing the earpieces. Some electronics supply stores, such as Radio Shack, sell voice enhancers that amplify the voice of the Therapeutic Listener so that the hearing-impaired Reviewer may hear the Listener better. The most common prosthesis is a hearing aid. Newer hearing aids fit better, have less feedback, and have longer lasting batteries. All such prostheses can be very effective in helping the Reviewers—and the Therapeutic Listeners—complete the Life Review process.

One more issue for Reviewers with poor hearing is that they may speak more loudly than people with normal hearing, thus possibly breaching the confidentiality of the visit themselves without even being aware that they have done so. Hence, the need for privacy is reinforced for someone who is hearing impaired. Listeners need to tend to these hearing needs and all others to enhance the therapy of the Life Review visit.

Vision

Vision is helpful but not essential to a Life Review. It certainly is not as important as speech or hearing. As stated earlier, people with impaired hearing often use their vision to enhance their hearing by lip reading and watching facial expressions, so these are considerations. Reviewers also see responsive messages that are sent through the Listener's body movements. Vision is important and enhances a relationship, but poor vision is not fatal to a therapeutic Life Review.

Listeners can help Reviewers who have compromised vision by enlarging the LRF. The enlargement of the form is most important before the Life Review starts, as part of full disclosure, when contracting with a Reviewer. Many prospects study the

> *Vision is important and enhances a relationship, but poor vision is not fatal to a therapeutic Life Review.*

form to help themselves decide if they want to participate in a Life Review. They rarely read the form after the agreement has been made and the Life Review begun; however, when they are trying to decide whether or not to participate, being able to see and read the form in its entirety is quite important.

Chronic Illness

Reviewers may have many chronic conditions at the same time, including strokes, amputations, diabetes, and arthritis, to name a few. Chronic diseases and any compounding effects can affect the Reviewer's ability to move around easily and to participate in long conversations. For example, those with chronic obstructive pulmonary disease (COPD) find it difficult to talk because of their labored breathing. Reviewers who have arthritis cannot sit for long periods in one place. As the Therapeutic Listener becomes aware of these varied conditions and monitors the Reviewer's comfort level, the Listener should adjust the delivery of the Life Review to maintain the highest levels of comfort throughout the visit.

Reviewer File

It is helpful to keep a file on each Reviewer that notes the person's habits, issues, and disabilities discovered during the assessment. Therapeutic Listeners who are guiding many Life Reviews may find it difficult to keep track of each Reviewer's habits, issues, and so forth. However, remembering their habits is like remembering their names and represents caring and concern. For example, adjusting your schedule to accommodate Mr. J, who takes a nap at 2 p.m. and enjoys a cocktail at 5 p.m., will make your review run more smoothly and demonstrate that Mr. J is important to you. Each individual file should be kept in a large manila envelope with an identifying number on the front. That big envelope can hold session tapes, assessment notes, and outcome measures and will be very valuable for Therapeutic Listeners to scan when they wish to refresh their own memories before each visit.

Next Visit

At the end of this first visit to a potential Life Reviewer, a concrete appointment should be set for the next visit, the first actual Life Review session beginning the following week. When Reviewer and Listener agree on the next meeting, the Therapeutic Listener should write the time and date on an appointment card as well as in the Listener's diary and put the card in a prominent place to help the Reviewer remember the appointment time. Before departing, answer any questions or concerns. As the Listener leaves, it is helpful to remind the Life Reviewer that they will talk about the Reviewer's childhood when the Listener returns the next week. This reminder will cause Reviewers to begin thinking about their childhood before the next visit and will effectively extend the time devoted to recalling the past.

Visit 2

CHILDHOOD

When I was younger, I could remember anything whether it happened or not.

—MARK TWAIN

This "application" chapter discusses the second visit of the Life Review process. It includes excerpts from actual past Life Reviews to provide examples of effective listening techniques from practicing Therapeutic Listeners. Remember to use the guidelines at the front of each subsequent application chapter as a reminder for how to prepare for each weekly session.

The Structured Life Review process consists of several disparate parts that come together to form a whole in actual application. Because these parts cannot all be illustrated at once, they will be spaced and explained throughout the next six chapters. These separate but complementary parts are:

1. Stages of Life from Erikson's Model
2. Questions from the Life Review Form (LRF)
3. Important Counseling Skills
4. Interviewing Techniques
5. Unique Characteristics of the Process
6. Types of Life Reviewers

Throughout the next chapters, look for these parts, which explain the visits for the whole Life Review process. You must apply all or some of these methods as needed throughout your various Life Review visits.

Preliminary Tasks

You must always take care of the Reviewer's comfort needs at the beginning of each Life Review session. For example, you may need to remind the Life Reviewer to consider using the bathroom before the conversation begins. You should also ask Reviewers if they can see and hear you before you start. Further, you should ensure that the chosen arrangements are comfortable by checking with the Reviewer. Also again check the light for glare and make sure there is a minimal amount of noise in the surrounding environment. Provide water within easy reach of the Reviewer because talking for 1 hour will make the Reviewer's mouth and throat dry. Most Life Reviewers are older and taking medication that contributes to a continually dry mouth. They may not recognize when they are thirsty.

The last part of preparation is the placement of the tape recorder. You should place the tape recorder in an unobtrusive place close to the Reviewer because it is the Reviewer's conversation that is most important to record. Once the recorder is in place and you are both seated, one facing the other, you should turn the tape recorder on. Attending to all these needs before or at the start of the visit will allow you both to concentrate on the Review and to ensure a successful and uninterrupted session. If necessary, make a checklist related to that particular site and Reviewer and use it to remind yourself.

Personal Issues for the Life Reviewer

If your Life Reviewer seems to be visibly upset about a personal issue, you should delay the start of the actual Life Review sessions until the person has had a chance to talk about the current concern. For example, people newly admitted to nursing homes take time to adjust to the idea of living in a nursing home and may wish to talk about their feelings regarding their relocation. You need to use the same listening skills that you use in Life Review when listening to the problems of a troubled Reviewer. After Reviewers have had an opportunity to vent, they will probably happily proceed with the Life Review. The attention you give to a Reviewer's personal concerns will serve the process of Life Review well. Also, you will bond with the Reviewer earlier in the Life Review, creating a feeling of safety for the Reviewer that will contribute to more openness during the next sessions.

Erikson's Model: Childhood

As was discussed in the chapter on "The Structured Life Review Process," Erikson's developmental model provides the foundation for the structure of the Life Review. The questions in the LRF also reflect that model, with particular questions addressing each of Erikson's developmental life stages. This visit 2 covers childhood. As Reviewers begin to recall their childhood, you need to be alert for comments that address Erikson's first stage—Trust vs. Mistrust; also, listen for the Reviewer's opportunity and ability to make choices during childhood, which represents the second stage—Autonomy vs. Shame— as discussed in the following pages. If you do not hear positive statements regarding these two stages, you may have to explore a little further with selected questions that will ask the Reviewer about Trust and about Autonomy as discussed below. (Note that the Background chapter provides further discussion of Erikson's stages.)

Trust

Trust vs. Mistrust is the first developmental stage in childhood. Questions such as, *"Did you feel cared for as a child?,"* will uncover issues of trust. You might not need to ask separate questions if the Reviewers respond to the first question about their earliest memory, saying something like Mr. B did in his response:

> *My first memory is of my Daddy reading to me every night before I went to sleep. It was our special time together and I always felt so warm and cozy when he had his arm around me to share the pictures in a book. He always let me choose the story, even if he didn't like it, and sometimes he really liked my choices. I always felt proud when I picked one that he liked.*

Here Mr. B shows that he felt safe during his childhood; he trusted his dad and enjoyed closeness and affection from him. His conversation reflects the love that was given to him by his parents and his personal sense of security as a child; hence he achieved Trust as a child.

Autonomy

Mr. B also demonstrated Autonomy, the second stage, when he talked about choosing the bedtime story his father liked. As Mr. B proceeded in his Life Review, he became more talkative and open. Mr. B spoke of being the family favorite and thought his father liked him the best out of three other children because he was the firstborn and also because he liked the same things that his father liked, such as history and reading. He was allowed to make choices. He was supported in his choices and felt pride in them. He also felt he was his grandmother's favorite, which served to pump up his self-esteem even more:

> *I was the favorite; I was the firstborn. My Grandma never would let my parents spank me—that probably means I became a brat. We moved near Grandma when I was three. I remember running next door to Grandma's house either to get potato soup or to run away from a spanking. She protected me.*

When asked if he was spanked often, he said, *"No more than the normal child, probably even less because of my Grandma."*

When you are conducting your Life Reviews, you should encourage Reviewers to search for positive memories such as Mr. B's. Such memories made Mr. B feel good and the memories assured his Listener that Mr. B had successfully traversed Erikson's first two developmental stages in his childhood. He trusted his dad and his grandmother and felt good about himself. In fact, Mr. B's Life Review started off positively, though slowly. He reported his feelings about certain events and became even more introspective over time. Your role is to keep promoting such memories to show your Reviewers their good fortune in childhood.

Mistrust and Shame

Not all Life Reviewers have had the positive experiences that Mr. B had, believing himself to be a special and loved child. You may hear some very traumatic stories as a Therapeutic Listener and they may be difficult for you to accept and respond to. Listening to stories of difficult childhoods will certainly not be as enjoyable as listening to stories about happy childhoods. Reviewers who believe they were unloved find the lack of parental love to be as damaging as being the loved child is beneficial. In an unhappy childhood, many children never gain trust or autonomy. The idea of being an unloved child stuck with Mrs. W during her entire life and may have been responsible for a life-time of depression and low self-esteem. Following are some examples of her traumatic childhood that surfaced during the Life Review.

> LISTENER: *"Tell me about your mother."*

> MRS. W: *I was the youngest of six. My mother would scream when she was mad, and I remember she would hit me severely around the legs and I can't let go of that. My sister taught me to hide in the closet when Mother was mad. No matter what, I never pleased my mother. I've tried all my life to please my mother; it's bothered me terribly through the years. My brother used to tease me too and told me I was adopted, then my mother would laugh when I cried. She never loved me because I was unwanted. She said she already had enough children.*

Mrs. W never felt loved and did not trust her mother or her brothers. When she reached out to them, she was rejected. Listening patiently to stories such as Mrs. W's and accepting her for who she is may be the best thing you can do as a Therapeutic Listener. Mrs. W told stories of being ashamed to be with other children, afraid that they would find out about how she was treated at home. She was ashamed to be unwanted. As she began her Life Review, she was finally sharing this feeling of shame with her Listener. And, despite Mrs. W's low expectations, the Listener empathized and cared for her, accepting her regardless of what she said. When you are the Listener, you must realize that Reviewers who share negative childhood experiences, such as Mrs. W, may have been influenced by them their entire lives. You will need to continue to listen and to accept such Reviewers as you encourage them to tell you more. There is healing in the telling and sharing that sometimes brings reconciliation later in life, when it was not achievable before. Hopefully, such Reviewers will begin to heal through the Life Review process, as did Mrs. W.

> *There is healing in the telling and sharing that sometimes brings reconciliation later in life, when it was not achievable before.*

Using the Life Review Form

The questions in the LRF are designed to jog the Reviewer's memory about specific stages of life's development. The first session of the actual Life Review focuses on childhood: family and home. For some Reviewers, those memories of childhood are very far away and difficult to remember. But often, once Reviewers begin to remember, more memories surface. The process is similar to priming a pump: hard to get started, but once started, the water flows steadily. Examples of suggested questions to use in the first Life Review interview are listed on page 82. Pay particular attention to the questions set in bold type.

Beginning the Process

Remember that the first Life Review session is only the second time you and the Reviewer have met. You are still in the get-acquainted phase of a relationship, making Reviewers somewhat cautious about their conversations and their disclosures. Think about a similar social situation and try to understand the Reviewer's beginning reticence. Reviewers are not quite sure what is expected of them and may be wary at the beginning of the Review when you and the process are still unknown. You should make every effort to put the Reviewer at ease.

Because you and the Reviewer are still strangers with only a tenuous connection, really probing questions will not be well received. Give anxious Reviewers time to voice any discomfort with the situation while you continue to assure them of privacy, confidentiality, and whatever else makes them comfortable. Usually the problem takes care of itself over time with only slight reassurance from the Therapeutic Listener. Following is an example of a Listener caring for and responding to a Reviewer's uneasiness at the beginning of the Life Review:

> LISTENER: *You know you were joking a little bit about me evaluating your interests; my job is not about evaluating anything. My job is to understand what your life was like.*

Suggested Questions for Childhood

- **What is the very first thing you can remember in your life? Go as far back as you can.**

- What other things can you remember about when you were very young?

- What was life like for you as a child?

- What were your parents like? What were their weaknesses; strengths?

- Did you have any brothers or sisters? Tell me what each was like.

- Did anyone close to you die when you were growing up?

- Did someone important to you go away?

- **Did you feel cared for as a child?**

- Do you remember having any accidents or diseases?

- Do you remember being in a very dangerous situation?

- **Did you play at any adult roles or games? Were you a leader or a follower as a young child?**

- Were you afraid of any adults?

- Was there anything important to you that was lost or destroyed?

- **Did you have childhood friends and playmates? A best friend?**

- Was church a large part of your life?

- **Were you given opportunities to make some decisions for yourself? What independent things did you do for yourself?**

REVIEWER: *And then try to figure out what ultimately I turn into.*

LISTENER: *No, no. That's your job. Any kind of evaluation is up to you, not up to me.*

REVIEWER: *All right.*

LISTENER: *So my only job is to understand what you tell me.*

Our Listener answered the questions to the satisfaction of the Reviewer, but this Reviewer was easily satisfied and eager to begin, despite his discomfort. You will find that it usually takes longer to make anxious people comfortable with you and the process. Time and familiarity contribute to feelings of easiness, but the process needs to begin before you can establish a firm easy relationship. Consequently, the first questions that you ask from the LRF must be nonthreatening and ones that can be answered either personally or impersonally.

First Question

You can open the Life Review with the first question on the form, *"What is the very first thing you can remember in your life? Go back as far as you can."* This first question is a non-threatening question to begin the interview and is good for priming the pump of memory. Even those with traumatic childhood memories can answer the first question without revealing negative events in their childhood; thus the first question is "safe." Life Reviewers can report anything that comes into their minds and their stories need not be personal if that is what they desire. Here is an example of answers and Listener responses to the first question.

Mrs. G, another Reviewer, chose a safe and entertaining response to the first question:

> MRS. G: *I remember sharing a bed with my sister. I always felt there were ogres and monsters in the room and just being able to touch her with my toe made me feel better. I had her check under the bed and in the closets before she went to bed. I was glad to have someone with me. My sister always took care of me.*
>
> LISTENER: **It sounds like you and your sister were very close.**
>
> MRS. G: *Oh yes, we were.*

Mrs. G's first memory created an atmosphere of lightheartedness. She also mentioned family in her first reply, giving the Listener the opportunity to ask about other family members more fully after exploring her relationship with her sister.

> LISTENER: **Tell me about the rest of your family.**
>
> MRS. G *(eagerly and excitedly)*: *Oh, I used to call my father "the old man"; it was a term of endearment. He had a soft spot for me, but he was very strict with my sister.*

To further explore Mrs. G's relationship with her father, you can use the technique of paraphrasing, described on pages 45–46, to encourage Mrs. G to continue and add more detail to the memories of her father:

> LISTENER: **He had a little soft spot when it came to you?**
>
> MRS. G: *Yes, now I don't know whether it was because I was the baby or because, whatever he was doing, I wanted to be near him and do things with him. Neither my brother nor my sister was like that. He played with me often. He would push me on the swing for hours, and he even had tea parties with me. He was very tolerant. He built me a playhouse and would stoop to come in the little doorway for tea with me.*

In her response to Listener paraphrasing, you will notice that Mrs. G expanded on her positive relationship with her father and affirmed that she and her father were close. As an alternative, you can use the suggested questions below to extend the conversation surrounding childhood to include family and home.

Once you get the Reviewer started and into the Life Review, the memories seem to bubble up spontaneously, unless of course the memories are unhappy ones, in which case they are not shared so easily. Because the Reviewer picks the memories in response to your questions, those unhappy memories may never come out or they may surface later, when the Reviewer feels safe. Remember that the Reviewer is in charge of the conversation and the content of the memories. You should not push Reviewers to reveal or explore adverse memories. Just be ready for the upsetting memories when they come.

Order of Memories

One thing you will notice is that Life Reviewers often move back and forth between memories of their childhood and their adulthood. Certain childhood memories can evoke related adult memories and often cause comparisons between the Reviewer's own child-

---

Suggested Questions for Family and Home

- What was life like for you as an older child?
- Tell me about your family.
- How did your parents get along?
- How did other people in your home get along?
- What was the atmosphere like in your home?
- Was there enough food and necessities for your family?
- Were you punished as a child? For what? Who did the main disciplining in your home? Who was the boss?
- Did you feel loved and cared for as a young child?
- Tell me about projects you started as a child.
- When you wanted something from your parents (or guardian), how did you go about getting it?
- Did you ever feel doubt, shame, or guilt as a young person?
- What kind of person did your parents like the most? The least?
- Who were you closest to in your family?
- Who in your family were you most like? In what way?
- Did you have any unpleasant experiences as a child?
- Tell me about your extended family: aunts, uncles, grandparents, cousins.

hood and the childhoods of their children. If Reviewers stray too far, you can easily put them back on track by reminding them of their own childhood after they have finished their current story. As long as you eventually cover all the developmental phases in the lives of the Reviewers, the Review will be complete. Moving back and forth in time while remembering is inevitable.

Responsive Comments

Remember, the LRF and its questions are just guidelines. By following the Reviewer's story with responsive comments, you can make the Life Review more intimate and interesting to the individual. Comments that are responsive to the Reviewer's story help Reviewers enlarge their stories and share details. Memories that Reviewers evoke on their own are equally as important as the memories suggested by the LRF, but you should still be very familiar with the LRF's contents and its ability to structure the Life Review. Your specific remarks should be fashioned to encourage Reviewers to talk about their emotions surrounding an event or to share the emotions they are feeling currently when looking back at the past. The earlier story of Mrs. G provides a good example of a Listener using responsive comments. The next story example demonstrates both responsive comments and order of memories.

LISTENER: *Did you enjoy your friends from school?*

REVIEWER: *They were fun. Four of us girls ran around together; we were the four L's.*

LISTENER: *Why the four L's?*

REVIEWER: *Because all our names started with L. We sat together at school. Sometimes we'd go shopping and get the same outfits, like we all bought black pleated skirts and wore them to school on the same day.*

LISTENER: *Sounds like fun. Are you still close?*

REVIEWER: *We were our whole lives, but now they're all dead. I'm the only one left.*

LISTENER: *You must miss them a great deal.*

REVIEWER: *Yes, we got together once a month our whole lives. We were in each other's weddings and raised our kids together. I guess I was lucky to have them as friends for such a long time. Laura just died last month. I really miss her.*

LISTENER: *That's so sad, tell me more about the L's.*

The previous story is a good example of the Listener using responsive comments to encourage the Reviewer to say more about her important friendships and then her losses. The preceding conversation also demonstrates a Reviewer's need to move back and forth in time to tell a complete story. Although she was discussing her childhood, the Reviewer needed to move into adulthood to fully describe her friendships. You should encourage both practices as needed to enlarge the life story.

Counseling Skill: Acceptance

The Participants chapter outlines the counseling skills and behaviors that make you a good Therapeutic Listener. The chapters here in Part II show you how to apply these skills. You must practice these counseling skills and interviewing techniques until they are a part of your natural listening and communication processes. One of the first skills you will need to incorporate into your repertoire as an effective Listener is Acceptance, both of Reviewers and of their stories.

Acceptance is a warm, open, and understanding climate that you create for the Reviewer. The atmosphere should be relaxed and nonjudgmental and immediately felt by Reviewers. In such a climate, many Reviewers will think: *"I can say anything here with this person."* Previously withheld stories may bubble past the boundaries that have held those stories back for a lifetime. Reviewers will seize the opportunity to unburden themselves when you make them feel welcome and safe, just as Mrs. W did when sharing her stories of childhood abuse for the first time.

> *Previously withheld stories may bubble past the boundaries that once held those stories back for a lifetime.*

To create a climate of acceptance, you must accept Reviewers as they are, without criticism or conditions. Reviewers need to feel the acceptance immediately when they first meet you and continuously over the next weeks. If you cannot accept a Reviewer because of issues in your own background, you must decline the opportunity to conduct the Life Review and find a substitute Listener. You will not be therapeutic if your personal value system gets in the way. It is essential that you regard the Reviewer with approval and warmth in order to be an effective Therapeutic Listener.

Interviewing Techniques

Interviewing techniques are described in an earlier chapter as additional skills to add to your behavior as an effective Therapeutic Listener. These techniques help to keep the conversation going and to direct Reviewers throughout the Life Review; they also help make Reviewers comfortable and encourage their memories. Mastering them is essential. For many Listeners, these techniques are second nature; for others, they must be learned and practiced before they become second nature. Either way, it always helps to practice them until they are yours.

Attentive Behavior

You must learn to communicate your attentiveness to the Reviewer through your words and actions. The actions involved in this behavior include eye contact, physical attention, and verbal responses. Attention is central to the interaction between you and the Reviewer and can only be achieved by really listening to the Reviewer. Close listening is synonymous with attending behavior when it is done properly. Attending to a Reviewer reinforces the Reviewer's inclination to keep on talking, just as the Reviewer did in the following example:

> REVIEWER: *She caught me philandering.*
>
> LISTENER: **What do you mean by philandering?**
>
> REVIEWER: *You know, having sex with another woman.*
>
> LISTENER: **How did she catch you?**
>
> REVIEWER: *She went to the office next door and heard us.*
>
> LISTENER: **What happened when she found out?**
>
> REVIEWER: *She threw a pitcher of ice tea at me.*
>
> LISTENER: **And then what happened?**

This Listener was demonstrating attentive behavior by repeating some of the Reviewer's words in the Listener's responses that directly followed each of the Reviewer's statements. There was no doubt that this Listener was listening closely. Attentive behavior such as this encouraged the Reviewer to talk in detail about his divorce leading up to his present feelings of loneliness.

Repetition

Repetition is a very potent tool in Life Review that helps Reviewers to dilute or get rid of old bothersome memories that may keep resurfacing when least expected. Sometimes these old troublesome memories are what cause Reviewers to get "stuck" in their Life Reviews, unable to move forward. Being stuck, wallowing in the guilt, can result in despair. On the other hand, continued repetition can result in catharsis—a truly beneficial result. Repeating a story sometimes gives the troublesome memory away. You can initiate repetition by asking Reviewers if they have talked enough about whatever is bothering them each time you meet, and then allowing time for the Reviewer to explore the issues again or to assure you that they would like to move on in their Life Review.

> *Repeating a story sometimes gives the troublesome memory away.*

Repeating happy memories has an opposite and beneficial effect. Reviewers relive the feelings of success, contentment, love, or whatever good emotions accompany the recalled happiness. Perhaps this is why high school jocks like to recall and talk about their touchdowns, winning baskets, or home runs. It feels good to relive those moments again and to get positive feedback from the Listener regarding old achievements. It only takes a minute to comment about an old success and to enjoy the feel-good sensations again, so remember that it is important for Reviewers to relive those good times more than once, if there is time.

To understand the use of repetition, recall Mrs. W's story of her childhood. In Mrs. W's Life Review, the Therapeutic Listener listened to the story of Mrs. W's mother every week throughout the Reviewer's recollection of her life. Mrs. W apparently needed to come to terms with this toxic relationship, so she told and retold the indignities that she had suffered and was still suffering. All of her life, Mrs. W was the outsider within her own family. As an adult, she remembered inviting her mother to visit for a holiday and being later turned down because her mother accepted another offer from a brother or sister. Mrs. W repeatedly concentrated on her feelings of worthlessness and of being unloved. She never trusted her family to love her or care for her because she was unwanted. Eventually, by repeatedly raising these troublesome childhood thoughts, Mrs. W was able to dilute the memories so that they became easier to handle.

If you were the Therapeutic Listener in that instance, you could encourage repetition by asking Mrs. W about her mother at the beginning of each session. The question will inevitably bring forth more unhappy memories of mother, but as the Life Review progresses, Mrs. W will be less and less disturbed. Unhappy memories will remain an important thread in Mrs. W's Life Review, but they will not be as disturbing. She may even begin to give those memories away or reconcile them for herself. You should encourage repetition in similar cases with hopes of getting rid of the negative emotion that surrounds disturbing childhood recollections such as these.

Reframing

Reframing is another very important interviewing technique to use when doing a Life Review. Reframing is actually a psychotherapeutic term adapted for use by Life Review to describe the process of changing one's thinking from a negative viewpoint to a more positive one. The Therapeutic Listener implements reframing by encouraging Reviewers to look at troublesome events differently than they have before, to change a negative memory or judgment to a more positive one. Reframing alters the perception of something by altering its context or description. In fact, reframing literally means to take the old picture out of its existing frame and to put it into a new frame that will require the Reviewer to look at the picture differently. The final decision to change one's thoughts belongs to the Reviewer but, when given the opportunity, the Therapeutic Listener can freely comment that the Listener now seems to see the story differently. We hope Reviewers will listen closely and then try out the Listener's view. Often, when events are reframed, they have a different meaning and become more acceptable to Reviewers. If you help Reviewers to see past events in your reframed way, they may also see them differently and accept them more easily. Once accepted, reframed thoughts can then be reintegrated; but first you need to help with the reframing. For example, Mrs. M was talking about the death of her son, which was very tragic and violent. The particular conversation started, as so many difficult conversations do, when the Therapeutic Listener was walking out the door.

MRS. M: *My son died 20 years ago when he was a child.*

LISTENER: *I am so sorry, would you like to talk about your son now?*

MRS. M: *We stopped to visit my husband in his office at the Army base. He had flags, bullet cases, guns, ammunition, and hand grenades in his office. Part of my husband's job was to dismantle live weapons. While we were there, my little boy picked up a hand grenade that my husband had examined earlier and it blew up in his face. My little boy blew up right in front of me.*

LISTENER: *How awful, tell me more about the explosion.*

MRS. M: *No one else was hurt but my baby died.*

LISTENER: *His death must have been so hard for you.*

MRS. M: *I should have been watching him better.*

Not only was this woman still grieving over the death of her son, but she was feeling guilty because she blamed herself for not watching and stopping her son from picking up the hand grenade. She also blamed her husband, whom she thought should have been aware that this was a live weapon and prevented the child from picking it up. Grief and guilt had been the constant companions of these parents for 20 years until her husband died recently. Now she carried all of the guilt.

The Listener encouraged conversation about the incident and, as Mrs. M talked about the event, both Listener and Reviewer began to think that the *death was not preventable.*

LISTENER: *How would your husband know if the grenade was live?*

MRS. M: *He tested it. He thought it was empty.*

LISTENER: *So he thought it was OK to put on his desk?*

MRS. M: *Yes, he had several that the boys played with when we visited.*

LISTENER: *Did you ever stop their play before?*

Mrs. M never thought the weapons were dangerous before the accident, nor had she ever stopped the children from playing with the weapons before. She began to think about her son's death differently, no longer blaming herself or her husband for causing the death. She reframed her own past thoughts accordingly: 1) No one realized the grenade was live; 2) the ease with which it blew up was astounding; and 3) the only way to prevent the death was to have no grenade present at all. However, dismantling weapons was her husband's job. He had to examine the weapons and have them nearby.

Mrs. M thought things through differently, facilitated by the Listener's pertinent questions. If you find yourself in similar situations as this Listener, remember that trying to clarify a story for yourself often causes the Reviewer to clarify the story as well and then view events differently. Also, by looking for a subtle, brighter side, the Reviewer can reframe the past based on new experience and new insight. Mrs. M began to see her son's death differently and no longer felt responsible for the accident. This less blameful view allowed her to accept this tragic death a little better than she had before. She still grieved, but she was healing and she had energy to move on in her life.

Reviewer Types

You will find it helpful to identify the distinct type of Reviewer whom you are visiting because you may need to handle each type differently. For example, the Therapeutic Listener conducting the Life Reviews in this chapter noted that two of the Reviewers, Mr. B and Mrs. G, were very different from one another, particularly in the way that they told their stories. They were contrasting types: one, Mrs. G, was a Storyteller; the other, Mr. B, started the Life Review as a Reluctant Reviewer. Consequently, different skills were needed with each Reviewer to elicit their life stories and to keep them on track throughout all the developmental stages of their unique Life Reviews.

Storyteller

Mrs. G was the Storyteller. It was easy getting her to talk by using just a few prompts. Her enthusiasm reflected her pleasure over the opportunity to talk about the past. Her stories were personal, about herself, and evaluative. She expressed how she felt about each incident. Each week when she was visited, she was eager to get started, and often the Listener had to stop her when the hour was up.

You will find that the Life Review process works best for a Storyteller like Mrs. G if you are well prepared each week and direct the memories of such a Reviewer as soon as each session begins. As a matter of fact, Mrs. G's Listener found that preparing Mrs. G a week in advance worked best, because she started talking as soon as they sat down together. The Listener's method was to note at the end of the present visit where Mrs. G needed to go the next week. As the Listener was leaving, she would inform Mrs. G that next week they would talk about her married years, for example. This way, Mrs. G was able to initiate the conversation (hopefully about her marriage) at the beginning of the next visit, not realizing that the Therapeutic Listener had already moved her along to this next developmental stage.

Reluctant Reviewer

In contrast to Mrs. G, Mr. B was more of a Reluctant Reviewer and had difficulty getting started each week. In the first session, for example, he reported his first memory with few words and only impersonal facts: *"The earliest thing I can remember was World War I. I was only a small child then but I can remember the Armistice."*

The Listener wanted Mr. B to round out his memory of the Armistice and asked another question about that particular event. He seemed to be less talkative than most Life Reviewers, and needed to enlarge his answers, so the Listener used an excellent prompt that would cause him to provide more information.

> LISTENER: *What do you remember about the Armistice?*
>
> MR. B: *I remember before it, my father reading the paper and telling my mother, "I'm afraid the Germans are winning." And I can remember my father, who was a minister, going downtown to say goodbye to the boys that were leaving for the war. I was my father's favorite son. I was the oldest, of course, and he and I had common interests.*

In response to the prompt, Mr. B brought his father into the Life Review immediately on his own, thus it was not necessary to seek this information with another specific prompt. As Mr. B started talking about his father, he became more animated and excited about his story and gave the Listener clues for the next topic or the next question. The Listener sensed the man's relationship with his father was a "hot button." For example, the Listener asked Mr. B what interests he and his father had in common and Mr. B spent 10 minutes talking about their common interests, which the Listener could address in more detail the following week. His answers to these questions also revealed a lot about himself that even he had not thought about in years.

Although Mr. B was a Reluctant Reviewer, he responded with memories that brought him great pleasure and he elaborated on each of the Therapeutic Listener's prompts. Mr. B just needed more coaching to get started and, over the course of 6 weeks, he began to talk more easily. With a Reluctant Reviewer like Mr. B, you will find it helpful to know a little history surrounding his lifetime to create questions when the conversation lags. Some examples might be: *Was immigration a major issue when he was growing up? What does he remember about the Depression? Did he go to the movies when he was young?* Many Life Reviewers have had what they think were boring lives and start out as Reluctant Reviewers. Your job is to find what interests the Reviewers and to start them talking, as the Listener did in this example.

> *Many Life Reviewers have had what they think were boring lives and start out as Reluctant Reviewers.*

End Visit 2

Summarize Session

Each Life Review visit generally lasts for about 1 hour. Time for the session can be monitored with a simple kitchen timer, a 1-hour tape that dings when the hour is complete, or a clock or watch that is set within the view of the Reviewer and Listener so both can be aware of the passing time. In an office setting, a clock set behind the Reviewer, but visible to the Listener, is another unobtrusive way to monitor the hour. The Listener should never keep glancing at a watch. This behavior connotes impatience and lack of interest, as well as rudeness, but it is alright to set the watch in front of both of you so that it can be casually seen during the ongoing conversation.

As the time for Visit 2 ends, you need to take the conversational lead away from the Reviewer to summarize the content of this session, while suggesting the content for the next session. Summarizing is important because it gives the Listener an opportunity to provide the Reviewer with feedback and to restate the highpoints of the session for the Reviewer's agreement. Summarizing also gives the Listener control at the end of the visit in order to direct the ending of the visit to a happy point and then to suggest next week's topic.

When you are summarizing the session for Mrs. W, for example, you need to note how difficult it must have been growing up in a family where she felt unwanted. You also need to praise her for the way she handled the difficult situations in her childhood: the lack of love and attention as a child. Show her how strong she has become. Point out how well she has coped and empower her. Then give *your* Mrs. W some new viewpoints to consider for next week's session.

When leaving, you could say: ***"When I return next week, we will talk about another part of your childhood, your adolescence and your friends. I want to hear about your friends, who you admired the most, and what you thought about school."*** Through the weekly summary, you can shift the ending of the Life Review to a happy note while focusing the Life Reviewer's thoughts on next week's topic.

Reviewers usually continue to review on their own between visits. The time between sessions provides solitary thinking time when Life Reviewers can edit and evaluate their stories and decide what memories they will talk about the following week. The Listener's summary informs Reviewers of the next area of discussion, while providing structure for the continuing Life Review process.

> *Reviewers usually continue to review on their own between visits.*

Next Visit

As you close this session you also need to affirm the next week's appointment. When the appointment time is agreed upon, you should write the time on an appointment card (in large, dark print) and put the card in a prominent place or hand it to the Reviewer. After you depart, you need to take a moment to make notes about the important issues that arose in this visit and any that you need to address during the following visit. Even though you have recordings to jog your memory, the notes are especially helpful when time has elapsed between visits and you need additional reminders. By commenting about important remarks made the previous week, you demonstrate attentiveness that shows Life Reviewers that they and their stories are important to you.

Visit 3

ADOLESCENCE

*Life is just a mirror, and what you see out there,
you must first see inside of you.*

—WALLY "FAMOUS" AMOS

The Life Review process will continue during the third visit and the questions will focus on the Reviewer's adolescence. This visit helps to reinforce the trusting relationship between the Therapeutic Listener and the Life Reviewer because the Reviewer probably is becoming more comfortable with the Listener's presence and questions. The Listener and the Reviewer are now at least acquaintances who are embarking on a friendly discussion. In this Life Review session, the Listener and the Reviewer will begin a dialogue about the Reviewer's later childhood and adolescence.

This chapter discusses and applies two more of Erikson's stages—Initiative vs. Guilt and Industry vs. Inferiority—using probing questions from the LRF about adolescence, school, and the Reviewer's feelings. It also covers the counseling skill of Caring and the interviewing techniques of Responding and Reflecting Feelings. The unique characteristic of Structure in the Structured Life Review is examined as well as the "External" type of Reviewer.

Preliminary Tasks

At the beginning of Visit 3, you should again tend to the comfort needs of your Reviewers. You need to return to that comfortable private spot for your dialogue. It is best to use the same seating arrangement as the previous session unless that arrangement did not work. Before starting, ask Reviewers if they are comfortable and can see and hear you. Also ask Reviewers if they need to use the bathroom. Set a glass of water within easy reach of the Reviewer. Finally, set the tape recorder in place and turn it on before starting your dialogue. Placement will depend on the quality of the first recordings. If the voice of the Reviewer was difficult to interpret, the volume and/or placement of the microphone needs to be corrected. Some older people habitually speak softly, especially in communal settings. If you cannot hear the Reviewer's conversation clearly on the tape, you can try a voice enhancer to increase the volume of the Reviewer's voice while recording on tape. Voice enhancers are not expensive and are sold in electronics stores such as Radio Shack. They look like microphones and can also be a helpful piece of equipment for Listeners to speak into when Reviewers are hearing impaired. Consider having one with you at all times. When these preparation are complete, the formal visit may begin.

Clarify Visit 2

Before this third visit, you will want to have reviewed the tape and your notes from the second visit. Then, at the beginning of this third visit you should concisely summarize and clarify what memories you think the Reviewer talked about in the previous visit. Ask Reviewers if there was anything else since you last met that they remembered from their early childhood that they would like to recall and share now. Reviewers may have talked about their father but not their mother. They may have discussed friends but not siblings. Often, the Reviewer's oversight or omission is simply a matter of running out of time. But the oversight may also be a deliberate avoidance of a topic, especially if the memories are difficult ones that have been pushed down over the years. Hence, a little inquisitiveness may pull out the rest of the story.

By summarizing and clarifying, you provide an opportunity to clear up any misunderstandings that may persist from the previous visit. For example, you may have some points of the Reviewer's story confused in your mind, and this confusion can grow if not sorted out early in the Life Review. When you ask for clarification, you ask Reviewers to revisit those memories, causing Reviewers to better clarify their own thoughts when they restate those parts of their story. You need to clearly understand the history that the Reviewer is sharing, because your understanding will influence the questions that you ask during the next weeks, which will in turn influence the rest of the Life Review. Unfortunately, it is possible to spend 6 weeks doing a Life

> *Reviewers may also be testing you to make sure you are really interested in them.*

Review without truly understanding the Reviewer's issues, if any. Remember, Reviewers may also be testing you to make sure you are really interested in them as individuals before sharing their really complex stories. By asking Reviewers questions about what you thought you heard them say, you can make them feel as though their life matters to you, while at the same time you are clarifying any vague issues.

Erikson's Model: Childhood and Young Adolescence

In this chapter, the third and fourth of Erikson's Life Stages are presented: Initiative vs. Guilt and Industry vs. Inferiority. These stages relate to the Reviewer's development during childhood and young adolescence. Briefly, Initiative is the third stage of life when children develop purpose and then add the ability to plan their own activities to their growing range of capabilities. Erikson states that those who are unable to develop the initiative to create and implement their own plans begin to experience guilt about their lack of motivation and abilities.

Industry, the fourth stage, is when one's work ethic begins to develop and manifest itself as the child becomes an eager participant in productive situations. Failing at this stage produces feelings of inferiority, such as when children fail to meet the goals they or others have set for them. You can ask about these two life stages with pertinent questions from the LRF, such as: *Did you enjoy starting new projects at home or at school? Would you describe yourself as a hard-working teenager? Did you ever feel inadequate when a project was too hard for you?* Or, Reviewers may just tell you stories about themselves that clearly reflect one or both of these stages without the help of probing questions from you, as Mrs. A did in the narrative in the next section.

Initiative and Industry

These two stages, Initiative and Industry, relate to establishing a sense of purpose and to forming a person's work ethic while developing competence. Mrs. A addressed both stages when participating in her Life Review. Mrs. A enjoyed talking about herself and voluntarily told the Therapeutic Listener how, even as a little girl, she helped her mother prepare for parties:

> We planned the menu together and then I helped prepare some of the party food. As I got older, I planned my own birthday parties and then my mother helped me get ready.

You can see that Mrs. A was proud of helping in the kitchen. Because of her early experiences helping in the kitchen with her mother, Mrs. A continued to take more initiative as she grew older, and she expressed joy in working. She showed the Listener that she had achieved both Initiative and Industry as a child. If you were the Listener in this instance, your role would be to reinforce Mrs. A's good feelings while encouraging her to enlarge her stories to include other influences in her life. You would not have to ask directly about Initiative and Industry because Mrs. A alluded to both in her stories of helping her mother.

Guilt and Inferiority

The opposite of Initiative is Guilt, which arises when a person is not able to complete a targeted job properly. A pattern of one's inability to complete required tasks may result in failures, and then feelings of guilt may surface over one's repeated failure. A similar pattern can occur if the child is repeatedly told that he or she is a failure or is worthless. Once feelings of failure and guilt set in, children may then experience the opposite of Industry, which is Inferiority. Feelings of inferiority may develop as a result of children's perceived prior failures and feelings of guilt that characterized the third stage, leading to a general feeling of being less then expected, which is debilitating and which tends to grow more oppressive throughout life.

You should not ask directly about feelings of guilt and inferiority, because Reviewers may resent the implications in your questions—that they *should* feel inferior. But you do need to be alert and listen for telltale clues about these stages. When you do pick up on feelings of guilt or inferiority through memories of failed efforts, explore the memories fully and look for extenuating circumstances that may have influenced those failed outcomes and contributed to the Reviewer's present negative feelings. For instance, maybe Reviewers were never allowed to try new things in the past because their parents were afraid the Reviewers would be hurt. Or, maybe Reviewers just lacked the skills for manual tasks at a young age, although they were strong in other areas. As the Listener, point out the effect of these possible past contributions on the Reviewers' accomplishments and feelings about themselves. Then, encourage Reviewers to rethink their past and their present views of themselves. Reviewers may have failed at certain tasks early in life for good reason and then overly focused on them, never recognizing their successes as they grew older.

For example, Mr. T, a retired history professor, talked about his high school experiences and revealed both past and present feelings of inferiority in his story. He started his review of late childhood by telling the Listener that when growing up he was slightly built and did not like or excel in sports. He was the eldest of four brothers and, by virtue of being the oldest child, more was expected of him. The community he lived in was football-minded and the high school students who were most respected were those who played on the football team. Mr. T's three brothers were all football stars in high school. Mr. T was only a good student. He talked about his lack of athletic abilities:

> I just wasn't able to play football and I wasn't good at other sports. My three
> brothers were all big football players and went to a big football college, but
> not so great academically. They all went there and they all later made a lot of
> money in their businesses. I always felt inferior to them. I couldn't even drive
> as a teenager, until my younger brother taught me. Even though I got a
> Ph.D., I never made a lot of money. And then when the war started, I flunked
> out of Officer Candidate School. My brothers all had commissions and were
> on active duty when the war started. I was simply reverted to the ranks.

This successful college professor was still comparing himself to his brothers and feeling inferior and guilty for not having achieved in the same manner as his brothers. He was not an athlete, nor was he a military officer. His Therapeutic Listener continued to work hard to turn his thinking around. He had been thinking negatively about himself his entire life. The Listener needed to help him to appreciate his achievements. By recognizing his own successes, he should then begin to feel pride in his own work and in himself and finally be proud of his initiative and industry:

> LISTENER: *Earlier, you told me that you became a sergeant during the war through hard work and your special knowledge of chemicals. Wasn't that an important achievement?*

> MR.T: *Yes, and my brothers couldn't believe that I was a sergeant because that was such a macho thing, but I did well with it and ended my time in the service with many achievements. It was a good feeling to be called a sergeant. People said that a sergeant had to be a rough and tough and mean old man. And some of them were. And my brothers were astonished that I had been made a sergeant because they thought of me as the impractical one, always reading history.*

> LISTENER: *So you were proud of your service and your brothers were proud of you.*

> MR.T: *Yes, I guess they were. The whole family was proud.*

The Therapeutic Listener totally turned around Mr. T's thinking about his success in life. Mr. T originally downplayed his success because he focused on his failures. The Listener remembered Mr. T's pride when he was talking about his military service and the Listener only had to remind him of this a few times before he began to adopt a more prideful identity for himself. As you read this example from Mr. T's review, you should recognize that the Listener's actions reinforce the importance of listening closely and then recognizing the nuance of feeling (pride) that finally accompanied Mr. T's particular story. If the Listener had not been alert to all of Mr. T's comments, she may have missed the feelings of pride in his military service, and missed a story that became a valuable tool in helping him to change his opinion of himself.

Using the Life Review Form

Most of the questions asked during the Life Review are from the LRF, but we also encourage asking other related, pertinent, and provocative questions. Do not be totally ruled by what is on the LRF. It is intended to be a guide. The flexible use of other probing questions that ask about the Reviewer's feelings and experiences broaden the review. Use the LRF to ensure that you address all of life's stages but be adaptive and creative depending on the Reviewer and the Reviewer's individual personal story.

Suggested Questions for Adolescence

- **Did you feel well guided growing up?**
- When you think about yourself and your life as a teenager, what is the first thing you can remember about that time?
- **Did you feel good about yourself as a teenager?**
- What other things stand out in your memory about being an adolescent?
- Who were the important people for you? Tell me about them (parents, brothers, sisters, friends, teachers).
- Who were you especially close to? Who did you admire? Who did you most want to be like?
- **Were there cliques or special groups in your day?**
- Did you attend church and youth groups?
- How far did you go in school? Did you enjoy school?
- **Did you have a sense of belonging at school or in groups?**
- Did you work during these years?
- Tell me of any hardships you experienced at this time.
- **Did you participate in sports and/or in school activities?**
- **Did you enjoy school activities? Why?**
- Do you remember feeling left alone, abandoned, or not having enough love or care as a child or adolescent?
- What were the pleasant memories about your adolescence?
- **Did you do well in school studies/academics? Did you work hard at school? Why/why not?**
- All things considered, would you say you were happy or unhappy as a teenager?
- **Do you remember your first attraction to another person?**
- How did you feel about sexual activities and your own sexual identity?

Questions About Adolescence

As you get into your third visit, your focus should be on the remainder of the Reviewer's childhood and the beginning of adolescence. Some people talk about adolescence with fondness; others don't ever want to visit that time again! Before you start this session, think of your own adolescence and try to remember what and who were important to you. Your own memories of what seemed important in adolescence may raise similar memories of importance to your Reviewer. During adolescence, children begin to measure themselves by a different standard than was used in childhood. Friends, and their opinions, become more important than the opinions of the family. The following questions are good probes for you to use to explore adolescence: *Who was important to you outside of your family (friends, teachers, and so forth)? Who did you admire?* The list on page 100 offers even more choices about adolescence and school for you to use in conjunction with or in addition to the family and home questions in the preceding chapter (see list on page 84).

A good example of using original questions to explore influential relationships outside of the immediate family was demonstrated by the Therapeutic Listener working with Mr. T. She asked him about the important people in his life when he was a teenager and an adolescent. Mr. T responded with a story of a principal who brightened a bad time for him.

> Mr. T: *The one man who was interested in me was the school principal. He very early seemed to realize I had interests of my own and he would stop and talk to me. And he was also trying to introduce some progressive policies at the school. He influenced me a great deal. One day he went to take a look at my program and saw that I would be going to college into a professional field of study. And he immediately saw that the program I was in at school would be useless and that I was wasting my time. So he went to work and rearranged my entire program.*
>
> Listener: *So he really advocated for you.*
>
> Mr. T: *Yes, I owe him a lot.*

You can see that most Reviewers enjoy recalling the people who guided them as they were growing up. Asking about special people is generally nonthreatening and is a good technique for Listeners. This technique can change the direction of a sad story and can act as a diversionary topic when needed. The next sections of this chapter offer other useful types of questions and techniques to enlarge your basic inventory of Life Review questions.

Probing Questions

Probing questions are those that dig a little bit deeper into the circumstances surrounding a memory. They are more invasive and so must be used carefully, with tact. Probing types of questions often bring out the rest of the story that the Reviewer didn't share before. They often reveal the Reviewer's feelings. Probing questions can cause discomfort and uneasiness, as they cause Reviewers to think a little more deeply about what they had experienced and what they just said. Probing questions may also cause Reviewers to change their thinking because, when Reviewers examine events closely in the present, they do so with the gift of hindsight, possibly generating a new view of the past. Additionally, when Reviewers seem to be discussing memories superficially, Listeners may need to press Reviewers to use more evaluation and insight, as the Listener did in the following example.

If you were the Listener reviewing with Mr. T, you would want to fully explore and exhaust his feelings of inadequacy that were apparently present during adolescence, and are somewhat prevailing still, by asking probing questions.

> LISTENER: *How can a retired history professor who worked so hard to get a Ph.D. feel inadequate?*

> MR.T: *I don't know. I'm always surprised when people tell me I've done good things.*

And then Mr. T embellished his answer with a story about a visit from his mother:

> *My mother was quite surprised by the respect shown to me around the campus. I think she was actually surprised when students chose to defer to me. She stayed for a few weeks and we had quite a good time doing things around town. I didn't earn as much money as my brothers, but it was enough to live well, and she seemed to think so too.*

You can see how the probing question caused Mr. T to again examine his past more closely. He finally realized that he already had parental approval. As Mr. T's Life Review progressed, there were fewer comparisons with other people where he found himself wanting. He realized the significance of what he had achieved on his own, though bookish and slight of build. If the Therapeutic Listener had not probed Mr. T about his feelings of inadequacy, Mr. T might never have reached his newly achieved comfortable stage of self-acceptance. You can learn a great deal from this example regarding the need to continue exploring events until the Reviewer reaches an understanding of why he believes the way he does.

> *Continue exploring events until the Reviewer reaches an understanding of why he believes the way he does.*

Questions About School

Questions about school experiences contribute to the picture of adolescence by bringing people outside of the family into the Life Review. Moreover, such questions are relevant and material because most Life Reviewers have spent a large part of their adolescence in school. The questions you ask about school encourage Reviewers to recall other connections and role models that influenced their adolescent lives and subsequent development. Peer approval is often more important than parental approval in adolescence; without such peer acceptance adolescents may have developed feelings of inferiority that need examining now.

Questions about school can initiate questions about friendships, giving Reviewers an opportunity to examine their first public persona and relationships outside of the family. Or, in some instances, as in the case of Mrs. W—the child who could never please her mother— questions about school encouraged a more positive life story that allowed her to be more than a humiliated child. She was able to describe moments of success outside of the home and, for a change, she was able to relate a more positive narrative than her earlier story of child neglect and abuse.

Questions about school are generally non-threatening but can lead to interesting revelations. Reviewers may choose to answer an open-ended question about school with whatever is important to them or with whatever they feel like sharing, allowing the Reviewer and Listener more time to establish an intimate and comfortable relationship before dealing with more personal questions.

> Questions about school are generally nonthreatening but can lead to interesting revelations.

LISTENER: *What was school like for you?*

REVIEWER: *I was actually bored in the first grade. I was in what they call the advanced reading circle. I don't know that I realized I was advanced, you know children, and you're in a circle. I remember getting home the first day of school and my aunt seeing something moving in my hair. I had head lice of all things. Mama fixed it and called the school, and then everyone was examined for head lice. My mother took care of the problem immediately.*

In response to such a Reviewer's memory, you, the Therapeutic Listener, should ask the Reviewer how it felt to have head lice or how it felt to be advanced in school. You could also explore the Reviewer's relationship with her mother, who took immediate care of the head lice. The Reviewer's story presents many new leads to other recalled stories that will enhance and enlarge the Life Review.

Questions About Feelings

By asking Reviewers how they feel about a memory, you cause them to think more deeply about it, perhaps getting them to determine the meaning of the memory to them and to their lives. We call this type of question "feeling questions" or "evaluative questions." Feeling questions encourage Reviewers to look more closely at their lives than they normally would. These questions tend to instigate more detailed descriptions about whatever event is under discussion and can help the Reviewer become more insightful. Unfortunately, many people do not look closely at the way past events personally influenced them; thus they lack understanding of why they are the way they are. By helping Reviewers to become more insightful about themselves through a Life Review, you will give them the ability to better reconcile their lives.

You can help Reviewers learn to look more deeply into their past by role-modeling the use of evaluative feeling questions. Soon Reviewers will be asking themselves those same questions: *"How did I feel? Was I sad? Did it really matter to me?"* As Reviewers develop a more introspective behavior, their Life Review memories will become richer, leading to more in-depth and ongoing self-evaluation of future memories.

Counseling Skill: Caring

To be an effective Therapeutic Listener, you need to incorporate selected counseling skills and interviewing techniques into your usual ways of listening and responding. Caring is an important counseling skill that creates a warm, open atmosphere, encouraging dialogue.

> *The ability to truly care may be the most important skill that effective Listeners put into practice with their Reviewers.*

Caring is the process whereby the Therapeutic Listener creates a compassionate climate by demonstrating feelings of concern, affection, and interest toward the Life Reviewer during the Life Review relationship. The ability to truly care may be the most important skill that effective Listeners put into practice with their Reviewers. Caring is an umbrella skill from which all other counseling skills evolve and then relate to one another.

Caring is both a skill and a personal trait. As a skill, caring can be learned; as a trait, it is probably inherent in one's personality and a part of a person's makeup. If sincere caring is not part of your natural makeup, you can learn that skill by trying to sincerely like people and by feeling interest, affection, and respect for your Reviewers as they talk about their lives. While listening, you must project your compassionate feelings toward your Reviewers so that they can feel them. Practice this also with others; you will be a better friend and relative as well!

When you truly care, you create a safe atmosphere of interest, closeness, and warmth that envelops Reviewers while they share their stories. Reviewers can then feel the compassion and respect of such caring Listeners. Caring also fosters trust between Listener and Reviewer. Conversely, if you remain detached from or indifferent to your Reviewers, they will sense this and will withhold important recollections while failing to form bonds of trust with you. In essence, without caring, you will be unable to create the proper receptive atmosphere and neither you nor the Life Review will be therapeutic. The next Listener portrays caring in this excerpt from a real Life Review:

LISTENER: *You may never be able to change people's opinions of you.*

REVIEWER: *I understand that.*

LISTENER: *But you can certainly change how you think about yourself. Even if you screwed some things up, you did more good than harm.*

REVIEWER: *Do you honestly think so?*

LISTENER: **Yes, yes I do. Sometimes it's hard to accept our human failings, but we all have them. You got caught in a crunch and became a scapegoat; the rest of us get to push our failings into a closet and don't have to parade them around like you had to.**

REVIEWER: *I've never done anything like this before but it helps, really helps. It really does, to be able to talk to someone who cares and to get it out. So there it is.*

Caring by words, deeds, and body language creates a warm, pervasive climate, something that one feels. You must smile and nod often to make your Reviewer feel cared for. Combine and apply all the skills, techniques, and listening practices that we have presented for you in this Handbook in order to become a Caring Listener, just as the Listener did in the previous example.

Interviewing Techniques

This chapter applies two more interviewing techniques to actual practice: Responding and Reflecting Feeling. Excerpts from actual Reviewers illustrate the application of these two techniques as teaching examples in the following pages.

Responding

Responding is the technique of directly and appropriately addressing the current recalled memories of the Life Reviewers so that they know they have been heard and understood right now. You must listen carefully to each word being spoken and responsively react with suitable body language or comments that encourage the Reviewer to recall and say more. Good responding requires you to closely follow the Reviewer's conversation and to react appropriately: soon, on topic, and in a caring way—in a word, responsively. By responding immediately and positively to the Reviewer's words, you show that you are listening and paying attention. Your appropriate and reactive responses often foster new awareness in Reviewers, whereas responses such as "*um hm*" do not shape the Life Review therapeutically. Your responses should be thoughtful and on target, and guide Reviewers as they tell their story, just as this Therapeutic Listener did for Mrs. R:

MRS. R: *When I was little, my Mother died. I never even knew she was sick. I had three older brothers but my Daddy didn't know what to do with a little girl, so he gave me to my Aunt and my brothers stayed with him.*

LISTENER: **Did you miss your Daddy and your brothers?**

MRS. R: *Yes, I felt like I wasn't wanted because the boys got to stay, my Mother was gone, and my Daddy didn't love me anymore. It was really lonely and I remember crying all the time.*

LISTENER: *Being lonely is hard, but how was it living with your Aunt?*

MRS. R: *Actually, not so bad. She didn't have any other children so I was special in her house. After a while I got used to being away from my Daddy and brothers. She bought me pretty dresses and walked me to school everyday. She was happy to have me and I got used to being there.*

LISTENER: *So you were special. Did you feel loved by your aunt?*

MRS. R: *She loved me a lot and always showed me that she did. I guess I was lucky.*

LISTENER: *So how do you feel about the move now?*

The Listener kept exploring this traumatic event in Mrs. R's life by responding to Mrs. R's story appropriately with multiple prompts and feeling questions. As the Listener and Mrs. R worked through the events of her childhood, Mrs. R began to see that her childhood move may have been the best thing for her, that her father still loved her and visited her often until the day he died, but that he couldn't care for her as well as her aunt did. The responses of the Therapeutic Listener caused Mrs. R to look at the past differently, in a more positive light. Her view changed from that of an abandoned child to that of a fortunate child who was loved by two families. Although Mrs. R did this evaluation herself and reframed her own thinking, the responses of this caring, responsive Listener prompted her to consider differently the events of her past.

Reflecting Feelings

Reflecting feelings is the act of giving back or returning the Reviewers' same feelings as they recall their life stories. This technique requires you to interpret the Reviewers' emotions while they are talking and then to respond by showing that you understand what they are feeling at the time. Mirroring, or reflecting their emotions, is one effective way to demonstrate that you understand what the Reviewers are saying and feeling.

Reviewers often do not state what they are feeling, but the emotions that they display through facial expressions, tones of voice, and body language can be perceptible parts of their story. By being attentive, you can interpret the changes in voice and body language of the Reviewer who is telling the story and then confirm your interpretation by reflecting your reading back to the Reviewer in clear words, tone, and body language that the Reviewer can confirm or deny. For example, in listening to a story about World War II, a Therapeutic Listener detected anger in the Reviewer's voice.

> *The emotions that they display through facial expressions, tones of voice, and body language can be perceptible parts of their story.*

LISTENER: *You sound angry when you talk about your Army experience.*

REVIEWER: *I guess I am, but I didn't realize it until you said it. I guess I've been angry for a long time.*

By sensing the emotions behind the Reviewers' memories, you will gain a fuller understanding of the Reviewers' experiences and, in turn, can help Reviewers to better understand themselves. You should not assume that you properly interpret every recalled memory. Rather, you should make reflective statements to seek clarification from the Reviewer of the Reviewer's feelings. Reviewers will either confirm or deny your interpretation. When they think about what you have said, Reviewers may also gain insight and get to know themselves better, thus enhancing their evaluation of what occurred in their lives.

Unique Life Review Characteristic: Structure

The Structured Life Review process is markedly different from other types of reminiscing because of its four unique characteristics: Structure, Duration, Individuality, and Evaluation. The first characteristic, Structure, is described in this chapter; the other characteristics are described in the next three chapters. The Integration chapter (Visit 7) summarizes the use of all four characteristics.

The unique **structure** that guides the Life Review process is the result of four components:

1. Erikson's model of life's development
2. The number of required visits
3. The LRF questions
4. The guidance provided by the Therapeutic Listener

Erikson's model provides the basis for the developmental format of the Life Review. His work is a logical way to approach looking at one's life. Thus, his model of eight, life-developmental stages, which is basically chronological, corresponds to the visits of the Life Review. Erikson's last stage of life, Integrity, occurring in maturity, reflects the ultimate goal of the Life Review, which is to accept one's life as it has been lived. By traversing Erikson's stages in retrospect and reconciling old issues in the present, most Reviewers reach the goal that the Life Review has established for them: to reach Integrity by reconciling and accepting their lives.

The second component of Structure—the number of recommended visits with each Reviewer—correlates with Erikson's developmental model: eight ages of man and eight visits. The eight visits of the Life Review provide structure and guide Reviewers developmentally and incrementally through the memories of their lives one week at a time, starting with childhood and ending with old age, corresponding to Erikson's stages.

The types and scope of the questions on the LRF constitute the third component of Structure. They again focus and guide Reviewers through each developmental stage while helping them search for their memories. The LRF's structured and focused questions assure that Reviewers will cover all phases of their lives. Finally, the questions on the LRF cause Reviewers to evaluate their lives to help them reach the last stage, Integrity, with the use of "feeling" (evaluative) questions (e.g., *"How did that make you feel?" "What was your happiest memory?"*).

The fourth and most important component of the process's unique structure is *you,* the Therapeutic Listener. It is incumbent upon the Therapeutic Listener to select key questions, respond to the Reviewer's particular life and recalled memories, and to guide Reviewers through their particular, individual lives by addressing each Reviewer's life stages. Although Reviewers are in control of what they cover and say in their Life Review, the Listener is the stable hand, guiding the process. The Listener must:

1. Ask the appropriate questions
2. Handle the variety of Reviewers
3. Keep the Reviewers on topic
4. Be certain to at least cover all the stages of the Reviewer's life

Since the structure of the Life Review is developmental, not strictly chronological, it is acceptable for Reviewers to move back and forth between developmental stages, especially if their story calls for it or they are reminded of other connected events. However, Therapeutic Listeners must ensure that Reviewers cover all the developmental phases of their lives in order to fully implement the requirement of Structure in the Life Review process. Further, the Listener guides the Reviewer to identify any issues and helps the Reviewer to rationalize or reconcile those life issues—thereby achieving Integrity.

Reviewer Type: The External Reviewer

External Reviewers talk about the past in an impersonal, observational manner, rarely including themselves in the memories they are recalling. They talk about events as if they were observers of life but not actual participants in their own lives. Thus External Reviewers never really seem to participate in an evaluative Life Review. Therapeutic Listeners have to encourage such External Reviewers to talk about themselves, and this is often hard work. Lifetime habits prevail in the way in which Reviewers describe their memories. They may naturally be shy or introverted, or they were taught as children that it was prideful or that it was rude to talk about themselves. When it comes time for a Life Review, the effect of such childhood lessons interferes with the storytelling and the personalizing of their lives. You have to find ways to overcome the tendencies of External Reviewers to leave themselves out of their recollections and stories.

One way to get External Reviewers to talk about themselves is to set an example through a story of your own. For example, in the following session, the Therapeutic Listener chose to disclose her own memories of her family for two reasons: first, to establish more closeness between the Reviewer and herself; and second, to role model talking about herself or her family in a personal way. The conversation with the External Reviewer went like this:

> LISTENER: *What do you remember about going to school?*
>
> REVIEWER: *The school was 2 or 3 miles away and was on top of a big hill. Everybody walked to school, there were no buses. There were only five teachers because everyone else was contributing to the war effort. The classes were big and had 2 or 3 grades in them.*

The Therapeutic Listener listened to this memory of school that was detailed but did not involve the Reviewer at all, and when she asked questions to try to involve the Life Reviewer, she received only terse answers:

> LISTENER: *How was the walk?*
>
> REVIEWER: *OK, I guess.*
>
> LISTENER: *Were any of the teachers special to you?*
>
> REVIEWER: *No.*
>
> LISTENER: *Did you like school?*
>
> REVIEWER: *OK, I guess.*

As the conversation continued to fail, the Therapeutic Listener was at a loss and decided to share a story she had heard from her father, who was approximately the same age as the Reviewer:

> *My father used to talk about going to school; he said it was uphill both ways! He didn't care about school a lot; he didn't even have shoes to wear so he would rather stay home because the other kids made fun of him. About the only fun he had was when he passed the apple orchard on his way. He said he and his brother would climb the fence and steal little green apples that were so good and tart, you wouldn't believe it. Sometimes they ate them, but other times, they would gather enough for a pie and their mother would bake one for them.*

While the Therapeutic Listener was talking, the Reviewer began to smile and continued the conversation:

> REVIEWER: *My brother and I used to steal apples on the way to school, but we got in trouble if we picked them off the trees—that was real stealing—so we shook the trees until the apples fell to the ground and then we could pick them up and take them. We were poor too; one year we had to share the shoes, so we took turns going to school.*

Visit 3

LISTENER: *Were you ever hungry?*

REVIEWER: *I don't know. Well, we had something to eat but it wasn't what we wanted all the time. I'd like a piece of candy or a cracker sometime, but we just never had that so it was no need to wish for it.*

The Life Review continued on a much better note as the Reviewer continued to talk about himself, poverty, and his family. With an External Reviewer, you have to remember to personalize events almost continually and to repeatedly probe for the Reviewer's involvement with follow-up comments such as, *"So you never felt like you went hungry?"*

You have to involve Reviewers personally in the process; Life Review is about them and is not therapeutic if they do not talk about themselves. Much of the therapy that happens in Life Review is the result of self-analysis and evaluation, particularly of incidents that have a great deal of meaning for the Reviewer. Reviewers who do not include themselves in their stories cannot evaluate and analyze their stories for meaning to themselves, thus bypassing a beneficial portion of the Life Review process.

End Visit 3

Summarize Session

As you get ready to finish the third visit, you should observe whether or not the present topic of conversation is an unhappy one. If it is unhappy, think about what you can say to bring out the lighter and brighter side of the conversation. Using Mr. T as an example for such a summary, you would note that he talked about being skinny and being the only nonathlete in the family, but that he was an excellent student and succeeded in school, his brothers probably envied his skill with scholarly things, and his parents, especially his father, admired his expertise in history. In the past and even in the present, Mr. T wasn't that proud of his scholarly achievements because he thought being athletic was more valued, but you could end the session on a happy note by praising his success in academics and reminding him of the pride he felt when his mother came to visit him at the college where he taught. As you are closing, leaving *your* Mr. T to enjoy these pleasant memories of his success in life, you need to remind your Reviewer that next week you will talk about his adulthood, his work, and his relationships.

Next Visit

As you pack your bag, negotiate a date and time for the next session of Life Review. Ask the Reviewer if the seating arrangement was comfortable and private enough; if it was, plan to repeat the arrangement the next week. Complete the visit by saying a pleasant good-bye and presenting the Reviewer with an appointment card in bold print. Again, make notes immediately after the encounter so that you are prepared for the next session.

YOUNG ADULTHOOD

*I tend to live in the past because most
of my life is there.*

—Herb Caen

The fourth visit of the Life Review process is a key visit because it is a possible turning point for the Life Reviewer. This visit occurs in the middle of the 8-week process when Reviewers are familiar with the process. Now that they have experienced part of a Life Review, some will be sorry they started and drop out; others will continue and be even more open. By now, most Reviewers may have developed a reasonable bond and trust with the Therapeutic Listener. They probably are enjoying and looking forward to the continuing process. During this fourth visit, the Reviewer recalls young adulthood, a time when important, independent decisions were made that may have influenced the rest of the Reviewer's life. Reviewers who continue are usually eager to begin Visit 4.

Preliminary Tasks

The same preparations as detailed in the "Getting Started" chapter need to be addressed at the beginning of each session. Therefore, you may look back at that chapter to refresh your memory regarding the details for the Reviewer's comfort, hearing, and vision, and the location's appropriateness. There is comfort in familiarity, so using the same seating arrangement each week contributes to a feeling of security and trust. A glass of water by the side of the Reviewer remains an essential courtesy. Finally, the proper placement of the tape recorder—turned on—assures good copy for listening to the session when it is over. Now you are ready to begin again!

Pivotal Session for Reviewer

The key determinant to Visit 4 may be a matter of the bonding that is taking place between Reviewer and Listener. Reviewers who bond with and trust their Listeners become committed to completing the Life Review by the fourth session. Such Reviewers have had enough visits to see where the Life Review is going and they want more. Some Reviewers are very eager to continue and become even more open and committed, enjoying the Life Review immensely. Committed Reviewers tend to lead the process from here on, and the Therapeutic Listener becomes more and more a sounding board and guiding hand, rather than an initiator. There seems to be a joint commitment to complete the Life Review that is exciting for both parties.

Conversely, those who drop out usually state that they don't want to remember or divulge any more. They may have decided the process is too invasive to their privacy and they choose not to stir up any more old memories. For years they may have successfully pushed down traumatic events. Living with those memories in the backs of their minds has been tolerable, but recalling and sharing them perhaps is not. Actually, those who choose not to participate further may not yet be ready to remember more, nor are they ready for therapy, which they also may refuse. It is noted that most of the Life Reviews in this book have been conducted as a part of research projects, and the participants were sought out as volunteers. Although fully informed, some did not realize that their memories would possibly hurt. They did not seek us nor did they particularly want to get therapy. We asked them to do a Life Review and they agreed, but once they began the process, some decided Life Review was not for them. They were just not ready to explore their lives and they had the right to refuse to do so.

Although Reviewers have the right to discontinue the process at any time, they will gain the most by completing their Life Review. You may tell them of others' good results and encourage them to remain until they finish the Life Review, if they think they can. A few of these people will persist in dropping out, but the experience to date may cause them to seek help later, if needed. You can leave them your name and contact number in case they change their minds and wish to contact you at a later date. Also, you might ask such Reviewers if there was anything about the process, including yourself, that led to their decision. This is a good way to get helpful feedback. Of course, you should learn from this feedback.

Clarify Visit 3

As you begin Visit 4, you will be prompting the Reviewers to leave childhood behind, unless of course something reminds them of an important childhood event that was not recalled or shared earlier. Before proceeding with Visit 4, however, you need to summarize and clarify the previous visit. Both you and the Reviewer need to gain clarity about the importance of events remembered in Visit 3 concerning childhood and the impact of childhood on the rest of the Reviewer's life. If needed, you can summarize highlights and state your impressions. Reviewers will correct false impressions if you summarize incorrectly, providing clarity for both you and the Reviewer.

Closure on Childhood

It is best to gain a clear closure on childhood memories before you continue to young adulthood. Childhood memories are the furthest away, most difficult to remember, and sometimes the most traumatic. Reviewers may need one more chance to recall and address such childhood issues, if any. By the fourth visit, Reviewers who continue on will probably trust you and the process more and be more comfortable sharing such issues or secrets. One Reviewer, Mrs. N, was asked if there was anything else she wanted to talk about in her childhood before beginning to address adulthood. She finally felt at ease with the Listener and shared this story of her childhood:

> *Childhood memories are the furthest away, most difficult to remember, and sometimes the most traumatic.*

MRS. N: *I remember my father as being good humored and laughing.*

LISTENER: **Was your mother like that too?**

MRS. N: *I don't know because there are four years of my life I don't remember. It started in the first grade and ended in the fourth grade. My mommy and daddy didn't get along. I remember them arguing a lot.*

LISTENER: **When they argued, what was it like for you?**

MRS. N: *I had the pillow on one ear and the covers over another. I couldn't sleep. Daddy forced pills down my mother and I could hear her voice getting slurred. He would bang her head against the headboard or the mirror or side table.*

LISTENER: **So this went on for a long time?**

MRS. N: *At least it went on for four years, then Momma left. I counted her dresses. She had 13 and I thought she would be away 13 days.*

LISTENER: *What was that like for you?*

MRS. N: *I don't know, I knew it was something she had to do. I found out later Daddy paid people to lie about my mother and he brainwashed me to testify against her. I don't know what I said. I lost those years and I don't know when Momma came back. She told me about helping with my homework, and I started to remember, but I don't remember the bad part and I don't want to.*

This story of childhood was pivotal to Mrs. N's entire Life Review. All of her life, she worried about having testified in her mother's hearing and wondering what she had said. She never seemed able to forgive herself for testifying against her mother. She did not feel comfortable sharing anything about what she thought was a disgraceful story until the fourth visit, when she trusted her Listener. She regretted losing her memory for 4 years, but she never wanted to explore her memories of those 4 years. The Therapeutic Listener advised her to see someone more qualified when she was ready to learn about those 4 years of her life. But as Mrs. N continued her Life Review, the lost memory took on less and less importance. She successfully proceeded to talk about her young adulthood.

Unfinished Business

People with unfinished business often will tell you something private and personal as you or they are going out the door. Reviewers do this on the spur of the moment but deliberately. They forgot, omitted, or lacked the courage to formally address the issue earlier, so they make a passing, departing comment. You should realize that such a parting shot is usually of an important nature that needs to resurface again when you and the Reviewer know each other better and the Reviewer is feeling more confident. For example, as Mr. Y, a big man, completed an hour of Life Review and was going out the door, he said, *"My father left me when I was 12 years old,"* and turned away before his Listener could respond. During the next visit, while summarizing the earlier session, the Listener noted Mr. Y's reference to being left and, before starting the questions on adulthood, the Listener said, *"I'd like to hear more about your father leaving you."* Mr. Y was eager to tell his story now, as he felt more comfortable by the fourth visit:

> *When I was 12 years old, my father left me on the side of the road and told me I was too big and he couldn't afford to feed me anymore. I was so scared; it was in the middle of the night. I didn't know where I was and I didn't know where to go. I knew my family didn't love me if they could just drop me off on the side of the road. I just kept hoping they would come back. I missed my brothers and sisters and my mother, but not my father because he hit me when he was drinking or when something went wrong. I had never been to school so I couldn't read or write. I still can't. Crying didn't do me no good, so when the sun came up, I started walking. I walked for two days. I didn't meet anyone. I ate grass but had nothing to drink. I was giving up,*

sitting in the grass crying, when a truck went by and then turned around and came back to see what was wrong.

The man driving the truck was a white man but he was kind. He listened to me and then put me in the truck and took me to his house. His wife gave me something to eat and drink. After hearing my story, he asked me if I wanted to live in the barn and work for him. He took care of the cemetery and was a gravedigger. I was big and strong and good at digging graves. So I worked for him and lived in his barn until I got sick and we both got too old to dig graves anymore. He was good to me and still comes to visit me here sometimes. He put money in the bank for me and got me a Social Security number, so now I have enough to live in this apartment. He was more like a father to me than my own father was. I never found my family again; I still don't know where they are, so I guess I was an orphan except for my boss and his wife.

The Therapeutic Listener listened attentively to Mr. Y's additional childhood story. Being abandoned as a child and losing his family was certainly traumatic unfinished business for Mr. Y. He had not talked about his abandonment much in the past, but talking about his childhood resurrected that event for him. The memory had been on his mind the whole time but he didn't feel comfortable enough to share the story until Visit 4. The Listener made certain that Mr. Y reviewed this traumatic event thoroughly for the next few weeks during the early part of each visit and then moved on to adulthood for the rest of the visits. Through repetition, Mr. Y was able to reconcile this untoward event and then to progress in his Life Review.

Erikson's Model: Adolescence to Young Adulthood

The fourth visit is structured to cover Erikson's fifth and sixth developmental stages: Identity vs. Role Confusion and Intimacy vs. Isolation.

Identity vs. Role Confusion

Erikson says this fifth stage is the end of childhood and the beginning of adulthood, leading to the development of a personal identity. A person's identity is one's view of oneself, influenced by the opinions of others, especially parents, teachers, and other role models. The developed identity, so dependent on the opinions of others, then influences each person's self-esteem. In other words, "I think I am OK if you think I am OK as well." If others do not reinforce the "I'm OK" feeling, then doubt occurs. Those uncertain persons experience confusion about their identity or role in society. Role confusion can grow and compound unless one's view of self is somehow positively reinforced throughout life, and even then it is difficult for an individual to figure out how he or she fits into the world as a whole.

One person who doubted his identity as a youth was Mr. T, who was mentioned in an earlier chapter for his lack of athletic and manly skills. While growing up, Mr. T felt belittled because he was not a football player and suffered role confusion for many years, feeling inadequate and unworthy. However, through his Life Review he finally realized that he had succeeded in life as a historian and professor and began to feel comfortable with that new identity.

If some of your Reviewers experienced role confusion in their youth, you can help them now by encouraging them to question and reframe their own picture of themselves at this point. Often, perceived failures in childhood, such as not belonging to a special group or not getting good enough grades in school, negatively influence a Reviewer's sense of self-esteem and then continue to be a negative influence on the Reviewer's growing sense of Self. To help such Reviewers, get them to examine their present identity by confronting their picture of themselves. Point out discrepancies between what they are really like in the present and their own personal view of Self based on the past. Then, help them to redirect their memories to focus on known successes, which may slowly get them to adopt a more positive attitude toward themselves. Like Mr. T and Mrs. R, they can reframe old conclusions, minimize the awkward events of the past, and paint a new, more positive picture of themselves in the present, finally realizing and embracing their true identity.

Intimacy vs. Isolation

As young people emerge from their identity struggles, they turn to encountering intimacy and relationships with others. Mastering these social skills is an important step toward becoming a caring adult who is less self-focused and more other-focused. However, those without a strong sense of themselves find relationships with others difficult to master. Rather than risk failure, they often put themselves in danger of becoming isolated. Sexual identity is a part of intimacy and primary to knowing one's self. Intimacy initiates the stage of being attracted to another and "falling in love." Mrs. H talked excitedly about discovering the opposite sex:

> *I hung out with a group of girls all through high school. I remember one girl*
> *inviting boys to her birthday party and the boys wanted to play spin the bottle.*
> *The girls made believe they weren't interested but we all wanted to try kissing.*
> *It was great. I've enjoyed it ever since. (Laughing)*

The Therapeutic Listener laughed with Mrs. H and said, *"Tell me about meeting your husband."* And the stories of relationships continued in this Life Review.

Erikson said that the opposite aspect of intimacy is isolation. People who do not form relationships easily with others find it increasingly hard to develop relationships as time goes on. Since relationships require both giving and receiving, people who start out as loners can find it increasingly hard to initiate and even harder to maintain relationships. Notably, if an isolated Reviewer enjoys sharing the Life Review relationship with a Therapeutic Listener, that Reviewer will be more likely to seek additional relationships when the Life Review is finished.

With the proper probing questions, you can help isolated Reviewers see that they are denying themselves pleasant relationships and closeness with others. Sometimes they isolate themselves through fear of being rejected and other times because they think they prefer to be left alone, or for other reasons. You need to help Reviewers gain insight into their isolated state and, once

> *You can help isolated Reviewers see that they are denying themselves pleasant relationships and closeness with others.*

gained, encourage them to reach out to others. A Reviewer who needs to develop social skills can reach out to others in service or volunteer work. There are many possibilities, such as joining a Big Brothers/Sisters Club to act as a big "sibling" to a child without a parent. Also, that Reviewer could volunteer to deliver meals on wheels to shut-ins and slowly develop social skills as a volunteer before socializing with peers.

Once you realize that your Reviewer is presently isolated, you can discuss those realistic options for him or her. Such Reviewers who then have to think about others often forget to dwell on themselves. Or, perhaps being a part of a group is even less threatening, and you may want to suggest that choice to a Reviewer. There are many group opportunities available: a church group, a book club if the Reviewer likes to read, an exercise group if the Reviewer is athletic, or a senior center. Encouraging Reviewers to make one or more connections as you later complete the Life Review in Visit 8 is a good way to end your visits and to help Reviewers become more involved with others.

As we complete these particular stages of Erikson's developmental model, consider what a traumatic time this must have been for people questioning their sexual identity. Not only did they question their own role in life, they probably shied away from intimacy with others while they figured out who they were and why they were different from their peers. Visit 4 is a good time for you to ask about dilemmas such as this and to open the door to such a discussion through your own questions and those on the LRF. Older people, such as the gay man who suggested we add questions on homosexuality to our LRF, would benefit from this direct approach.

Using the Life Review Form

The Visit 4 portion of the LRF centers on young adulthood. As you begin this fourth session of Life Review, you need to continue the good job of helping Reviewers recall the past while allowing for individual differences that are common among Reviewers in adulthood. The questions listed on page 118 may work for your Reviewers or they may need other questions customized to their interests.

All Reviewers do not need specific tailored or customized questions. Some Reviewers become so involved in telling their life story that they just need guidance and appropriate responses to what they say. Reviewers such as these do not need more questions, but should be directed ahead each week as they keep on talking to make certain they cover

Suggested Questions for Young Adulthood

- Now I'd like to talk to you about your life as an adult, starting when you were in your 20s. What were the most important events in your adult years?

- As an adult, did you do what you were supposed to do in life?

- What was life like for you in your 20s and 30s?

- Did you think of yourself as responsible?

- What kind of person were you? What did you enjoy?

- Tell me about your work. Did you enjoy your work? Did you earn an adequate living? Did you work hard during those years? Were you appreciated?

- Were you happy with your choices?

- Did you have enough money?

- Did you form significant relationships with other people?

- Did you marry?
  - ☐ (yes) What kind of person was your spouse?
  - ☐ (no) Why not?

- Do you think marriages get better or worse over time? Were you married more than once?

- Did you have children? Tell me about them.

- What important decisions did you make during this time?

- On the whole, would you say you had a happy or unhappy marriage?

---

all of life's developmental stages. At the end of each hour visit, you should summarize that visit and provide future direction for the Reviewer by introducing the topic for the next week's visit.

Customize Questions

Other Reviewers need more coaching and/or an individualized focus. For instance, some Reviewers have never married, thus the questions on the LRF regarding marriage are inappropriate and should be ignored or adjusted. Alternative queries can include questions about intimacies, friendships, work, or hobbies. Some people go to college, some to work; others get married, or join the military, or learn a trade. Many Reviewers have had successful careers that dominated their adulthood, and talking about these careers will in turn dominate their Life Reviews. Your questions should reflect the Reviewer's choices in life as closely as possible. Follow up with what you already know about your Reviewer and build on the clues that Reviewers give you as they talk about their lives.

The following excerpts from Miss C's Life Review illustrate a Life Review that is different from that of many other women because Miss C focused on work and never married or had her own family:

> LISTENER: *Tell me about your life as a young adult.*

> MISS C: *Well, in my day there was no money for college, so I went out looking for a job. The one thing I loved more than anything else was clothes, so I went to the biggest department store to try to get a job in the dress department, and I did. I worked there for 40 years before I retired, and when I retired, I was head of buying for the store.*

> LISTENER: *What an achievement; to do that today you would have to go to college first. Tell me more about those years?*

Miss C recalled how much she enjoyed displaying the merchandise, finding the right dress for the right person, and matching accessories to the dresses. Miss C thoroughly loved her work and loved talking about it. After exhausting the details of Miss C's work life, the Listener then asked what she did for fun when she wasn't working. Miss C responded with stories of going to USO dances with her girlfriends and dating one particular man whom she loved. Miss C said she had to say "No" when he proposed because she couldn't move to another town with him while caring for her mother. After some time and much fruitless persuasion, he moved away without her.

In this example, the Therapeutic Listener obviously did not use the marriage questions that are part of the LRF, but instead concentrated on Miss C's career, using questions that corresponded to Miss C's chosen lifestyle.

Examine Past Decisions

When reflecting on their lives, Reviewers often are troubled by the decisions they made in the past that influenced their particular life course. They are often not certain that they made the right decisions when they look back at them. But when they talk about them in the Life Review they can achieve a kind of clarity and perhaps realize that they did not really have the freedom to make alternative decisions. For them, the way things were, had to be. You can help them examine their past decisions closely by discussing these decisions in the Review, as the Listener did for Miss C when she responded to Miss C's statement regarding her need to care for her mother: *"Do you think you made the right decision to stay behind and care for your mother?"*

> *Reviewers often are troubled by the decisions they made in the past that influenced their particular life course.*

Visit 4

Miss C thought about the Listener's question and then confirmed in her response that she really had no other viable choice, she could not follow her boyfriend to marry him, and caring for her mother was the only decision she could have made at the time.

When you work with such a Reviewer, your insightful comments and questions will help Reviewers examine their options, and hopefully reconcile them to the choices they made. You need to help Reviewers find what is positive in those choices. Or, help Reviewers at least realize that maybe they did not have another realistic choice at all by asking questions that explore the circumstances surrounding the decision. As Miss C discussed her decision from all viewpoints, she became firm in her belief that she had done the right thing by staying with her mother. Miss C even identified good results from staying behind, such as being fortunate to find such compelling work for so many years. She said she enjoyed being an aunt to her sister's children, but, even more, she liked the freedom to work, to spend her money on clothes, and to do what she wanted to do.

Miss C's story is a good example of someone finally coming to terms with a decision made long ago. Doubt about the decision was apparent in her Life Review when she talked about her lost love, and that doubt hovered in the back of Miss C's mind for many years. However, when she finally began to explore the decision with another person, she reconciled her doubt, confirmed her choices, and felt good about them.

Reviewers need to acknowledge their decisions as their own choices in order to actually accept their lives as they were lived. Helping Reviewers accept the decisions that affected their life course is a part of the fourth session of Life Review that addresses young adulthood, the time such big decisions were generally made. Your role is to praise the good decisions while helping Reviewers reconcile poor decisions that took their lives in a seemingly difficult or less desirable direction. For most Reviewers, it is too late to reverse erroneous life decisions, but never too late to accept them or amend them, as Mr. L did:

> *For most Reviewers, it is too late to reverse erroneous life decisions, but never too late to accept them or amend them.*

MR. L: *I worked in a grocery store my whole life. It was my father's grocery store and I started sweeping up when I was 8 years old and kept sweeping till I was 60. I was the oldest of seven children and, when my father died while I was in high school, I had to stay and run the store with my mother so we could support the family. Some of my brothers and sisters went to college and I kept thinking that my turn would come, but then I got my girlfriend pregnant and had to get married and support my own family, so I stayed in the grocery store.*

LISTENER: **What is it you think you missed because of your responsibilities?**

MR. L: *I was always good in math and I would have liked to go to college.*

As Mr. L explored the story of his life, the Therapeutic Listener helped Mr. L to accept his past decision by reminding him that he said his wife and children were his greatest blessing and that he would not have changed that outcome even if he could. The years he spent in the grocery store made his wife and children possible. Mr. L finally realized he had little control over the earlier decision to work in the grocery store, and that decision enabled him to marry and have a good family, but now he could make other choices—and he did.

Mr. L continued his Life Review while also arranging to finally take accounting classes at a nearby college. Not everyone is fortunate enough to be able to overcome and build on a difficult decision as Mr. L did, but by talking about it with a sympathetic Listener, Mr. L began to see other possibilities and explored them fully, amending an earlier decision and finally living out his dream. The Listener helped Mr. L see that in reality he had it all!

Clearer Adult Memories

The memories of adulthood are easier to access in a Life Review, because they are more recent, and the events remembered are usually the most significant ones. Knowing when memories are clearest can be helpful to you as you plan your Life Review visits. Just as you adjust your approach for different types of Reviewers, you may also wish to adjust your methods for accommodating differences in recall. When talking about adulthood, ask about important events—such as weddings, children, promotions—rather than everyday proceedings, such as what that Reviewer did just 3 weeks ago. Know that memories will be richer in adulthood for most people, unless they have dementia, in which case long-term memories are more easily accessible. Be satisfied with memories of the first part of life when working with those who have dementia, and explore the whole adulthood fully in those who have no cognitive losses.

Counseling Skill: Unconditional Positive Regard

Unconditional positive regard means to accept the Reviewer wholeheartedly, without limits or conditions, regardless of the Reviewer's background, or who they are, or what they say. If you accept Reviewers as they are and were, and take them for themselves, they can learn to accept themselves, if that is a problem. For example, Reviewers may be criticizing themselves for past mistakes and talking about old issues that they have never resolved or accepted. Consequently, such Reviewers may expect to receive a similar cold, closed, or critical response from their Listeners. When they do not get that expected response, but instead receive the acceptance of the Listener, it is a pleasant surprise. Then, many such Reviewers may go on to describe even more egregious life events—true or false—to test you further

> *If you accept Reviewers as they are and were, and take them for themselves, they can learn to accept themselves.*

Visit 4

or to make sure that the open, tolerant response from you is still there regardless of what they say. When Reviewers finally realize that they are not being judged, but fully accepted, they often also become empowered and accept themselves, and are more open to you, the Therapeutic Listener.

Mrs. F tells a difficult story and is surprised to receive unconditional positive regard as a response.

> MRS. F: *I got drunk for the very first time when I was 10 years old. I remember my father pouring a shot and handing it to me and showing off to everyone that I could gulp the shot of whiskey without making a face. By the time I was 15, I was drinking heavy. I don't remember much clearly after that except passing out after drinking. I would start drinking in the morning and then try to sober up before my husband came home. When the kids came, I was a little better but not much. I always liked to party.*
>
> LISTENER: **Alcoholism is a terrible illness; tell me more about your struggle.**
>
> MRS. F: *Then I got into drugs and did cocaine. I knew it was wrong, but I couldn't stop. Every Friday when that paycheck came, we'd party. I got two DUIs and had to go to jail; then they took my family away from me.*
>
> LISTENER: *Is it hard to stay clean now? How long has it been?*

Mrs. F responded that she had been clean for 5 years but was still ashamed of her past; yet she chose to continue the sordid narrative of her early adulthood. She did not shock or drive away the Therapeutic Listener. The Therapeutic Listener accepted all parts of Mrs. F's life and encouraged her to talk more about the bad times. Continued introspection on the Reviewer's part and acceptance by the Listener caused Mrs. F to also be proud of winning her struggle with addiction. For 5 years, she had been a sober, caring mother and wife, but she was especially happy to have had the opportunity to review her life and share her past struggles with the Therapeutic Listener. Unconditional positive regard granted her absolution.

Interviewing Techniques

Sharing Behavior

Sharing is a technique used by Listeners to get or keep the Life Review ongoing. At times, awkward silences occur; the Review stalls or the Reviewer stops talking for any number of reasons. The Therapeutic Listener must keep the Reviewers on topic and continuing to talk about their memories. The Listeners can use any of several options to keep the Review going: a follow-up question related to what the Reviewer was specifically talking about when he or she stopped talking; another question related to the stage of life being discussed; or the Listener could "share" by telling an anecdote about a notable event, historical fact, or a person, place, or thing relevant to the Reviewer's life at the specific date or time being remembered. Sharing is particularly helpful if the Reviewer becomes quiet because of an embarrassing revelation that he or she just made during the Life Review.

For example, many Reviewers can recall difficulties they had with bed-wetting as children, and for some, the revelation is still embarrassing. They never realized at the time, or even now, that bed-wetting was pretty common and that they were not the only bed wetters. Remember the Children's TV host, Mr. Rogers, and his tendency for sharing stories about bed-wetting (and other childhood foibles) and learn from his example. Lots of children found solace in Mr. Rogers when they heard him on the educational channel talking about wetting the bed. When he shared stories about bed-wetting, he made millions of little boys and girls who were bed wetters feel better about themselves. Mr. Rogers understood the value of appropriate "sharing."

Paraphrasing

Paraphrasing is a restatement of the Reviewer's words to clarify what was apparently said, meant, or intended when the original statement is not clear. The Listener uses different words to restate the Reviewer's apparent meaning or intent. By restating what you think the Reviewer has said in your own words, the Reviewer hears your interpretation and can correct or agree with what you said, clarifying any misunderstanding. This is illustrated in the Life Review of Mrs. D, who was talking about the early years of her marriage:

> MRS. D: *Well, after we got married, we went to visit his family and they didn't like me. His Momma wanted him all to herself; he was a Momma's boy.*
>
> LISTENER: **You said they didn't like you?**
>
> MRS. D: *Well, they treated me nice the first time we met, but then we took a trip together and I should have seen the signs. We visited him after he went in the Army and his Momma never left us alone. She wanted to be with him every minute and didn't want me to be there.*
>
> LISTENER: **So you felt like his mother wanted your husband to herself and you were in the way. That's why they didn't like you.**
>
> MRS. D: *Yes, yes, that's it, and I was right. They never grew to like me.*

By listening to her own words restated, Mrs. D obtained a clearer understanding of the past situation and of her own thoughts and feelings. She realized that she attributed her unhappy marriage to not being accepted by her husband's family. Paraphrasing acted as a mirror for her that reflected the understood meaning of the verbal content of her words. Not being accepted by her in-laws may have influenced the failure of her marriage.

Paraphrasing can clarify the mutual understanding of the Reviewers' words, and help Reviewers evaluate the effect of such understanding on their own thought processes. Paraphrasing should be used as an interviewing technique so that the Listener is also clear on the impact of what the Reviewer just said. Then the Reviewer can validate the paraphrased conclusions and understandings.

Unique Life Review Characteristic: Duration

The Structured Life Review process has an optimum total time and a recommended length and frequency for each visit. These time factors are unique to this Life Review process and contribute to the therapeutic benefits accruing from the process, taken as a whole. Research has validated that the duration should be 6 to 8 weeks with about an hour devoted to each weekly visit. Moreover, the weeks should be consecutive whenever possible. However, Listeners conducting the Structured Life Review process are encouraged to use common sense and flexibility in implementing these recommended time considerations.

It takes the recommended time to hear the story of an entire life and to complete the preliminary and closing duties. Clinicians from various disciplines differ on the amount of time they think is necessary for them to hear Reviewers tell their life stories. Some clinicians, often nurses with numerous tasks to complete, say that 8 hours is a long time to spend on one person. Others, psychiatrists especially, think 8 hours is a minimal amount of time for listening to an individual's life story. Because 8 weeks has always been effective in the past with good outcomes, we recommend an approximate 8-week time span, which makes the Life Review unique when compared with other, shorter or longer reminiscing interventions.

This schedule provides time between visits for Reviewers to think about what they have said and to decide what they plan to talk about during the next visit. You should encourage Reviewers to use the time between visits to think about their lives, to review on their own, and to evaluate the meaning of past events for their lives. These scheduled intervals contribute to the inherent effectiveness and uniqueness of the Structured Life Review. Reviewers may even want to jot down notes for the next visit with you so they can remember the thoughts they wanted to share. By thinking in between sessions, Reviewers extend the Life Review process, which becomes even more valuable. Encourage your Reviewers to do so.

Although the structure of the time span may seem stiff and unwieldy, the advantage of a prescribed duration is that Reviewers know what to expect from their Listeners when they start the process. They can plan on the amount of time they will need to spend on the Life Review. That in itself is unique and very important to working adults or those with full schedules. The set duration also differentiates Life Review from other forms of therapy and other forms of reminiscing. Finally, the Life Review is probably billable to Medicare and other insurance companies as a short-term therapy because of its structure and time limitations—a final and helpful uniqueness.

Reviewer Type: The Creative Reviewer

Creative Reviewers are those who resemble Storytellers because their stories are told with enjoyment, skill, and enthusiasm; enjoyed by everyone who hears them. Creative Reviewers often have reputations as Storytellers and, when asked a question, they respond with a story. Some would say they are long-winded. Unfortunately, they differ from Storytellers in that they embellish the truth to create a better story for the enjoyment of others and occasionally to make themselves look better or different. Over time, they begin to believe the stories themselves. Their stories are fact dressed up with a little fiction to make them sound better, but to the Creative Reviewer they are truthful.

Although Creative Reviewers take liberties with truth when constructing their stories, they have no dark intent. When you are listening to their stories in the Life Review, listen as you would with any other Reviewer, being responsive and empathic. The only problem you may have is moving the Reviewer along to correspond to the structure of the Life Review as the stories get longer. Creative Reviewing is only a problem if Reviewers create a story to hide certain facts from you and from themselves as well. Deliberately concealing facts is stressful and actually causes anxiety as Reviewers wonder if they are giving themselves away and strive to maintain the facts of their stories.

Remember to enjoy the Life Review with the Creative Reviewer and do not concern yourself with trying to determine if a story is true. Determining truth is not your role and it is also unnecessary. Be a good Listener and concentrate on using your skills, while being responsive and helpful. Probably most of what you hear is true; enjoy it.

End Visit 4

Summarize Session

As the fourth visit ends, the Listener should summarize the high points of the visit for Reviewers and clear up any misinterpretations of either the Reviewer or the Listener. At this time, it would also be helpful to reframe negative thoughts and steer the conversation toward a happy ending for that visit. Remember Mr. Y, who had unfinished business. The Listener in this case said she was so sorry to hear the sad story of his childhood, but was he not fortunate to be found by such a good man who became his boss and looked after him the rest of his life? Mr. Y had not thought of the event in that way, but after reconsidering said, *"You're right, I was lucky,"* and he left the session thinking about his good fortune.

Next Visit

The last bit of business is to make an appointment for the next visit, leaving an appointment card behind. Depending on the content of the presently completed fourth visit, direct the Reviewer to think about family, work, and the Reviewer's contribution to the next generation for the following week in Visit 5.

Visit 5

OLDER ADULTHOOD

I think that somehow, we learn who we really are and then live with that decision.

—ELEANOR ROOSEVELT

As you begin the fifth visit of the Life Review process, the atmosphere is like that of visiting an old friend. By now you should have bonded with the Reviewer and established a trusting relationship. The Reviewer may be anxious to share the rest of the story and you should be eager to hear the conclusion. This visit is enjoyable for you both; to the casual observer you probably look like two old friends visiting one another and catching up on their lives. There may be no new expectations, just more of the same. You can relax, enjoy the dialogue, and let the good therapy happen.

Preliminary Tasks

At this point, preliminary tasks should be second nature. Reviewers may even take care of the tasks themselves before your arrival and be sitting in the appointed spot waiting for you with a glass of water! You can quickly assess the comfort of the situation based on your earlier visits and fix any deficiencies before you begin. Remember to arrive early to deal with any unexpected setup issues and also to make Reviewers feel important and know that you care about them.

Clarify Visit 4

You should start the session by noting where the last session ended. By now, Reviewers often start the sessions themselves because they may have been reviewing privately all week and are eager to share new insights or reaffirm old ones. Since Visit 5 is a continuation of Visit 4, recapping the last session should provide a starting point for the fifth session. You need to ensure that there is no unfinished business from the last visit and that earlier topics have been explored thoroughly before you ask additional questions to expand the Reviewer's picture of adulthood.

Erikson's Model: Older Adulthood

Generativity is the seventh stage in Erikson's model. It addresses the period of older adulthood.

Generativity vs. Stagnation

Generativity is the process of passing down knowledge, wisdom, love, or a part of oneself to the younger generation. Generativity takes place later in life when people have acquired knowledge and experience to transfer to others. The most common way to be generative is through raising children, where it is expected that parents will hand down knowledge and love while caring for their children. How-ever, people who do not have children can find generativity in other ways. Aunts and uncles often enjoy caring for and teaching their nieces and nephews about their own special skills and experiences. Coaches of Little League teams do the same thing by volunteering for a generative-type activity. Teaching, mentoring, and passing on the skills, wisdom, and insights gained from a lifetime are what it takes to be generative, whether at home, in communities, or in your work.

> *Generativity takes place later in life when people have acquired knowledge and experience to transfer to others.*

Many occupations are generative, such as teaching school, where the requirements of the position are to impart knowledge and mold the younger generation. As you listen to Life Reviews, you will notice that people can be generative in even less obvious ways, such as Miss C, the woman discussed in Visit 4 who became a buyer in a department store. Throughout her Life Review, Miss C talked of young store clerks to whom she taught the business of merchandising. She became a mentor to many of them as they sought her counsel regarding being single, having a career, or choosing an apartment. Her dialogue was full of "generative" examples when she talked about her work.

Miss C enjoyed these relationships and they fulfilled her need to care for others. Generativity is a hidden need, often not fully recognized by Reviewers, that involves sharing, caring, and giving. This is how a society evolves and thrives. But all people are not necessarily generative and they become stagnated. Stagnation and self-absorption characterize older people who make no attempt to reach out to others. Sometimes those with multiple personal problems become so absorbed in their own troubles that they do not have time for others. Through their own selfishness, they miss the opportunity to care, and hence the opportunity to be generative. Doubtless you have met people like that and may recognize Dr. E in the following example:

Dr. E was a surgeon who was very absorbed in his own life and troubles. He seemed to be an unhappy man, attentive to everything and everyone who had wronged him, but seldom thoughtful of the welfare of others.

> DR. E: *Mrs. Doe was referred to me by a general practitioner for internal bleeding. During the surgery, the medical resident cut the common bile duct by mistake and we thought she would die.*

> LISTENER: **Is that what caused you to lose your practice?**

> DR. E: *No, I had to testify against the doctor and then he sued me for defamation and testified against the surgery I did. I lost my practice; nobody would refer patients to me. After that, I worked in the Emergency Room and got caught fooling around with a nurse and got fired. After that, I felt like life was a haze. I put all the money I had left into opening an abortion clinic and lost that too.*

> LISTENER: **I guess the question becomes how do you make sense of all of this?**

> DR. E: *The establishment was just too big for me and beat me down. There is no question in my mind that a hatchet job was done on me. So I retired. I rarely see anyone from the hospital, or anyone from my family. They don't visit, but I have my own routine.*

> LISTENER: **Do you try to contact your old friends and family?**

> DR. E: *They know where I am.*

You can see that the Listener was trying to get Dr. E to see events more responsibly and to reach out to others. The Therapeutic Listener tried to let in some light for Dr. E by asking him how he made sense of everything that had happened to him, but Dr. E did not bother to look more deeply. Instead, he attributed his present situation to everyone but himself. Basically Dr. E presented himself as a narrow-minded, self-centered man with some resemblance to a Bleeding Reviewer. Although married with children, his Life Review showed that he spent little time and attention on his family. Apparently he was never generative; Dr. E seemed to have never cared for others except for their impact on

Visit 5

him. He was the perfect example of a stagnated person—unhappy, but not aware of his own contribution to his unhappiness.

You will find that working with such persons as Dr. E becomes tiresome week after week. Often Reviewers like Dr. E remain obtuse, even though you provide opportunity for them to develop insight through the Life Review. Their basic personality traits and patterns of response get in the way of the opportunities offered through a Life Review. Be assured, however, that they do benefit from talking about their lives, even if they remain stagnated.

Using the Life Review Form

This week the questions we recommend from the LRF address older adulthood and concentrate on family, work, and relationships. The questions correspond to Erikson's Stage 7—Generativity—and are listed below. The bolded questions particularly ask about the generativity experiences of your Reviewer. These questions guide both you and the Reviewer through each section of the Life Review while focusing your thinking.

Suggested Questions for Older Adulthood

- Is there anything else you would like to add about your marriage?
- **In your entire life, what relationship stands out as most important?**
- **Tell me more about your children. Did you enjoy being a parent?**
- Would you call yourself a spiritual person?
- Tell me about your friendships and relationships.
- Was sexual intimacy important to you?
- Did you have hobbies or major interests?
- **Do you think you have helped the next generation?**
- What were some of the main difficulties you encountered during your adult years?
  - ☐ Did someone close to you die? Go away?
  - ☐ Were you ever sick? Have an accident?
  - ☐ Did you move often? Change jobs?
  - ☐ Did you ever feel alone? Abandoned?
  - ☐ Did you ever feel needs?
- Have you remembered anything else you'd like to talk about?
- **What piece(s) of wisdom would you like to hand down to the next generation?**

Work and Family

The preceding week of dialogue will help you to choose the questions to ask during this visit. If the Reviewer concentrated on family during the last session, then you should move on to other questions about work, hobbies, or relationships. You may also encounter people like Mr. S, who spent the entire fourth visit talking about his work as a conductor on the railroad and wanted to talk more about his work during this fifth visit. He did not have many memories about anything else, even family. His work absorbed him, which is not uncommon for men of his generation.

> LISTENER: *Mr. S, let's go back to your earlier years of young adulthood. Tell me about becoming a father.*
>
> MR. S: *You know, that memory is not very clear. I remember getting the baby's room painted before he came home from the hospital and I remember my wife getting up to feed him in the middle of the night, but I was on the Chicago run then and was only home once or twice during the week. I had just been promoted so felt I couldn't ask for a different run to be home more.*
>
> LISTENER: *I understand your boys were good ball players. Did you teach them?*
>
> MR. S: NO, *I was a supervisor then and was away during the week overseeing the railroad in different cities.*

The Listener continued to prompt about family, but Mr. S never contributed additional details and had a hazy memory of family life. He saw his role as the breadwinner, which he did well. You will run into many Reviewers whose lives consist only of work, especially older Reviewers who were not as active in family life as fathers are today. Fathers of past generations are proud of the way they provided for their families, because being a provider was what was important then. They may have actually practiced generativity in their own minds by providing monetary support to their families in accordance with the expectations of their day. Allow your Reviewer to enjoy his successes at work, and join the Reviewer in that dialogue as the Reviewer completes the fifth visit with more memories of pride in work.

Relationships

Lifelong friendships and relationships outside of the family are important to most Reviewers. In many studies about aging, the most important contributor to an older person's well-being is the existence of a significant other or a confidante. Lasting external relationships are especially important to older people whose world has been narrowed by retirement, deaths, and decreasing social opportunities. Old relationships that influence a Reviewer's history are always meaningful to the Life Review and current relationships influence the Reviewer's present satisfaction with life.

Visit 5

Ask about the Reviewer's closest friends, along with memories of the friendships. Listening to "best friend" stories is usually a happy time. If the best friend has passed away, the stories may be sad but still meaningful, and you can help the Reviewer grieve again. One Reviewer, Mrs. J, talked about a lasting and ongoing friendship that was very important to her throughout her life that had grown even more important over the years.

> MRS. J: *During the war, we kind of had to fend for ourselves while our husbands were gone. My next-door neighbor, Sally, was always there for me, helping out when one of the kids got sick, and I did the same for her. We babysat for each other and often visited each other at night when the children were asleep. It was nice to talk to another adult after having only children to talk to all day. We often went out together with the kids on the weekend and we became each other's families. After the men came home, we didn't need each other so much, but we still remained close and our families did too.*

> LISTENER: *Do you still see each other?*

> MRS. J: *Oh yes, and we talk on the phone once a month. When my husband died, Sally came down to be with me. It felt good to know she was there for me. We've even talked about becoming neighbors again, now that she is alone too.*

As you listen to Mrs. J talk about her friend, you realize the importance of this friendship throughout Mrs. J's life and the influence this relationship has had on her life and her Life Review. Mrs. J was closer to Sally than she was to her brothers and sisters, and spent much more time with Sally. You should encourage these memories of important relationships because they bring joy to the Reviewer and often shed light on past decisions. One confidante is more important to an older Reviewer than a number of acquaintances, and the memories, besides being something to treasure, are usually meaningful to the Life Review.

> *Listening to "best friend" stories is usually a happy time.*

Other Reviewers may have had even more intimate relationships, such as that of a lover that is still a secret and may need to remain a secret to protect the feelings of others. You can give the Reviewer an opportunity to share this kind of memory when you ask about relationships outside of the family, and the Reviewers will decide which memories to reveal. Often, simple questions instigate a variety of surprising memories, some best left to rest. People who have had affairs outside of marriage often retain feelings of guilt and want to talk about their feelings and reasons for straying. These revelations are difficult because there is little you can do but listen as Reviewers rationalize their past decisions. The act of sharing the past with you helps Reviewers as they try to absolve themselves of guilt.

Outside Interests

Some Reviewers run out of memories during Visit 5, having recalled their intimate past fully in the preceding weeks with little more to say about it. If this is the case with your Reviewers, you may enable him or her to recall more by asking about outside interests, such as hobbies and volunteer work. A Reviewer may be consumed by an interest outside of job and family, but has never had an opening to begin that dialogue. The Therapeutic Listener needs to make sure an opening is provided to talk about whatever that interest is. If the reviewer is a golfer, the golfer will certainly enjoy talking about a hole-in-one; the fisherman will talk about "the one that got away." Hobbies, community work, and personal accomplishments make great topics for those who were never employed outside the home or who do not have families. Those stories may also initiate other memories that need to be examined. Regardless of their connections to other memories, they bring a great deal of enjoyment in the telling and thus satisfaction with the Life Review.

One Reviewer, Mrs. K, a "stay-at-home" parent, exhausted the topic of family during her fourth Life Review visit, leaving the Therapeutic Listener to search for other meaningful topics for the remaining visits. Mrs. K had never worked outside of the home. Her family seemed to be her whole life and her other interests were unknown. Because the fifth visit is the last session of recall before Reviewers begin to evaluate their lives, it is important to elicit those last memories that may seem unimportant but that may lead to other more important memories of older adulthood.

When you are listening, you may find yourself in a similar situation, at a loss for interesting topics. If so, you will have to do some groundwork to learn about the Reviewer's interests so that you can proceed with pertinent questions. Also, look around the room(s) for possible memorabilia, knickknacks, or personal items. For example, this Therapeutic Listener noticed a bowling ball in Mrs. K's living room and commented on its weight. Her chance remark initiated stories of Mrs. K's successes at bowling.

MRS. K: *I bowl with a lighter one, 12 pounds.*

LISTENER: **Twelve pounds sounds heavy to me.**

MRS. K: *It is heavy; the first one I got was almost 13 pounds. I was using two balls and sometimes I couldn't get the new one to do right until I broke it in. I have a double carrier on wheels that holds both balls and my shoes.*

LISTENER: **Then you must be serious.**

MRS. K: *One time I bowled over 200—you know, in one game. I tried out for the Senior League and I got to be pretty good.*

Mrs. K's pride in her bowling prowess was evident, so the Therapeutic Listener continued to express her admiration for Mrs. K's athletic accomplishments, maintaining that she herself could never bowl like that. Outside activities, such as bowling, add an additional element to the Life Review and can be a source of pride that engages Reviewers

Visit 5

and adds to their feelings of accomplishment. Those prideful feelings are important to the success of the Life Review for the Reviewer. Therefore, in the fifth visit, when rounding out adulthood, you should broaden your search of the question-base to provide opportunities for Reviewers to talk about their interests and achievements outside of the home.

Forgotten Memories

Once Reviewers start searching their own mental databases for memories, they are surprised at the number of memories that they find there. Many forgotten memories tend to present themselves again during a Life Review, possibly because one old memory evokes another that was long forgotten. Some bring joy to the Reviewer and others cause sadness, but because they have been lurking below the surface, they may be important to the Life Review. Reviewers often say, *"I don't know why I thought of that now."* Before the opportunity to share "new-old" memories ends, questions such as, *"Have you remembered anything else you would like to talk about?"* can open this avenue for Reviewers, as it did for Mrs. O:

> MRS. O: *I haven't thought about my sisters and brothers in a long, long time. My sister Mary and I had a falling out almost 40 years ago about some disagreement between our children. I think it was about one of the weddings; my daughter didn't have any of her children stand up for her and Mary was insulted. The children made up fast, but I haven't talked to Mary for a long time. I guess you could say we've been estranged for 40 years. Talking about my childhood made me realize how much fun Mary and I had together. We were very close as children and I miss her. She's the only sister I have left.*
>
> LISTENER: **What would you like to do about your relationship with Mary?**
>
> MRS. O: *The whole thing is so foolish; I've been waiting for her to say I'm sorry for 40 years. I guess I could call and say, "I'm sorry."*

Mrs. O asked the Therapeutic Listener to look up her sister Mary's phone number at the end of the session. As the Therapeutic Listener was packing her bag, Mrs. O made the call to Mary. Mary was glad to hear from her sister, and as they laughed and cried and made plans to visit, the Listener let herself out the door.

> *Recalled long-forgotten memories often provide an opportunity to mend old fences.*

Recalled long-forgotten memories often provide an opportunity to mend old fences, which is a way of taking care of unfinished business. It is not unusual for people to mend fences as a result of the insight they gain when doing a Life Review. Reviewers get a sense for what is important in life and realize the foolishness of past grudges and slights. Often they want to mend relationships while they still have an opportunity and can take steps to do so. When you act as Therapeutic Listener, it is important to remember that lifetime solutions can arise from sidebar memories that don't seem that significant at the time. Hence it is best to consider all memories essential to the Life Review and to follow the lead of the Reviewer.

Counseling Skill: Empathy

Empathy is the fourth counseling skill that Listeners need to learn and to adopt—a skill that combines understanding and compassion for the feelings of the person who is reviewing. An empathic Therapeutic Listener is receptive to the emotions accompanying the Reviewer's narrative and expresses a mutual concern. In fact, the Listener should feel what the Reviewer feels, appreciating the depth of the experience, and let the Reviewer see these responsive emotions.

Empathy is often confused with sympathy, but they are different. Empathy is feeling *with* someone, whereas sympathy is feeling *for* someone. Empathic understanding puts Reviewer and Listener on an equal emotional footing, sharing feelings, whereas sympathy can be more like pity and places the Reviewer in an inferior position. In empathy there is no hierarchy: The Therapeutic Listener senses the Reviewer's distress and the Reviewer, in turn, is aware of the Therapeutic Listener's responsive compassion.

It is difficult to teach someone how to develop empathy. For some, feeling empathic when listening to a Reviewer's problem is second nature. For others, having empathic feelings can only be learned through the continued practice of caring, attentive listening, and responsiveness to the Reviewers' feelings as they relate their emotions. With practice, you can learn to be sincerely in touch with yourself and with the Reviewer, so that you can genuinely feel and mirror the Reviewer's feelings. Being in real touch with the Reviewers' experiences—and feeling what they feel—creates a more permissive atmosphere for Reviewers to be open, as Mr. P was when recalling the daughter he had lost in an automobile accident when she was 17. As he talked about his daughter's death, his eyes filled with tears.

> Mr. P: *My daughter was walking along the highway to go home after visiting a friend and a drunk driver mowed her down with his car. When she called for a ride earlier, I was too busy to go get her and told her to wait until I finished mowing the lawn. She didn't wait and started walking instead. If I had gone, she would still be here.*

> Listener: *How awful for you Mr. P, to lose your daughter when she was just a teenager. Losing a child is just about the most grievous death there is and I guess people feel the loss forever. She was such a beautiful girl—I can see by that picture over there.*

Visit 5

MR. P: *I still think about her all the time; she was such a good girl, smart and talented besides being beautiful. Her Mother always thought about her too, actually died thinking about her, called to her when she was crossing over.*

LISTENER (WITH HER OWN EYES FILLING WITH TEARS): *Mr. P, I can't imagine how difficult it would be to lose your daughter and then to lose your wife. What do you do to keep yourself going?*

Mr. P spent the rest of the session talking of his losses and the strength he got from his religion to deal with them. The Listener continued her empathic responses, particularly when Mr. P said he felt responsible for both tragedies because his wife just wasted away after they lost their daughter. He said he'd still have them both if he had gone to pick up his daughter when she called him for a ride.

How would you have handled this situation? Think for a moment. In the actual Life Review, the Listener encouraged Mr. P's thoughts with attentiveness and empathic responses while helping Mr. P to look at events just a little differently. She reminded Mr. P that his daughter chose not to wait for a ride from him, and that his wife was already sick and dying with lung cancer before a car hit his daughter. Clearly, the deaths were not his fault. Mr. P's grief continued but became a little less potent as he shared his story and received warm, empathic responses from the Listener in return. Finally, he was able to absolve himself from blame for the two deaths and finished his Life Review at peace with himself.

Interviewing Techniques

Self-Disclosure

Self-disclosure is the actual sharing of a personal story by the Therapeutic Listener for the purpose of getting a stalled conversation started or for the purpose of allowing the Reviewer to get to know the Therapeutic Listener better. The following Therapeutic Listener knew that her Reviewer had exhausted the experience of family and was ready to move on to the evaluation portion of Life Review. Although the Listener didn't know a great deal about Mrs. Q, the Listener recognized that such a lively and interesting woman must have additional interests outside of the family. Therefore, the Listener decided to share a personal experience of her own with Mrs. Q to model an example:

After my family grew up and left home, I needed something to do to fill my time. So I went to the knitting shop and signed up for a class in making squares. We go to class once a month and learn how to knit a new square, and then at the end of the year we put all the squares together to make an afghan. Now I'm hooked and wish I had more time to knit. I really love knitting.

The Listener's self-disclosure served the intended purpose and Mrs. Q responded:

> *Oh, I love knitting and needlework of all kinds, but I enjoy quilting the most. I even won a Blue Ribbon at the State Fair for one of my quilts.*

As she talked, she glowed with her success and showed the Listener many of her quilts, still talking of her achievements as the hour ended.

Mrs. Q enjoyed the opportunity to talk about her quilts and basked in the process. Self-disclosure was a good technique to use with Mrs. Q, and the preceding example shows good, controlled use of self-disclosure by the Therapeutic Listener. The one danger of self-disclosure is that Listeners can forget their role as Listeners and talk too much about themselves, using the Reviewer as a sounding board. When self-disclosure is not tightly controlled, the Life Review sessions can become therapy sessions for the Listeners. So when using self-disclosure, you must constantly be in touch with the extent of your storytelling, and keep the disclosures to a minimum, just as the Listener did in this session.

> *Listeners can forget their role as Listeners and talk too much about themselves.*

Encouragement to Talk

Encouragement to talk is the technique of making appropriate rejoinders and encouraging comments to the Reviewer to keep the Reviewer's memories coming. This technique is helpful just to let Reviewers know that you are listening and following their story as they talk. You can practice this technique with an "Uh-huh" here and there, following the Reviewer's statements. However, the technique is much more effective with responsive comments, such as "*So you were young*" or "*I understand*" or "*Go ahead*," accompanied by the Listener's feelings that reflect the same emotional tone of the Reviewer.

Encouragement is especially useful when a Reviewer is hesitant. Even during the fifth visit, Reviewers can become tentative when they are telling a difficult story. Ongoing encouragement can keep Reviewers talking and moving along, such as in the following example where the Reviewer was disclosing a history of drug abuse to the Listener.

LISTENER: *Tell me how you got started taking drugs.*

REVIEWER: *He'd be there with his paycheck and we would party all weekend.*

LISTENER: *How long did that go on?*

REVIEWER: *The drugs? Probably heavy for a year. We wanted to give it up, but our friends would come to the house with drugs.*

LISTENER: *So away you'd go again.*

Visit 5

REVIEWER: *He was going to counseling and lying about the drugs, but they knew.*

LISTENER: *Of course they did.*

REVIEWER: *But we finally decided to stop using together.*

LISTENER: *Can't have been easy.*

The Reviewer continued to talk freely for the next 2 weeks, disclosing a complete story of drug addiction and then success in conquering the habit. The Reviewer concluded that it felt good to share the story with someone else. As the story progressed, even those small comments by the Listener were unnecessary. The story just came out. However, with Reluctant Reviewers, repeated and multiple encouraging remarks may be necessary.

Unique Life Review Characteristic: Individuality

We have discussed aspects of the Life Review that set it apart from other forms of reminiscing. One more unique characteristic of the Structured Life Review process was validated by research as specific to the success of this process: Individuality.

Individuality means conducting a Life Review on a one-to-one basis with one other individual: one Listener and one Reviewer. The privacy and bonding provided by Individuality contributes to feelings of safety that allow Reviewers to unburden secrets, such as the woman describing her drug abuse in the example in the preceding section.

When there is a one-to-one interaction, the Therapeutic Listener's full attention focuses on one Reviewer, making that Reviewer feel special, with something important to say. Although many Reviewers are self-effacing and doubt the importance of their lives, they begin to feel pride in the lives they have lived when someone else is interested in their memories and helps them to recall them. Although individual interventions take more time than group interventions, they are essential to the soul-searching and sharing that unfolds in a Life Review.

Individual interventions also create bonding in that the Therapeutic Listener becomes a significant other to the Life Reviewer. This bonding and feeling of trust is especially important for Reviewers who are loners and do not make friends easily. The relationship that evolves from a one-to-one intervention may be the first time that a particular Reviewer has experienced a real connection with another person.

Reviewer Type: The Denying Reviewer

The Denying Reviewer is among the Reviewer types that are described in this Handbook. This is a Reviewer who does not really engage in examining the past insightfully; thus the Denying Reviewer is one who undergoes little change.

Generally, Denying Reviewers have lived their lives avoiding responsibility for their difficulties and misfortunes while refusing to face the hard truths and the realities of their lives. These types of Reviewers often need to keep up a continual façade for themselves, as well as toward others, as they talk about their lives. They often use their own fictional views of past events to avoid the truth. For them, only seeing what they want to see works as a major defense mechanism that has served them well throughout a lifetime, particularly during difficult times.

Denying Reviewers enjoy participating in the Life Review as much as anyone else, but they gain little insight because they are concentrating on keeping up the façade. Instead of gaining insight, the Life Review gives them an opportunity to talk about themselves and to reaffirm myths that have kept them going for many years. Sometimes Denying Reviewers actually reinforce existing defense mechanisms. Although they accept the interactions of a Life Review, the Life Review may not be as therapeutic for them as it is for other Reviewers who want to honestly examine their past behaviors, discussions, and events.

You need to learn how to handle Denying Reviewers, because denial has long served them as a defense mechanism and you do not necessarily want to strip that defense mechanism away. Encourage Denying Reviewers to tell their stories and then accept their stories at face value. Give them an opportunity to reveal their true selves through normal Life Review questioning, but do not challenge their answers. Their stories are true to them and to you; it doesn't matter whether they are actually fact. Probably, Denying Reviewers should be left with their myths and not be forced to recognize reality. They may need to keep their convictions intact as a sort of safety net against reality.

> *Denial has long served them as a defense mechanism and you do not necessarily want to strip that defense mechanism away.*

Life Review is not the time to change such Reviewers because you probably do not have enough skills to do so, and even if you did, there is really no point in forcing hard reality onto someone late in life. Most Listeners are not educated or skilled enough in psychotherapy to therapeutically unveil a lifetime of self-serving stories. You have to remember that in a Life Review relationship, the power belongs to Reviewers to tell their life stories in the way they want to. You may feel discouraged listening to a Denying Reviewer, but your role is to leave them intact, as in the following Life Review involving Mrs. Z:

> *All her life, Mrs. Z talked about her wonderful childhood and delightful family. In her Life Review, she recalled parties on her birthdays and special cakes her mother had made for her parties. She maintained this beautiful story of her life as she talked of the dresses her mother made for her and how lucky she was to have such a clever, loving mother. Occasionally, she would mention strife at home between her mother and father, causing her brother to run away. But when she was asked about that incident, she would say her brother was just wild and then go back to talking about her happy life.*

Visit 5

She talked of her marriage in the same way, though she had eventually left her husband, and admitted he was an alcoholic. Mrs. Z said:

> We used to go to New York to the baseball games and we had such a good time, staying at the Waldorf, which we couldn't afford. We'd go out to dinner at a special restaurant and have several drinks. It was a fun time. Sometimes he drank too much, but it was all in fun.

Mrs. Z apparently needed to look at her life through such rose-colored glasses. As long as she maintained this stance, the Listener had to accept it. Mrs. Z finished her Life Review without a true examination of her life's issues. She gained little therapeutically but enjoyed telling her life story the way she wanted to tell it. In many ways, she probably served herself by reinforcing her own defense mechanisms.

End Visit 5

Summarize Session

As you come to the end of the fifth visit, take time to summarize the session for your Life Reviewer. You do this by reiterating the topics discussed during the visit and then seeking confirmation from your Reviewer as to whether or not you are correct. If some stories were sad, try to focus on a happy portion of the story or something special that the Reviewer shared earlier, so that you may end the fifth session on a happy note.

Next Visit

After summarizing the fifth visit, you should make an appointment for the next session. When making an appointment for Visit 6, you should remind Reviewers that there are only two more meetings after that left for them to talk about their lives. If you have the LRF handy, show them the questions in the last section of the form, the evaluation portion, and tell them those questions will be the focal point for the next 2 weeks. Tell Reviewers that next week you are going to ask them to evaluate their lives and to talk about the best and the worst parts of their lives using these questions.

As before, make an appointment card reminding Reviewers of the agreed upon time for next week. Make a reminder in your own book, and when you depart, make notes of the session in your own book as well.

Visit 6

SUMMARY AND EVALUATION

All truths are easy to understand once they are discovered; the point is to discover them.

—GALILEO GALILEI

The sixth visit is entitled Summary and Evaluation because it is the time in the Life Review when Reviewers are asked to take a close look at their past lives to summarize key memories and evaluate them. Summarizing causes the Reviewer to look at life as a whole—not as individual, separated events—and this leads to evaluation. Evaluation is the self-assessment of the way one has lived one's life, and that should lead to reconciliation of events that cannot be changed, and then to final acceptance of the life as it was lived. The result is Integrity. During this visit, the Therapeutic Listener asks evaluation-type questions to help Reviewers come to a place in their Life Review that enables them to order and accept their lives. This chapter also discusses the counseling skill of Congruence, the interviewing technique of Summarizing, the unique characteristic of Evaluation, and the type of Reviewer known as the "Bleeding Reviewer."

During this visit, you will want to remind Reviewers that the Life Review process will soon be coming to an end. Reviewers generally accept the completion of Life Review graciously, though some may express regret. Most Life Reviewers are eager to move on in their lives when they have completed the enjoyable task of Life Review. They often seem to gain new energy and look optimistically toward the future. Some Reviewers have things they still want to do, such as learning to paint or visiting a foreign land. Others may have problem relationships to mend that surfaced when doing the Life Review. Still others may be too ill or lack energy to tackle new challenges, but still obtain a new internal peace as a result of Life Review. They can rest more easily knowing they have finally "finished" their business.

Preliminary Tasks

There are no additional tasks for you to think about before you begin the sixth Life Review visit. You only need to remember to inform Reviewers of the pending finish at the end of two more weeks. For example, you could say, "*Well, remember last week was my fifth visit, and after today I have only two more visits to talk about your life. So, let's begin.*" It is important to mention closure at least 2 weeks in advance to prepare Reviewers for the end of the Life Review. If you prepare Reviewers for the completion of the process, they will participate more freely and accept the end more readily than if the ending is abrupt.

Clarify Visit 5

Clarification examines the details of the preceding session to arrive at a crystal clear understanding of what has been recalled by the Reviewer. Clarification is especially important when changing life stages or topics, as when shifting from childhood to adulthood in Visit 3 and again during this sixth visit. During this visit you must move the Review from questions about adulthood to questions that cause Reviewers to summarize and evaluate their whole life, such as, "*What were the happiest moments in your life?*" or "*What do you think about the way you lived your life?*" Regardless of the need to move on, you should always ask for clarification of memories and events that were discussed the week before that you did not thoroughly understand, as this Listener did:

> LISTENER: *I was wondering about your relationship with your father. I remember you talking of a turning point when you stood up to him and said, "You're not going to do this any more." And that your determination influenced you as an adult. Is that right? I want you to straighten me out here. How did that influence you?*

> REVIEWER: *Remember, he was a drunk and he beat my mother until I called the sheriff and then he never did it again; he never touched me either, but I was always afraid of him until then.*

LISTENER: *So, by standing up to him, you learned he could not hurt you anymore.*

REVIEWER: *I finally felt like I had some control over my life.*

In this instance, the Listener was not sure what the Reviewer meant when he mentioned a "turning point." When the Reviewer clarified his meaning, the Listener found out that the Reviewer, in standing up to his father, gained confidence in himself and felt a greater sense of control over his life. When you are not sure of a point that might influence the rest of the review, ask the Reviewer to tell you about that aspect again to help you understand before you move on to the next life stage.

Erikson's Model: Oldest Adulthood

The final stage in Erikson's model is Integrity (accepting one's life as it was lived). Acceptance is pivotal to gaining Integrity. Thus the Structured Life Review includes an intermediate stage of Acceptance, discussed in this chapter, as the first step in reaching the final stage of Integrity, which is presented in the following chapter.

Acceptance

Acceptance occurs when the Reviewer objectively considers past life events and adopts them as an inevitable part of life. Often, Reviewers realize through the Life Review that they had no control over some unexpected events in their lives. For example, most people do not plan to flunk out of school, get fired, or get divorced. But those events may happen with regularity and need to be reconciled and accepted over time. An unexpected death in the Reviewer's family or of friends is one of those difficult events over which Reviewers have no control. Although sometimes never truly accepted, such sad events may become more tolerable over time by talking about them in the Life Review process. Mrs. L talked about accepting the deaths of her children:

> *Reviewers realize through the Life Review that they had no control over some unexpected events in their lives.*

MRS. L: *Did I tell you that my children are dead?*

LISTENER: *You did not; tell me about them.*

MRS. L: *Well, I had one son and one daughter, beautiful children. My daughter died first. We were going to the store to get groceries and it was a very narrow street where we parked. When we were done, the children went ahead to the car and all of a sudden a 16-wheeler went by and just sucked my daughter up*

Visit 6

under the wheels. I didn't know what to do, but I didn't want my son to see her, so I grabbed him up and went home and left her body there.

LISTENER: *And then what happened?*

MRS. L: *By then everyone in town knew about it; my neighbors went down and covered her with a blanket and called the funeral home. I stayed with my son and told him how she was with God now and God must have had a reason for taking her.*

LISTENER: *How did your son do?*

MRS. L: *Terrible. He stopped talking, and when he went to school, he couldn't control his bowels. We grieved and grieved together and became very close. My husband was overseas and could only come home for a week, so it was just John and me coping together for a long time. My daughter would have been 63 today.*

LISTENER: *And you still grieve for her?*

MRS. L: *I think of her often, but God must have had a reason for taking her, for taking them all. I am lucky to have a strong faith to rely on. I can't change things so I have to accept them.*

LISTENER: *And how long did you have your son?*

MRS. L: *Until he was 21. It was his birthday. He was at MIT, but he came home to celebrate. We had a great night, all his favorite food and his friends, and then we put him on a plane and never saw him again.*

LISTENER: *How awful for you and your husband. You sound like a very strong woman to endure all of that.*

MRS. L: *Well, God gave us two angels to love for a while, that's what I have to think. After we lost them, we did youth work for the church and that helped.*

Mrs. L's Life Review took place during the Christmas holidays, which was also the anniversary of her children's deaths. She talked about dealing with her depression that usually came upon her during holiday time. The Therapeutic Listener assured Mrs. L that it was normal to have anniversary reactions for such grievous events as the deaths of her children. Mourning was understandable and acceptable and the Listener was glad that Mrs. L had an opportunity to share her grief. The unfortunate timing of the Life Review during the Christmas season nevertheless offered an opportunity for Mrs. L to relive the past and again grieve for her loved ones, with the Therapeutic Listener acting as a support system. As a result of sharing her burden, Mrs. L said she was doing better this year and thanked the Therapeutic Listener for being there for her. She was better able to accept the deaths of her children during this particular Christmas season and hopefully in the future as well.

Denial

To correspond with Erikson's framework, Denial is seen as the opposite state of Acceptance (Acceptance vs. Denial). Denial is the subconscious dismissal of a past event that is too shameful or too hurtful to even think about and may well be the opposite side of acceptance. Thinking about such events hurts; denying their existence allows one to get by, but the hurt is never fixed. The Reviewer's perceived realities of these hurtful occurrences are often faulty or inadequate, even when the Reviewer is presented with incontrovertible evidence that the event did indeed occur, such as an untimely death, or abuse as a child, or a failed marriage. Sometimes, Reviewers cannot even admit the occurrence of these tragedies to themselves; thus they continue to deny everything about them and go on living. Continual denial means that these prevailing problems never get fixed, just pushed down out of sight and mind a little more each time they try to surface.

Denial is closely associated with depression. Reviewers who are depressed often refuse to acknowledge that they are depressed, while denying the fact that they are rejecting a troubling past that may have caused the depression in the first place. Although the Listener may present old facts in a new light through reframing, Reviewers may still negate the impact of the past from their lives. Reviewers frequently say, "*I just can't think about it.*" Thus they are rejecting still another opportunity to reconcile an old issue, to change, and possibly to heal. The story of the Denying Reviewer in an earlier chapter (Mrs. Z) is a classic example of someone in denial, as is this story told by Mr. X:

> MR. X: *I was brought up in an orphanage; my parents couldn't afford to feed me. I learned how to fight there to make sure I got my peanut butter sandwich for lunch. Then my sister got me out and I lived with her.*
>
> LISTENER: **Was it hard to live in an orphanage?**
>
> MR. X: *No harder than anything else I had to do.*
>
> LISTENER: **Is life still hard?**
>
> MR. X: *I do what I want, have a few drinks, go dancing, find women. I guess it's better. My mother and sisters are dead and I never knew my father. I like my freedom.*

Mr. X said his present state of well-being was just fine, even though he tested as depressed on a paper-and-pencil measure of depression. He was also managing his drinking by switching from 100-proof vodka to a lesser proof, but still drinking the same quantity as frequently as he did before. He had recently been fired for drinking on the job. When the Listener's questions were too tough, he would recite a joke or poem in response to the question, to divert the Listener. He just did not want to remember anything that was the least bit difficult or painful. The Therapeutic Listener worked to get Mr. X to acknowledge his tough childhood, but was unsuccessful. An 8-week Life Review was not enough for Mr. X and did little to help him change his viewpoints. He also refused a referral to see someone else who could help him. Mr. X claimed to be okay in his denial, although denial really was not serving him well, as evidenced by his depression scores and his constant drinking. You will work with other Reviewers like Mr. X. Not all Life Reviews have successful outcomes, no matter how hard you work at it. The Mr. Xs of this world often wish to be left alone to try to solve their problems—or not—in an ineffective manner. Since the Mr. Xs are in charge of their own Life Reviews, you must let them maintain control and possibly flounder.

Using the Life Review Form

The questions in the summary/evaluation section of the LRF differ from the questions in its preceding sections. The summary/evaluation questions do not ask about developmental life stages (childhood, adolescence, and so forth) as the questions did in the first 4 weeks of the Life Review; instead, they are more thought-provoking and cause Reviewers to consider and value certain key events that may have molded their lives. These more thought-provoking questions used in Visits 6 and 7 teach Reviewers to use self-examination and cause them to gain new insight into their lives.

You may use the questions from the list on page 147 interchangeably with those listed on page 162 (Visit 7) during the next 2 weeks as long as you try to ask *all* the questions in the summary/evaluation section of the LRF, not just selective ones, as done with the earlier sections of the LRF in Visits 2 through 5. A time frame of 2 weeks usually allows you to exhaust the summary/evaluation questions in this and the next chapter. Of course, there are occasions with Reviewers who are Storytellers when it becomes impossible to ask all the summary/evaluation questions. If that happens, you must judge accordingly, use specific questions selectively, and try to finish in the appointed time.

Flexibility

Because this Life Review is so structured, you may think that you cannot make any changes and must rigidly follow the set schedules. Fortunately, this is not so. The recommended schedule is structured to teach you how to do a typical Structured Life Review and to offer you a framework for optimum results. As you become more skilled in guiding the Life Review process, your instincts will tell you when you should change from the usual format. Some Reviewers may need more time; they may wish to repeat a troubling event, or they may need to spend more time talking about adulthood or a death in the family, for example. Each Reviewer is an individual with individual needs and differences. Follow our guidelines and your best instincts to help each Reviewer differently and individually.

Gaining Insight

The questions in the summary/evaluation section of the LRF help Reviewers determine why they lived the way they did, why they made certain decisions, and why they chose the partners and friends whom they chose. This summary/evaluation section causes introspec-

Suggested Questions for Visit 6

- On the whole, what kind of life do you think you've had?

- If everything were to be the same, would you like to live your life over again?

- If you were going to live your life over again, what would you change? Leave unchanged?

- We've been talking about your life for quite some time now. Let's discuss your overall feelings and ideas about your life. What would you say the main satisfactions in your life have been? Try for three. Why were they satisfying?

- Everyone has had disappointments. What have been the main disappointments in your life?

- What was the hardest thing you had to face in your life? Please describe it.

- What was the happiest period of your life? What about it made it the happiest period? Why is your life less happy now?

- What was the unhappiest period of your life? Is your life more happy now? Why?

- What was the proudest moment in your life?

tion and appraisal that often develops new insights that have become possible with the added assistance of hindsight gained from the process of an ongoing Life Review. At this point, the Reviewer's former perceptions of past events may change (usually in a positive way) and the change may be surprising to both the Listener and the Reviewer. For instance, Mrs. U had repeatedly described her life as one that was difficult, but now in the summary/ evaluation section of the Life Review she expressed a different and new understanding of her life:

LISTENER: *On the whole what kind of life do you think you've had?*

MRS. U: *I think I've had a good life.*

LISTENER: *Have you?*

MRS. U: *Yes, I've had a lot to face, but I've gotten through it and I haven't buckled under.*

LISTENER: *So because you've successfully faced bad times, you feel like your life was good?*

MRS. U: *Yes. It's like, after W died, and you know it really got to me; I was very depressed. But I said, "I'm going to be a participator, not a spectator, and get off my duff and, you know, make a life."*

> *Reviewer's perceptions of past events may change (usually in a positive way) and the change may be surprising to both the Listener and the Reviewer.*

LISTENER: *That's admirable, you were able to survive.*

MRS. U: *Yes, yes I did.*

Most of Mrs. U's Life Review memories were about difficult times and about being unhappy. So it was surprising to have Mrs. U sum up her life as a good life towards the end of the Life Review. Earlier, when she reviewed each particular life event, she described them negatively. Because of Mrs. U's negativity, the Listener found Mrs. U's present positive response, *"I think I've had a good life,"* difficult to believe.

When you are listening to a Life Review, if you get a surprising answer such as this one, explore the answer fully until both you and the Reviewer understand the reason for the Reviewer's apparent changed outlook. As Mrs. U talked about the bad times in her life, she gained insight into her own strengths and abilities to handle those bad times. As she summarized and evaluated her life during the sixth visit, she discovered that she was proud to have survived the many bad times. As a result, Mrs. U decided her life was good. This final positive assessment of her life made Mrs. U feel proud as she concluded her Life Review. The Listener was pleased to leave Mrs. U in a better frame of mind. The Life Review had done its work.

Repetition

Repetition, the reiteration of a memory recalled earlier in the Life Review, is one of the hallmarks of the Structured Life Review process. The Listener needs to encourage the retelling of a troublesome or noteworthy story over and over until the Reviewer no longer seems to be disturbed by recalling that particular memory. Repetition helps Reviewers to work through unpleasant past events a little bit at a time, over time.

Because of the therapeutic outcomes that result from a repetitive review, some of the questions in this section of the LRF may seem to be asking the same things over again. Take for example the following two questions: *"What have been the main disappointments in your life?"* and *"What was the hardest thing you ever had to face in your life?"* Although both questions may be asking about difficult parts of life, each question approaches those difficult parts in a different way and thus may elicit different responses. These seemingly repetitive questions offer the Listener the opportunity again to retell a troublesome story. While some Reviewers may interpret them as the same question, Mrs. U, the Reviewer who said she had had a good life at the end of her Review, shows us how the questions were different and held separate meanings for her:

LISTENER: *Everyone has had disappointments in life. What have been the main disappointments in your life?*

MRS. U: *Well, W's alcoholism. And I would have liked more time with him after he sobered up. And being such a dysfunctional family.*

LISTENER: *I know you worked hard to make family life better. Can you tell me what the hardest time was?*

MRS. U: *That's easy. When my son was a POW and we never knew what was going on.*

LISTENER: *I can't even imagine how hard that would be. You showed a lot of courage to get through that.*

When you are in the summary/evaluation section of the LRF, sometimes it is best to break up the similar questions with other different questions and then later return to *"What was the hardest thing you had to face in your life?"* You also might say, *"You told me about the disappointments in your life, but now I want to hear about the hardest thing you ever had to face"* as a way to clarify your intent to the Reviewer.

Self-Examination

Questions in the summary/evaluation section encourage self-examination by Reviewers by causing Reviewers to scrutinize the past closely and then to make judgments about certain times and events. Self-examination is the process of looking closely at the past to appraise the impact on the present of the way one's life was lived. Self-examination contributes to new perceptions, reconciliation, acceptance, and, ultimately, Integrity. For example, during self-examination Reviewers often realize that they were responsible for their own life course. With this realization, they accept the outcomes more readily. Or, Reviewers may recognize instances where they had no control over their lives, again allowing them to accept the outcomes and present circumstances as something that had to be.

Revisiting Key Events

Revisiting key events is different from repetition in that revisiting is more targeted and specific to a few singular events. Key events, such as the death of a parent or abuse as a child, that influenced the earlier part of life and were discussed early in the Life Review should be raised again during the summary/evaluation portion of the Life Review. The purpose of revisiting these events is to encourage Reviewers to talk about them one more time in order to assess their continuing and lasting impact on the Reviewer.

You will find that most Reviewers naturally revisit past events on their own when they sum things up and recall their greatest disappointments and hardest times during the summary and evaluation portion of the Life Review. If your Reviewer does not return to an

Visit 6

earlier event that caused great distress when first remembered, then ask about it at an appropriate time during the summary/evaluation sessions to make sure the Reviewer has reconciled the memory, as Mr. Y did during his Life Review. As described in the chapter on young adulthood, Mr. Y had been abandoned as a child and left by the side of the road by his father. He talked about being abandoned several times every week during the beginning of the Life Review. He did not, however, mention that memory again toward the end of the Life Review when asked about the hardest thing he ever had to face.

LISTENER: *Mr. Y, what was the hardest thing you had to face in your life?*

MR.Y: *When my boss's wife got sick with cancer; it was awful. He couldn't do anything for her and I couldn't do anything for him. He's still sad and likes to talk about her when he visits. I listen, but it's been 20 years since she died.*

LISTENER: *Was that harder than when your father left you by the side of the road?*

MR.Y: *Yes ma'am, yes ma'am, because I couldn't fix it.*

It seems Mr. Y had reconciled his childhood abandonment. With reconciliation, Mr. Y was able to move on to other memories. His greater concern in his later life was his boss's grief because he could not help him. Often Reviewers reconcile old issues on their own before they reach the summary and evaluation section of the Life Review, as Mr. Y apparently had. But if the Reviewer has not reconciled the old issue, the Listener needs to revisit the pivotal event again, after acknowledging the Reviewer's present, more pressing concerns. The Reviewer's additional comments will reveal the present state of the issue.

Counseling Skill: Congruence

Congruence is the last but not the least counseling skill to apply to the Life Review process. Congruence is a sense of accord between Listener and Reviewer that delivers the message "I understand" to the Reviewer. Congruence requires the Listener to feel and project back the emotions of the Reviewer. When there is congruence, there is a felt agreement and conformity between the Listener and the Reviewer as one talks and the other listens closely. A Therapeutic Listener demonstrates congruence by expressing and reflecting feelings that parallel the apparent feelings of the Reviewer. If the Reviewer is telling a happy story of childhood, the Listener reflects the emotion of happiness by smiling and nodding while listening to the story. To be congruent, you must be open to and in touch with the Reviewer's current, described experience. While listening, be fully engaged in the story. You should understand and accept the Reviewer's outlook unconditionally, as the Therapeutic Listener working with Mrs. W did when relating to Mrs. W's story. Recall Mrs. W, a Life Reviewer who was abused by her mother (see Visit 2):

MRS. W: *My mother never came to any of my school events, even when I won and got medals.*

LISTENER: **Did it bother you when she didn't come? Did you want her there?**

MRS. W: *Yes, I would have liked her to see me.*

LISTENER: **It would have been nice to have your mother enjoy your success. How did it feel when you won?**

MRS. W: *I felt great! I felt like I proved something, not so much to my mother as to myself.*

LISTENER: **How exciting. It must have been great to achieve recognition. I'm thrilled to share that moment with you, but I am sorry your mother missed it.**

The Listener matched Mrs. W's excitement over winning, and shared her disappointment over the mother who never saw her success. The Listener praised Mrs. W's achievements. The Therapeutic Listener understood the joy of sharing special moments and now actively shared those with Mrs. W. They were in harmony and congruence.

> *The Therapeutic Listener understands the joy of sharing special moments and actively shares those.*

When you find yourself in a similar situation, remember to listen closely to the Reviewer's exact words; try to understand the situation and respond in kind. If you can feel true agreement between yourself and the Reviewer, you are on your way to manifesting mastery of the Congruent counseling skill.

Interviewing Technique: Summarizing

Summarizing is a technique by which the Therapeutic Listener condenses all or part of a Reviewer's Life story into an understandable whole that can be communicated back to the Reviewer. The Listener returns the essence of the story to the Reviewer, perhaps in clearer terms, which serves to clarify the memory for both Reviewer and Listener.

When you summarize, you sometimes create your own interpretation of the heard words for clarification and affirmation by the Reviewers, or, if necessary, correction by them. Although you should have summarized every weekly session for your Reviewer at the end or beginning of each visit, now in the concluding 2 weeks of Life Review, you will offer a more in-depth summarization of key points to create a picture of the Reviewer's total life as it was remembered. Through this technique, you provide a "snapshot" of how a life was lived. In the following example, the Listener is urging the

Visit 6

Reviewer to single out his proudest moment as one way to contribute to the summarization of the Reviewer's life:

LISTENER: *What do you think was the proudest moment in your life?*

REVIEWER: *Being overseas.*

LISTENER: *What made you proud about that?*

REVIEWER: *I was an engineer and did important work. And then we traveled all around to different places in France and made good friends in France; I learned to speak French and I didn't have a problem getting around. I was very proud of the way I adjusted to being in a foreign country. It was a good time.*

LISTENER: *You seem very proud of your work and adapting to a foreign environment and learning a foreign language. Sounds like those were good years for you.*

REVIEWER: *They were—some of the best.*

When asked what age he would choose if he could pick any age from his past, this Reviewer said 19, when he went overseas. The Listener recapped the vignette with the statement, "*It does sound like those were good years for you. You seem very proud of them.*" And the Reviewer reaffirmed that being overseas made him proud.

The technique of summarizing is facilitated through the questions in the summary/evaluation section of the LRF. Summary questions such as, "*What was the happiest period of your life?*," encourage Reviewers to make assessments of what was best. As Reviewers progress through the summary, they reveal a clear, more complete picture of life as it was lived, readying themselves for evaluation.

Unique Life Review Characteristic: Evaluation

The unique characteristics of the Life Review are those features that make a Structured Life Review process different from other ways of reminiscing. Four unique characteristics have been validated by research. Of the four, Evaluation is probably the most important characteristic contributing to the therapy of the Life Review. Evaluation, as a unique characteristic, is the same as the specific insightful examination taking place in Visits 6 and 7 of the Life Review. In fact, evaluation as both characteristic and technique is foundational to the process underlying the Structured Life Review.

Evaluation is the process of weighing and valuing life's events while making connections between them. Although the process of Evaluation in the Life Review is ongoing, there is a specific emphasis on a collective evaluation of the entire life during Visits 6 and 7 of the Review. The Therapeutic Listener leads the Reviewer through this final evaluation by encouraging the Reviewer with insightful questions (called feeling or evaluative questions) and comments from the summary/evaluation section of the LRF (see pages 147 and 162). These questions for Visits 6 and 7 help Reviewers determine the effect of their decisions on their lives, to appreciate successes, and to accept any setbacks. While considering the questions in this summary/evaluation section, Reviewers decide whether they should or could have done things differently or are content with their choices and able to accept their earlier decisions and actions because it was the best they could do at the time. Evaluation provides Reviewers with an opportunity to create a clear and complete picture of life, both past and present, as they end the Review. They are asked to closely consider certain events in the past, to make connections between the events, and to think about how those events made them feel. Questions such as, *"How did that make you feel?"* or *"What was the hardest thing you had to face in your life?"* or *"Did you live your life as you hoped to live it?"* encourage Reviewers to examine memories from several angles and to make judgments about themselves and their lives.

A summative or collective evaluation of the whole life is additional to the ongoing use of evaluation throughout the Review and begins during this sixth visit and continues through Visit 7. There are numerous examples of "feeling questions" causing self-examination throughout the application section of this Handbook (Part II) that illustrate how Reviewers practice specific evaluation with the encouragement of the Therapeutic Listener. Additionally, the following is an example of a Reviewer's actual summative evaluation of his life, occurring near the end of the Life Review process:

LISTENER: *Today I'm going to ask you to evaluate your life.*

REVIEWER: *Well, I think I've had a fairly good life. The money came slowly and we couldn't take vacations or travel, but I managed to get the kids through college and then we had some vacations.*

LISTENER: *What would you change if you were to change anything?*

REVIEWER: *I don't think I would change any part of it. I've had two good marriages and raised three children. And they're respectful of me. They know me and they take care of me as a family should.*

LISTENER: *What were your disappointments?*

REVIEWER: *I guess the biggest one was not going to college myself. Now it doesn't bother me, but years ago it bothered me because I was the only one without a college education. I went nights for a couple of years but I never got a degree.*

LISTENER: *Do you think you would have done better with a college education?*

REVIEWER: *That's debatable. I was very fortunate in business, but without a college education I didn't succeed as far as I'm concerned, because everyone who worked for me had a college degree.*

LISTENER: *Well that's remarkable, that you managed people with degrees, but you didn't seem to need one.*

REVIEWER: *I guess so. I'm over it now.*

As this Reviewer continued to evaluate his life during the end of his Life Review, he seemed surprised by his success and his happiness. He concluded that he didn't really need a college degree and had made out better than expected in his life, especially in his business, which he had recently sold for several million dollars. He accepted his life as it was lived and was a brilliant example of someone reaching Integrity.

Reviewer Type: The Bleeding Reviewer

Bleeding Reviewers are Reviewers whose memories are dominated by negative events in their view of the past. Such Reviewers may see themselves as victims of life and repeatedly talk about how tough life was for them. When encouraged to evaluate their lives, they often continue their negativity. Bleeding Reviewers may be pessimists who have difficulty seeing the "good" side of anything.

> *Bleeding Reviewers may be pessimists who have difficulty seeing the "good" side of anything.*

Remember Mrs. W, an unhappy woman, who told distressing stories to the Listener about her childhood. She epitomized a Bleeding Reviewer. Although she had reason to be disheartened about her childhood, she refused to let go of the bad events and carried her poor relationship with her mother into adulthood. Despite the best efforts of the Therapeutic Listener, Mrs. W's negativity about herself continued throughout her Life Review. Mrs. W's stories of her mother dominated each conversation as she worked things through in her mind. The Therapeutic Listener was patient and continued to project acceptance and positive regard throughout the Life Review. With acceptance, Mrs. W was feeling approval for the first time; yet she clung to her negative approach, although she recognized it was negative. Eventually, she spoke out loud about her inner struggle to overcome her negative thoughts, which in itself was a big gain for Mrs. W. She needed to resolve her bad memories of her mother and move on. She finally demonstrated a bit of learned insight in her last sessions:

> MRS. W: *I don't like this feeling that goes on inside of me all the time. I keep saying why can't I be satisfied? Why can't I accept things the way they were? Why do I always have to upset the apple cart and think negative thoughts? And being negative—I don't want to be negative, I want to be positive.*
>
> LISTENER: **Do you feel you have benefited from these visits?**
>
> MRS. W: *Yes, yes I did because there's a lot of things that you've asked me that I've answered that I've never really thought about. I've looked maybe in one way through the years. But once you've asked these questions, and it gave me a chance to think about them, I find that I look at lots of things differently than I have been looking at them all these many, many years.*

The Therapeutic Listener brought about change in this Bleeding Reviewer, who recognized her negative ways of thinking and wanted to do something about them. When you are listening to a Bleeding Reviewer, it is important to maintain a positive outlook yourself, while providing unconditional positive regard throughout the Life Review. Your continual optimism may be the key that prompts the Reviewer to let go and eventually make a change. The use of interviewing techniques such as Acceptance and Unconditional Positive Regard may be a pleasant first-time experience for the Bleeding Reviewer, who may not always have received such positive responses from others.

> *Your continual optimism may be the key that prompts the Reviewer to let go and eventually make a change.*

You will find that working with Bleeding Reviewers requires a great deal of patience that is only occasionally rewarded by success. When someone is as troubled as Mrs. W, you may need to suggest further counseling with a professional when the Reviewer completes the Life Review. We can only hope that Bleeding Reviewers such as Mrs. W will have gained enough insight through doing the Life Review to follow up on a referral. No matter how difficult Bleeding Reviewers make it to dialogue with them, once you start a Life Review, you are responsible for seeing it through to the end. Just keep using the positive skills you have learned in this Handbook.

End Visit 6

Summarize Session

As you summarize at the close of the sixth visit, note which questions you used during this part of the summary and evaluation visits so that you don't repeat yourself during Visit 7. Also point out the positive highlights of the Review to the Reviewer and show the Reviewer the rest of the questions you will use to complete the Life Review during your next visit. It is always important to leave on a happy note. Quickly go over some of the more notable statements the Reviewer made and remind the Reviewer that you will continue with similar questions during the next visit.

Next Visit

Remember that you can use the summary and evaluation questions interchangeably between Visits 6 and 7. Keeping notes will make it easier to do that. There is one more session for the Life Review and a final session for closure. Remind the Life Reviewer that there are only two more visits left. Make a date for the next meeting. As before, write the information on an appointment card in dark ink with large print to give to the Reviewer.

Visit 6

Visit 7

INTEGRATION

One's first step in wisdom is to question everything—
and one's last is to come to terms with everything.

—Georg Christopher Lichtenberg

Visit 7 is the last Life Review interviewing session with your Reviewer. This chapter presents additional directions for using the evaluation section of the LRF and suggests ways to examine your own methods of listening. As you embark on Visit 7, remind the Reviewer that you will visit only one more time after this session and that this Visit 7 actually ends the Life Review process. The final visit will be for closure and good-byes. As you will see in this chapter, you and the Life Reviewer will complete important work during this last session, which uses evaluation techniques to lead to Integrity.

Preliminary Tasks

Tasks remain the same and should be a matter of habit for both you and the Reviewer. The Reviewer will probably be waiting patiently in the appointed spot, eager to begin. You only need to check on glasses of water and to turn on the recorder, and you are ready to begin.

Clarify Visit 6

It is quite simple to clarify Visit 6 and move smoothly into Visit 7 because both sessions use the evaluation questions on the LRF. Clarification serves as a reminder of what was covered the week before. Tell the Reviewer what you think you heard during the previous session and ask the Reviewer to correct you if you are wrong. If you ask in the following manner, Reviewers will correct and clarify for both you and themselves:

> LISTENER: *I enjoyed our visit last week but I am confused about one or two events that I'd like to understand. Last week you said you kept your marriage a secret and then later you said you got married a second time. Were you married twice?*

> REVIEWER: *Oh, the wedding was getting married to the same man again, but now we could tell everybody. My Daddy brought me down the steps. It was in July before air-conditioning and we were hot, but we were so proud. I could finally let everyone know I was married.*

> LISTENER: *So that was your proudest moment, when you got married the second time and you could tell everyone.*

> REVIEWER: *Yes, I loved Martin and wanted everyone to know.*

While clarifying, the Listener provided an opportunity for the Reviewer to relive the moment and feel proud yet again. The Listener also showed true interest in the Reviewer's life, because the Listener really wanted to understand about the Reviewer's marriages. Finally, the Listener clearly understood that the Reviewer was married twice, but to the same man.

Erikson's Model: Oldest Adulthood

The last of Erikson's stages is Integrity vs. Despair. The eighth stage of life, Integrity, is the same as the goal of the Life Review because the definition of Integrity—accepting the life as it was lived—matches the description of the desired outcomes of the Life Review. The opposite condition of Integrity is Despair. Together they form the last stage of development in Erikson's model.

Integrity

Integrity means to accept one's life as it has been lived, with few reservations. Reviewers need to understand their life course in order to reconcile and accept their lives. Erikson et al. (1986) said that at this stage people achieve wisdom by ultimately integrating all of the life parts into a whole, then knowing and accepting that whole. The act of integrating requires a merging of separate pieces until a balanced whole is reached. The process of bringing life into balance requires a review and a coming to terms with the way the life has been lived thus far, a reconciliation. Integrity implies a feeling of satisfaction with one's self—a reconciliation of decisions made—and an acceptance of the life as it was lived. Integrity is coherence and solidarity. Mr. D exemplifies a man who has reached Integrity:

LISTENER: *How did your life change when you retired?*

MR. D: *Well, I got to travel more, the beach and the mountains. I would have liked to go to Europe, but Virginia was afraid to fly so we stayed nearby.*

LISTENER: *What else changed?*

MR. D: *Well, I played golf more and saw the grandchildren more. Our daughter makes sure we see a lot of her and them. She's adopted you know. We couldn't have our own. I guess it all worked out. I am a lucky man.*

Note that many of Mr. D's activities were not of his choosing. He never got to Europe, but accepted that. He couldn't have children of his own, so he chose to adopt and was happy with his adopted daughter and his grandchildren. Mr. D accepted his life as it was lived, despite being denied some wishes, and he had no regrets.

Mr. D seemed to have reached Integrity on his own, but you can help Reviewers reach the goal of Integrity in this part of the Life Review with the evaluation questions that cause the Reviewer to examine life's parts. During this final interview visit, Reviewers can examine, evaluate, and consider past events from both new and old angles until they feel satisfied with what they have done in life or until they have reframed and reconciled their thinking. Your pointing out what was good and how they overcame past defeat helps Reviewers to recognize their previously unappreciated strengths. Your job is to continue to highlight the good until Reviewers begin to see the good in themselves.

> *Your job is to continue to highlight the good until Reviewers begin to see the good in themselves.*

Despair

Despair is caused by a lack of Integrity and exists in Reviewers as hopelessness and depression. Despairing people are disheartened and discouraged. They cannot reconcile untoward events, nor can they recognize where they have done good during their lifetime. Butler once said that he thought depressed older people were stuck in an internal Life Review, unable to resolve their problems. Continually being overwhelmed by unsolvable problems leaves people with unfinished business, which in turn creates anxiety, melancholy, and general ongoing unhappiness.

Visit 7

> *Continually being over-whelmed by unsolvable problems leaves people with unfinished business.*

Every skill and technique that you learn to apply in these chapters is helpful to those in despair. With despairing Reviewers, you must work harder—using reframing and repetition in conjunction with acceptance, empathy, and caring, to name a few of the skills you have learned—to get Reviewers to see the past in a different light in order to help them move on. Rarely do you make great change in the despairing, but sometimes you *can* turn them around to consider their past differently, and usually you can create a little change. Mr. M.'s Therapeutic Listener is working toward that small change:

MR. M: *I had an affair when I was first married and left my family for another woman. I had three little girls, the youngest was three. I regret that I deserted them. I wish I'd done things differently.*

LISTENER: **What would you have done differently?**

MR. M: *Well, I would have tried to put the other woman out of my mind and then worked it out with my wife and my girls; they were still small. I was not a nice guy.*

LISTENER: **We all make mistakes.**

MR. M: *Yeah, I could have even lived a double life for my girls.*

LISTENER: **Would that have been better?**

MR. M: *It would have been dishonest, but now I'm estranged. I haven't seen them for 20 years.*

LISTENER: **That sounds like that's really hard for you.**

MR. M: *It is, especially when it is their birthdays. My oldest would have been 39 last week.*

LISTENER: **Have you tried to find them?**

MR. M: *Yeah, yeah, but I was rejected. They're all mad because I deserted them and they had a hard time of it.*

LISTENER: **What keeps you from trying again?**

MR. M: *Rejection.*

Mr. M went on to describe himself as a functional drinker (one who could still work while drinking), who had been homeless at one time and slightly disabled, and he thought he had made out worse in life than he expected. Now he was a loner, shunning social contacts. The Listener made small gains toward bringing some light into his life through the

Life Review and in getting him to see that reconciliation was still a possibility for him. The big guilt of deserting his family remained in the forefront, but he was slowly considering trying a new approach, like personal letters of regret and flowers to each of the girls on their birthdays with the hope that one of them would call him back.

Using the Life Review Form

This is the next-to-last visit of the Life Review and the last opportunity to complete the questioning portion. By now you should have asked the first half of the questions in the evaluation section of the LRF (see list on page 147 in the preceding chapter). Now, it is time to complete the rest of the evaluation questions, presented on page 162, while using the additional instructions below. Remember to use all of the questions suggested for Visits 6 and 7.

Encourage Understanding

As you help the Reviewer to complete the Life Review, your goal is to help make a sum of life's parts so that the Reviewer can envision the whole life and understand its meaning. You can do this by enumerating the good things in the Reviewer's life that you listed from your notes from the preceding visit before you started this session. This preparation is important. Give the Reviewer time to relish the long-forgotten achievements and then begin to show how one affected the other, building a picture of a life that Reviewers can accept. Include the bad times and show how the Reviewer conquered them, and how sometimes the bad times brought the good times. By doing your homework prior to Visit 7, you will be better prepared to help Reviewers put their lives together.

Reviewers need to understand where they have been and why, and to accept some inevitable life turns. You help Reviewers to do this with insightful queries and responses; "so what" questions inspire further exploration. Completing a Life Review allows people to "unstick" themselves so they can begin to look ahead. Sometimes the Life Review gives Reviewers the insight and strength to try again to reconcile things that are still unresolved.

REVIEWER: *A great deal of what I've told you, I've never told anyone else.*

LISTENER: *I understand, but you know, if you'll bear with me, I think I'll ask similar questions again.*

REVIEWER: *You're going to see if my answers are different?*

LISTENER: *No, but the way you think about things may have changed.*

REVIEWER: *Well, that's true.*

LISTENER: *Yes, and sometimes you shift about the way you think about something. Even though it was painful, and you understand it in one way, you can shift and understand it in a slightly different way.*

Visit 7

Suggested Questions for Visit 7

- If you could stay the same age all your life, what age would you choose? Why?
- How do you think you've made out in life? Better or worse than what you hoped for?
- **Did you live your life as you had hoped to live it?**
- Let's talk a little about you as you are now. What are the best things about the age you are now?
- What are the worst things about being the age you are now?
- What are the most important things to you in your life today?
- What do you hope will happen to you as you grow older?
- What do you fear will happen to you as you grow older?
- **Are you happy with your life choices and decisions?**
- What do you want for yourself as you look toward the future?
- Have you enjoyed participating in this review of your life?
- Do you have any comments or suggestions?

REVIEWER: *You know you're right. I mean the death of my sister pained me a great deal, it was painful. I thought about it 24 hours a day. Her death was a real case of malpractice. Talking about it helped me to see I couldn't change it. Finally, I just had to let it go, but it still crops up now and then—but as time goes on, not as often.*

LISTENER: **Good. You will still think about your sister's death, but in a better way.**

You can see that by the last visit this Reviewer was moving toward understanding the way things had to be and accepting them as a part of his life. This kind of thinking also moves Reviewers toward viewing life as an integrated whole.

Review Significant Successes Again

This last session of the Life Review provides a perfect opportunity to remind people of their significant past successes so that they may relive those gratifying moments again. When you are asking them about their greatest satisfactions or their proudest moments, remind them of what they said before. For instance, remember Mrs. W who had a difficult childhood: When the Listener asked her to talk about her greatest satisfactions, she replied almost traditionally that her children were her greatest satisfaction. The Listener asked Mrs. W to tell her more about her children, but added, *"Wasn't your athletic success also a great satisfaction?"* Mrs. W replied, *"Oh that was fun, but it didn't make me as proud as my children did."* The Therapeutic Listener, using the evaluation section of the LRF, continued to remind Mrs. W of other past successes in her life, leaving her with a more positive feeling about her life and about herself as she completed the Life Review.

Reframe Difficult Times Again

You have one last opportunity to help Reviewers create an acceptable picture by again reframing their life events that troubled them in the past. The initial reframing earlier in the Life Review may not have been immediately successful. Your Reviewer may still be trying to reconcile and accept certain life events. Since this visit is your last chance to help Reviewers look at events in a different and more positive light, you should ask about or at least be alert for the mention of events that still disturb Reviewers and that surface when you ask about disappointments or sad times while using the questions on the LRF. The question, *"What was the unhappiest period in your life?,"* may still generate turmoil when your Reviewer answers you. If Reviewers still feel disturbed, seize the opportunity to go over earlier issues again. Questions such as, *"Do you still feel that way about . . . ?"* may instigate additional reframing, or at least inform you of the Reviewer's prevailing perceptions. A good example is Mr. A, who was asked about his disappointments:

> LISTENER: *What would you say were your biggest disappointments in life?*
>
> MR. A: *Well, first not going to college, but I did alright with the education I have. Then of course when my first wife died and I had to raise my daughter alone; that was hard. And then my mother died and we were all alone.*
>
> LISTENER: *You seemed to have done a great job raising your daughter. What an enormous job.*
>
> MR. A: *Yes, yes, it was and she's a good daughter even today.*

In this example, the Reviewer seems to have done his own reframing at an earlier date and has now accepted all those hard times. He first mentioned his lack of education, then his grief. He seemed to reconcile his misfortunes on his own with only a little help from the Listener. Though he wanted things to be different, such as the opportunity to go to college, he was satisfied with the way his life had turned out and felt he had done a good job.

Establish a Future Emphasis

Reviewers who look to the future have optimism and hope, two traits of people who are not depressed. Therefore, a future orientation contributes to their state of well-being. A

> *When people finish reviewing their lives, they often have renewed energy and you need to help them refocus this energy toward a new interest.*

shift needs to take place that refocuses the Reviewer from the past to the future. There are many comments and probes in the LRF that help to point Reviewers in a future direction. Questions such as *"What do you hope will happen to you in the future?"* or *"What kinds of things would you like to do with the time you have left?"* (hobbies, friends, projects, and so forth) help to shift thinking. When people finish reviewing their lives, they often have renewed energy and you need to help them refocus this energy toward a new interest, as Mr. A did when he began making plans for the future immediately after completing his Life Review:

LISTENER: **Do you have plans for the future?**

MR. A: *Well, first I need to get healthy after this hip operation, and then, you know, I'd like to live in a little shack at the beach. Get up in the morning, have a swim, and then cook myself a steak at night.*

LISTENER: **Wouldn't that be a little lonely?**

MR. A: *Maybe, but just for a few years, then I'll go to a retirement place where they feed me.*

LISTENER: **You seem to have thought about this; maybe you could rent a place for a year.**

MR. A: *Yes, yes, I could afford that.*

The future brings different choices for each Reviewer, sometimes future dreams and sometimes preparation for the end of life. Reviewers who have resolved their unfinished business and now feel at peace with themselves are often also ready to die. When you review with frail, elderly people, you should not be afraid of such an outcome. Readiness for death is a good outcome whether it is immediate or years from completion of the Life Review. Today, millions of government dollars are being spent on promoting palliative care and creating hospice care for the dying. The Life Review is an excellent tool to use in this endeavor. Many older or ill people will be forever grateful to have had an opportunity to express the last word on who they were while they were still here.

Counseling Skills: Review All

Review and practice all of the skills that you have learned in this Handbook until you become confident in using each of them. This last visit is your opportunity to put together all the skills you have learned to use in response to Reviewers' needs. The following excerpts show the Therapeutic Listener demonstrating each skill in response to a Reviewer's comment. Although the phrases are presented out of context, the Listener response is easy to understand.

> *The future brings different choices for each Reviewer, sometimes future dreams and sometimes preparation for the end of life.*

1. Example of Acceptance:

   REVIEWER: *I've been fortunate in my decisions, most of the time, that I've done the right thing.*

   LISTENER: **Well it certainly sounds that way to me. You make a decision and you stick with it and feel good about it. That's an admirable trait.**

2. Example of Caring:

   REVIEWER: *Our church is important to us. We really miss not being able to go anymore.*

   LISTENER: **It must have been hard to leave your church when you moved? I can understand how difficult that loss is for you.**

3. Example of Unconditional Positive Regard:

   REVIEWER: *I am having a real hard time getting over this surgery. I've always been independent.*

   LISTENER: **Yes, you always were independent and you adapted readily and well to many disastrous events throughout your life. So you will again. You've had lots of challenges and survived them.**

4. Example of Empathy:

   REVIEWER: *I'm sorry. I should be over it by now, but whenever I think of the way my son died, I get angry and feel sad again.*

   LISTENER: **He had a horrible and untimely death, whenever I think of it, I feel sad too.**

5. Example of Congruence

   REVIEWER: *Well, you know I always hated speaking in public. I guess I was shy, but I got over it.*

   LISTENER: **I understand that feeling; I don't like speaking in public either.**

As you read these examples, look back and listen to your own Life Review tapes. (If you are new, review the one that you are presently completing.) Ask yourself if all your responses were therapeutic when you had the opportunity to use skills such as these. If the responses were not as good as they could have been, think about how you would

Visit 7

respond now, given another chance. Remember these colloquial sayings: *Practice makes perfect; Hindsight is always clearer;* and *You get better over time.* They apply to your development as a Therapeutic Listener.

Interviewing Techniques

Integrating

The last interviewing technique that you need to apply in your role as a Therapeutic Listener is the technique of Integrating. When a Therapeutic Listener integrates events as a technique, it is different than when the Life Reviewer reaches the goal of Integrity, a state. As confusing as this sounds, the skilled Therapeutic Listener who integrates well for the Reviewer may help the Reviewer to reach the state of Integrity more quickly.

To integrate means to put things together. You take all of a Reviewer's experiences and help the Reviewer to blend them together into a congruent and adaptive whole, to help the Reviewer understand the entire life as it was lived. You help the Reviewer to consolidate, merge events, and then assimilate them, showing how one life event may have initiated the next life event. You can implement the integrating technique by asking pertinent questions to try to understand the whole yourself and then playing it back to the Reviewer to see if your understanding is correct. The questions in the evaluation portion of the LRF direct Reviewers toward integrating separate life events into an understandable whole. When a Reviewer hears your interpretation played back, the Reviewer may correct you, advise you further, or take a different look as well, just as the Reviewer did in the following narrative:

> LISTENER: *Tell me more about the death of your brother.*
>
> REVIEWER: *The first thing I remember is my brother dying. He had a little casket and a little wagon, all white, and they came and took him away. I used to hide among the pots and pans in the kitchen so they wouldn't get me too.*
>
> LISTENER: *What a scary feeling. Why did you think they would get you?*
>
> REVIEWER: *I don't know, I was a kid, but I'm still afraid of hospitals and never went to a wake until recently.*
>
> LISTENER: *Did anyone explain what was going on back then?*
>
> REVIEWER: *No, my parents were Swedish and didn't speak English good, so we never talked. My father worked all the time, so I never remember talking about anything.*
>
> LISTENER: *How did you feel about that?*
>
> REVIEWER: *Sometimes I was lonely, and I always wondered about my brother. Well, I found out later he probably had the flu, but when he died, no one told me.*

LISTENER: *Do you remember him at all?*

REVIEWER: *No, they had the wake in the house and a friend hid with me in the pots and pans that time.*

LISTENER: *Sounds like you thought about it a lot.*

REVIEWER: *It stayed with me. Maybe that's why I'm afraid of funeral homes and hospitals.*

LISTENER: *Could be. You didn't understand death as a child and that made you afraid of dying yourself. I imagine your fear contributed to your dislike of hospitals and funerals.*

The Listener related the early death of the Reviewer's brother to the Reviewer's fear of hospitals by communicating the Listener's own understanding of events and asking for clarification. The Listener's request for clarification not only helped the Listener to understand more clearly, it also gave the Reviewer an opportunity to rethink the past and gain greater clarification for himself. The Reviewer in this example finally realized that his fear of hospitals and funerals might have evolved from witnessing a death he did not understand when he was 4 years old. He was tying events together and integrating them, trying to make an understandable picture for himself.

Review of Techniques

After learning this last technique, Integrating, consider all of the interviewing techniques and make them part of your repertoire, using them selectively as needed. To be effective you must continually and consciously practice, just as you do with the counseling skills. Some techniques will become second nature; others will require more attention and practice from you. You can use them in normal conversation as part of good listening practices. Then, every once in a while, check the list of interviewing techniques in Part I so that you will remember and use all of them.

Unique Life Review Characteristics: Consider All Four Together

There are at least four characteristics that make a Structured Life Review uniquely different from other forms of life review and reminiscing. As previously discussed, these are: Structure, Duration, Individuality, and Evaluation. As you complete the particular Life Review that you are presently conducting, think about all four of these unique characteristics in connection with this Life Review. Does your work incorporate all of these characteristics together in one Life Review? If your answer is yes, then you have a good grasp of the concepts that have been presented in this Handbook. You are ready to proceed to conduct more Life Reviews and to implement this combined knowledge of the

Visit 7

characteristics on your own. If your answer is no, then be sure to follow the Handbook closely when you do your next Life Review.

Reviewer Type: Recognize Your Reviewer's Type

In this chapter, think about the type of Reviewer you may be visiting, then identify your particular Reviewer by type, selecting the most helpful skills and techniques to elicit that Reviewer's life story. Then, when you proceed to your next Reviewer, identify the type again, as soon as you can, so that you can select helpful techniques in advance of the visits. For example, with a Storyteller, you would need to provide immediate and future directions to structure the review and keep the process on target. Therefore, you should have a tentative plan in your head, using good probes at the end of each session to keep the process moving. With a Reluctant Reviewer, however, you might need to identify some stories to share to get the Reviewer talking. Prior planning with this Handbook will help your Life Reviews to be more effective.

Of course, there are some Reviewers who do not fit any of the types described in this Handbook. They may be answering your questions easily, staying on target, and contributing entertaining stories. In such a case, don't try to categorize them—just enjoy the visits, making sure to supply lots of feedback to the Reviewer—so that the Reviewer will receive and enjoy the therapeutic benefits of a Structured Life Review.

End Visit 7

Summarize Session

As you summarize Visit 7, you should sum up the Life Review experience in its entirety. Share your pleasure in knowing the Reviewer's life story and in the opportunity to make the visits. Thank Reviewers for their time. Tell them where you think they have made great gains and ask them if they agree. Use the next-to-last question in the LRF to see how Reviewers enjoyed the process. In the following examples, notice that each of four Reviewers answered the question about enjoying the Life Review differently, and each of the answers provided the Therapeutic Listener with a little more perspective about how well the Listener had conducted the process.

Life Review #1

LISTENER: *Have you enjoyed participating in this review of your life?*

REVIEWER #1: *In what?*

LISTENER: *Have you enjoyed talking about your life?*

REVIEWER #1: *I don't know, it's given me a chance to talk.*

LISTENER: *Did it make you think about a lot of new things?*

REVIEWER #1: *I always think about things but I usually put them in a little box and lock them up.*

LISTENER: **Was remembering helpful or painful?**

REVIEWER #1: *Sometimes both.*

Life Review #2

LISTENER: **Have you enjoyed this review of your life?**

REVIEWER #2: *Yes, yes, and you've helped me finish my book of my life for my grandchildren. You've made me think back over things I've forgotten. Now my granddaughter will know us and our parents because it will be there in a book for her.*

LISTENER: **That's such a nice thing to do. She'll appreciate it as she grows up.**

Life Review #3

LISTENER: **Did you enjoy this Life Review?**

REVIEWER #3: *No, I haven't. I was sorry to dredge up the past. I don't like remembering those times. It's best to leave them alone. But I did enjoy having a visitor.*

LISTENER: **Well, I enjoyed visiting you a great deal and thank you for your time.**

Life Review #4

LISTENER: **Did you enjoy participating in this Life Review?**

REVIEWER #4: *These visits have meant the world to me. I've remembered things I've long forgotten. I've told you things I never told anyone else. I got to think about me for a change.*

LISTENER: **So the time you've spent recalling your life has been helpful?**

REVIEWER #4: *More than I could ever imagine.*

These selected excerpts include a variety of responses both for and against the Life Review process, from the negative to the positive to the superlative. Most people love talking about the past and doing a Structured Life Review. Others volunteer to do a Life Review and then regret doing it for numerous reasons. Hopefully, your experiences with Life Review will be as rewarding as our own experiences have been, encouraging you to do more.

Visit 7

Consider Referrals

Most Reviewers do not need referrals, but if you find a Reviewer more troubled than expected, you may want to talk to him or her about getting additional help. Because you have trained yourself to be a Therapeutic Listener, and through this training are more aware of an individual's emotions, you should be perceptive enough to realize when people need more help than you can give them. Refer them to a professional counselor or psychotherapist who is more qualified to treat the seriously ill and who can prescribe medication that may be necessary for your Reviewer. Your suggestion may motivate your reviewer to think about the possibility of therapy. You may never use our advice for making referrals, but if you do need it, you have it (see page 172 in Visit 8).

Next Visit

As you arrange the next, and last, visit in the same manner you used for earlier sessions, remind the Reviewer that you will be back one more time for a good-bye visit. The last visit is important for closure and separation and may not take the whole hour. While you are separating during the final visit, you may also want to use the time to evaluate the impact and the outcomes of the process of the Life Review on your Reviewer. If you intend to use paper-and-pencil measures to assess the outcomes of the Life Review, tell the Reviewer about the measures beforehand, during this seventh visit. Explain why and how you will use them during the next visit.

CLOSURE AND OUTCOMES

*We don't receive wisdom; we must discover it
for ourselves after a journey that no one can
take for us or spare us.*

—MARCEL PROUST

This eighth and final visit provides an opportunity to tie up loose ends, to make referrals, to test for outcomes, to wrap up the Reviewer/Listener relationship, to close the Life Review process, and to thank Reviewers for their time. This visit is particularly for the benefit of Reviewers, to help them with closure and separation while allowing time for social visiting. During this visit, you should also set aside time for measuring the outcomes resulting from the Life Review process and for providing and explaining any previously promised health materials and referrals.

Bringing an end to the Reviewer/Listener relationship takes place during Visit 8. You must be sure Reviewers are satisfied with the amount of time you have spent with them and with the Life Review process as a whole. Visit 8 provides time to focus on each individual Reviewer's needs, leading to completion as well as closure.

Because you have been preparing Reviewers for closure by mentioning the end of the visits during Visits 6 and 7, closure is usually expected and accepted by Reviewers when the time arrives. Closure is actually anticipated, because Reviewers know that the Life Review is conducted for a prescribed amount of time and they know when they have completed the process. Because Reviewers are fully prepared and have completed the task of Life Review, separating from a Life Reviewer should be relatively easy. Often, Reviewers are looking forward to moving on to other things, freeing you to end the process easily.

Professional Referrals

Now is the time to finalize referrals to other professionals or health care providers. If you have been following these visit guidelines, you should have mentioned the need for such a referral earlier in Visit 7, giving the Reviewer time to think about the possibility of seeking additional help. For some troubled people who have participated in a Life Review, the need is clear for more help and counseling than the Life Review can give to them. Because of the bonding that takes place during the 8-week Life Review process, the Reviewer may value your advice enough to seek additional help. Be forewarned, however, that such suggestions are not always well received; some Reviewers may be insulted and even momentarily angry.

Regardless of the Reviewers' response to your advice, you need to tell them if you think they need more help. Some reviewers will argue with you, telling you that they are fine as they are. But later, they may take your advice and follow up on your referral. Suggesting a referral for the Reviewer to seek additional help loses nothing and may gain much. When you make such a suggestion, follow the suggestion with a card listing a few professionals' names and telephone numbers for the Reviewer to consult in the future. Of course, you need to prepare this information in advance.

During your visits, you may also have mentioned other types of helpful agencies for referral. You may have suggested an adult day program for a resident with Alzheimer's disease, or legal aid for someone with a law issue. Life Reviewers who are older are grateful for any help given because most of them do not know what kind of help is available in the community for the varied problems associated with old age. You, on the other hand, will hopefully be familiar with such helpful information. If you do know the helping agencies in your community, then be clear and provide the Reviewer with detailed written instructions as follow-up to your suggestions. Although sharing information is not a part of the Life Review itself, it is often a part of the interaction between Reviewer and Listener because the Life Review relationship is a "helping" one.

Contact Information

When you complete a Life Review and separate from a Reviewer, there is often no way to find and contact that Reviewer again, especially if the Reviewer moves or is discharged from the present facility. Therefore, you need to get the names of one or two contact people from your Reviewer before you complete the final Life Review visit. Getting contact people is especially helpful when working with older people who often move from home to hospital, to assisted living, or to a child's home. The best contact people are the Reviewers' children or other relatives because they usually know the whereabouts of their parents or relatives and know how to reach them. One would think recontacting an older person is easy, but most institutions do not require follow-up information or forwarding addresses from people they discharge, or else will not divulge such information to you. Death notices are not always current, and often old friends and neighbors have not been notified of their friends' deaths. Thus, you can avoid not knowing where old Reviewers are by asking for at least two contact people who will most likely always be in touch with them when you complete the last visit.

A business card is the best way for you to remain available to your Reviewers if you would like to be in touch with them after the Review is finished. Sharing your card is a gesture of friendship that keeps the doors open. You may wish to stay in touch to confirm follow-up on a referral, or just to find out how your Reviewers are doing. Recall also that 6 months after a Life Review is a good time to posttest for therapeutic results. Leaving a card with your essential information will make you available—and is your personal choice.

Thank You Note and Other Cards

Common courtesy requires a thank you note at the end of the 8-week session to thank Reviewers for the time spent with you. The note should be handwritten, personal, and mailed with a proper stamp. A thank you note will make Reviewers feel they have given something back to the world by spending time describing their lives to you, the Therapeutic Listener. If your Reviewers are older, their present opportunities to give back are limited, making their participation in the Life Review even more valuable to them. Thank you notes make the Reviewer feel appreciated and valued.

In our many years of conducting Life Review, it has been our practice to send birthday cards to Listeners after completing the Life Review process. We collected some demographic information when we began the process, which included birth dates. We created a tickler card system by the month that reminds us to send a card on each Reviewer's birthday. We were very surprised at the amount of pleasure this greeting card system gave our Reviewers. Many were alone and our card was the only card they received for their birthday. Regrettably, for some, it was the only birthday card they had ever received.

The effort was not costly because we produced the cards on our computer, and the cost of the stamp was insignificant when compared to the amount of goodwill and good feelings produced. If you wish to stay more closely in touch with your Reviewers, you can also send them holiday cards, such as Christmas, Valentines Day, and so forth. With continuous card contact, Reviewers are easier to locate should you wish to visit them or retest outcomes one more time. How long you keep in touch by greeting card is up to you, but sending a card at least once after the Life Review is complete makes a difference, particularly a birthday card, which is the most personal.

Assessment and Findings

Visit 8 is the time set aside for assessment of the entire Life Review process with your particular Reviewer. There are many ways to assess: with measured outcomes, by observation, and by asking the Reviewers for their opinions on the process. Often Listeners get continuous feedback from their peers and supervisors in ongoing supervision throughout the process. Thus you are always assessing your technique and making yourself a better Therapeutic Listener as you go along.

Tested Outcomes

Tested outcomes are achieved with reliable and valid paper-and-pencil measures, mostly used by researchers to measure participants' state of mind before and after an intervention (see Appendixes). You can use these tests to measure the effects of the Life Review. During the eighth visit, you need to repeat any paper-and-pencil pretests that you may have given Reviewers at the start of the Life Review process to assess their current well-being. Repeating the tests at the end of the process provides an objective measure of any change that has taken place within Reviewers as a result of the Life Review process. To get a numerical outcome, you subtract the posttest score from the pretest score, resulting in a change score that indicates the extent of change in your Reviewer over the 8-week process (see, e.g., Haight et al., 1998). If you did not use pretests before you started, you can still get an idea of how your Reviewer is doing at the end of the Life Review from the posttest score. But you cannot objectively measure change that may have taken place over the 8 weeks without first doing a pretest.

The tests we have recommended are short and easy to understand. They have shown change in Reviewers in our completed Life Review research projects. They measure outcomes such as mood, mental function, and general well-being. The Geriatric Depression Scale (GDS) is a good example of a test for measuring mood (see Appendix F). Other reliable and valid tests are also in the Appendixes for your use.

Reviewer Feedback

It is helpful to ask Life Reviewers what they thought about the process they just shared. The Reviewer's evaluation is an important critique for the ongoing use of the Life Review and provides the Therapeutic Listener with useful feedback. Even though the next-to-last question on the LRF asks how the Reviewer enjoyed the process of Life Review, some Reviewers may wish to provide a more in-depth critique or supply additional information, such as the Reviewer at the beginning of this Handbook who talked about the need to discuss sexuality in the Life Review. (See the last LRF question asking for comments and suggestions.)

Also, Reviewers may provide important insights to Therapeutic Listeners about the way the Life Review was conducted and about the Listener's techniques. A Reviewer's assessment of the Life Review process may influence the way you practice the Life Review in the future. In fact, if Reviewers are critical of your responses or state that they were uncomfortable at certain times during the Review, you will have to look to yourself for change. You can do this by critically relistening to the Life Review tapes to identify your mistakes and change your procedures and practices accordingly. The Reviewer's assessment gives you an opportunity to be a better Listener the next time you do a Life Review.

Observed Outcomes

Aside from paper-and-pencil tests, there are many other observational and subjective ways to measure change in a Reviewer after the completion of the Life Review. Just by observing, the Listener can readily note change in the Reviewer's emotions, activity level, outside interests, and appearance, especially if the Listener has notes that compare the Reviewer at the beginning of the Life Review with the Reviewer at the end of the Life Review. (The baseline assessment form in Appendix D is useful for this comparison.) Simply asking Reviewers to tell you how they feel now is another way to measure, as is being alert to making notes of observational change. Generally, the quantity and quality of benefits from a Life Review vary for each person. However, there are common outcomes from the Life Review process that can have positive effects on all Reviewers. They are listed in the box above to help you recognize them and are explained in the following paragraphs.

Coherence and Understanding. The first of these observable outcomes is felt rather then seen and is a sense of coherence and an understanding of why life was lived the way it

---

Reviewer Outcomes

Coherence and Understanding: Accepting life as it was lived

Self-Acceptance: Accepting oneself as is

Finding Meaning: Identifying a reason for being

Reconnection: Getting in touch with again; re-establishing a link

Shared Experiences: Undergoing an event in common with someone else

Bonding: Establishing a relationship based on shared experiences

Catharsis: Cleansing oneself of lifetime burdens

Future Orientation: Looking ahead with expectations

New Energy: Renewed vigor and enthusiasm

Peace: Feelings of contentment

Good Death: Accepting life as completed and being ready for its end—death

was. Understanding seems to create contentment and feelings of peace in Reviewers, and this understanding or final coherence helps Reviewers reach Integrity and is necessary for Reviewers to accept their lives. Life Reviewers gain an understanding of life's events as all the recalled pieces in a Life Review come together to form a whole, just as in a puzzle when the pieces are finally in place and form a complete picture. Reviewers who understand the reasons for "things" and have questions answered in their minds begin to accept their lives. Once Reviewers understand the "whys" of their lives, they can begin to accept the facts and circumstances. Past unresolved experiences can be reinterpreted in a new way, finally leading to an acceptance of the way one's life was lived under the past's prevailing circumstances.

Self-Acceptance. With understanding and acceptance of life comes acceptance of oneself—another important outcome in a Reviewer who has completed a Life Review. Self-acceptance for Reviewers means confirming that the way they have done things in the past is the way they should have been done, leading to a respect for oneself and a belief in oneself throughout life. People who are "achievers" in life are those who believe in themselves and in their own abilities. Others who do not believe in themselves may not be successful, sometimes because of childhood messages or personal failures.

> *The Life Review provides an opportunity for Reviewers to disprove past negative evaluations, to reinterpret the past, and to verify who they are in the present.*

The Life Review provides an opportunity for Reviewers to disprove past negative evaluations, to reinterpret the past, and to verify who they are in the present. Self-acceptance means Reviewers now approve of themselves and their past actions as they were examined in the Life Review, with reconsideration and reconciliation of parts of the past. The recalled memories may look different over time and be more acceptable now. What may have been a problem in one's teenage years is now seen as not so bad or as more suitable, or something that had to be, given the circumstances of the past time. Self-acceptance appears as a kind of satisfaction and contentment and a display of confidence. People who like themselves are no longer at war with themselves; they project serenity and confidence.

Finding Meaning. Finding meaning in life happens within a Life Review as Reviewers examine the past and recognize their purpose in life or their reason for being. Some Reviewers identify multiple purposes that changed over time, while others focus on what they see as their main purpose. Without purpose, some say, there is really no reason for being, no motivation, no compelling reason for doing well, and no meaning. A Reviewer's purpose in life can arise from many arenas, such as one's profession, or can be less grand but still compelling and important to the Reviewer. A person's purpose often goes unrecognized to that person until that person becomes a Reviewer and looks back on life. As that purpose is recognized, clarity occurs for Reviewers who, with hindsight, can determine what was or was not important to their entire life, and thus find its meaning.

For example, consider the Reviewer whose main occupation was parenting and who may have felt less than successful because she was "just" a stay-at-home mother without education or job skills. Throughout life, she may have felt she had never accomplished anything important, especially when comparing herself, for example, to her attorney sister, or her husband, perhaps a successful businessman. Finally, later in life, when participating in a Life Review, she realized her real purpose was to successfully raise children. Instead of feeling that she had never accomplished anything, she may now appreciate the importance of raising her children—perhaps four very successful and well-adjusted adults who dote on their mother. Those who do not appreciate the importance of their roles frequently feel they have not done much in life as they measure themselves with prevailing work-world standards. But when looking back, they realize that their purpose gave meaning to their lives.

Attaching meaning to the way and why one's life was lived is important to most people. Many believe there has to be a reason for why things happened the way that they did. After completing a Life Review, Reviewers often see the purposes that gave meaning to their lives; then they realize their individual importance and place in the world. With this recognition, Reviewers often feel content and somewhat more satisfied with the way they lived their lives, allowing them to recognize their reasons for being, while letting them look forward to the rest of their lives with anticipation.

Reconnection. Another outcome of the Life Review is reconnection. Reconnection means to be in touch again with people, hobbies, relatives, or networks from the past, whose earlier associations may have been lost or forgotten over time. Life Review enables Reviewers to reconnect with their past in many realms: old friends, old abilities, old achievements, and old relationships. The Life Review offers a link to people and things that have been lost from the Reviewer's past by recalling how important those earlier relationships and activities once were to the Reviewer. An older Reviewer whose world is narrowing may wish to revive some of those earlier relationships once reminded of them through the Life Review. Reconnection with others is especially important for those who live alone, have few outlets, and have become loners over time. Often "loners" have lost the desire to connect with others and the Life Review reminds them of how much better it is to have someone else in their lives. Many Reviewers learn to relate to another person again (the Therapeutic Listener) and begin to value relationships through experiencing them in the Life Review.

Recalling an old network of relatives and friends encourages Reviewers to reach out to those friends again or to establish new friendships if old friends have moved away and are not available. The good memories resurface, encouraging many Reviewers to want to experience those earlier good feelings again. Reconnection is also a way to "mend fences" and repair relationships that have suffered because of past misunderstandings.

Siblings may have fought with each other, both being too proud to give in and call one another. These meaningless feuds often continue for years until one of the parties dies, and then it is too late to repair the relationship that once was so important. Reviewers who talk about these old misunderstandings often see how foolish they are and find the strength to be the one to reconnect, happy to mend the relationship while they still can.

Reconnecting with past skills and abilities is equally as important as reconnecting with past friends. Reviewers recall how they used to solve problems and adapt to misfortunes, reminding themselves of how capable they used to be and can be again. Reviewers also remember hobbies they enjoyed in the past that may forge new interests in the present, such as playing golf, painting, or carving wood. The Reviewer who reconnects with the past and relives good times becomes full of possibilities for the future.

Shared Experiences. The Life Review offers Reviewers an opportunity to share both good and bad memories with a Therapeutic Listener for several weeks; in effect they share a meaningful experience when they participate in a Life Review just by verbalizing memories. A shared experience in the Life Review can simply be the Reviewer's disclosure of a meaningful event or confidence to the Therapeutic Listener. If the disclosed experience was a difficult one, then sharing the experience with the Therapeutic Listener makes the Reviewer's burden easier to endure, because once shared with another, the burden becomes lighter. Conversely, if the experience shared is a happy and prideful memory, the happiness doubles with sharing, and both Reviewer and Listener can relive the happy moments again, together. Being able to use another person as a sounding board makes a big difference in the heaviness of a burden or the amount of happiness enjoyed.

Although a confidante usually fulfills this need for sharing, in later life many people no longer have confidantes. A Therapeutic Listener can fill the need as well, sometimes better than a confidante. Listeners are strangers and bring objectivity to the process. People often think they must keep up a façade with their confidantes, family, and those they know and love the best. In a Life Review, the Reviewer can disclose anything without fearing repercussions because of the "stranger relationship." The Therapeutic Listener is a stranger whom they may never meet again. You need to help Reviewers recognize the value of strangers as listeners so they may use the opportunity to disclose and share their burdens during a Life Review.

> *The Life Review is a partnership, a time-limited friendship, and a relationship in which Reviewers consider Listeners to be personal confidantes.*

Bonding. Bonding is the psychological attachment of the Reviewer to the Listener based on affection and trust. Reviewers may have shared their darkest memories with Listeners but can see that Listeners still offer unconditional positive regard. The Life Review is a partnership, a time-limited friendship, and a relationship in which Reviewers consider Listeners to be personal confidantes and so trust the Listeners with their secrets. For many Reviewers, the Life Review is a first-time bonding experience, enjoyed for the connection and the feelings of closeness with another. Bonding usually emerges during the fourth Life Review visit as a result of trust in the relationship. When Reviewers finally feel trust in the Life Review relationship, they delight in the opportunity to communicate their thoughts with another, which forges an even stronger bond.

Some people who are Reviewers never experienced bonding with another person in their earlier relationships. They never had the feelings of affection and safety that one often feels in a Life Review. For people experiencing bonding as a new phenomenon, bonding may take a little longer. But Reviewers who recognize and enjoy the experience of bonding often seek similar experiences with others in their future relationships. As a result of the Life Review experience, some Reviewers will relate more easily to their contemporaries and want to develop their own peer confidantes. They may have learned in the Life Review that it feels good to have someone available to confide in.

Catharsis. Catharsis is a purging and cleansing of one's stresses and problems, resulting in an emotional release and final relief by freeing oneself from internal issues. This cleansing often happens without specific awareness. Reviewers just know they feel better and may give credit for feeling better to the Therapeutic Listener. Reviewers actually provide catharsis for themselves by letting go of pressing issues. The Listener is not really responsible for this release and relief, except for leading the Reviewer in the right direction by encouraging the Reviewer to talk about troubling events until the events are no longer bothersome. The Reviewers really do the rest.

Catharsis often takes place through the repeated telling of a recalled difficult memory. The acts of repetition allow the Life Reviewer to examine the event from many different angles, to have the story accepted by the Listener, and finally to better understand and accept the story themselves. Repetition diminishes the pain until the pain of the memory is small enough to let go. After experiencing such catharsis, Reviewers are often emotionally freed up enough to move on in their lives.

Future Orientation. The Structured Life Review process provides a future orientation for Reviewers as they complete the recall and reorganization of the past. After dwelling on the past for 8 weeks, Reviewers are ready to put the past behind them and move on to other matters in the present. Sometimes these matters are activities they have always planned to participate in but just never got around to, and sometimes Reviewers are just more hopeful and optimistic because they can envision a future and look forward to it.

There is a freeing quality as a result of resolving past issues or in realizing how lucky the Reviewer was to have such a good life. Some Reviewers no longer seem burdened with old unsolvable problems. This freeing up provides motivation. Reviewers can then make plans for new activities, or renewing relationships, or reaching out to family members. Reviewers can also plan to accomplish certain tasks that they have never been able to finish before but that have taken on new importance as a result of the Life Review. The future offers many opportunities to unburdened Reviewers.

New Energy. Completing a Life Review leaves those who have done so with new energy to get on with life and to accomplish other things. People with energy have a zest for life. This new energy may be related to the future orientation resulting from the Life Review. The new energy can wipe away any existing apathy that may have persisted before the Life Review was begun. Feeling energetic is often tied up with feeling optimistic. Reviewers can gain optimism as well as new energy by getting rid of old baggage. Reviewers with new energy make plans and exhibit excitement for living.

> *The future offers many opportunities to unburdened Reviewers.*

Peace. Peace is another probable outcome of the Life Review process and indicates feelings of serenity. Reviewers who complete the process often develop new feelings of tranquility, equanimity, and composure. They now know who they are and where they have been, and by virtue of this knowledge, they can direct where they are going. People at peace with themselves exhibit contentment and readiness to face the future.

Good Death. The feelings of contentment and peace gained from a completed Life Review may play out differently for those who are very elderly and/or ill. If one is old, frail, and sick, the future may bring inevitable death, but it is hoped the death will be a peaceful one. A peaceful death is another good outcome of the Life Review. Many hospice centers use a form of Life Review or reminiscing as part of their care. Some make a video that families continue to enjoy after their loved ones have died; others use an interview format such as ours. Regardless of the format, doing a Life Review helps to create closure for Reviewers and makes it easier for them to accept death.

In the early 1800s, the writer Leo Tolstoy described a peaceful death resulting from a life review (Tolstoy, 1960). Tolstoy wrote of the death of Ivan Ilych, "who passed his life in review" during the last days of a long excruciating illness, and then lay back in peace, called for his family to make amends, closed his eyes, and died. Through his Life Review, Ivan took care of his unfinished business and disturbing thoughts. Having done this, he was able to die at peace.

Summary

The preceding descriptions are of outcomes we have observed in people who have completed a Life Review. These observed, subjective outcomes have not been tested by research, but have been reported by many Listeners who have seen them and by many Reviewers who have experienced them. They are the combined anecdotal reports of many Listeners and Life Reviewers. As such, they are not empirically tested, but they are equally as important as the evidence-based outcomes reported in the literature listed in the Annotated Bibliography. Visit 8, then, is the last visit between Reviewer and Listener and completes the activity of one Structured Life Review process.

PART III

USES AND OUTCOMES OF THE STRUCTURED LIFE REVIEW

VARIED USES FOR THE STRUCTURED LIFE REVIEW

A life reviewed is a life renewed.

—ANON.

This chapter outlines a large variety of uses for the Structured Life Review process. Because the Life Review is therapeutic, practically everyone who participates in a Life Review benefits from the process. The applications discussed below are the most common uses, based on our experience.

The range of possible uses is wide. In the past, the Life Review has been used successfully and mainly with older people, particularly after a significant or traumatic event, such as relocating to a senior living facility, being admitted to hospice, and/or developing dementia or depression. Other reasonable uses might be for people who are

- grieving after a death or loss
- enduring a long hospitalization
- introverted, lonely, or estranged
- experiencing a severe setback, such as job termination, unplanned retirement, or a denied promotion

In other words, the Life Review is useful for anyone experiencing a great stress or a failure in meeting an important goal. Potential uses are only limited by the imagination.

Uses based on experience are described in detail in the following pages, with suggested alterations to the process for certain groups, such as those with dementia. Other potential Reviewers and settings are listed thereafter.

Newly Relocated

The Structured Life Review is especially useful for older people who have to relocate from the homes they have enjoyed for a lifetime to a place providing more care. Newly relocated individuals not only need to get used to new places and new friends, they also need to adjust to losing the old familiar places and conveniences. The choice to move is usually forced by circumstances beyond their control, and so relocating is not really a choice. When newly relocated older people enter a new environment, particularly if it is an assisted living environment, they have many adjustments to make. They need to adjust to the place itself, the meal schedule, and numerous close neighbors. Often newly relocated individuals feel isolated because everything is so foreign. They need to talk out their issues with someone, but often there is no one they really know to trust.

The Therapeutic Listener can be that trusted person and ideal sounding board and soon becomes someone the new person can reach out to and confide in. Often, relocated Life Reviewers need an extra visit added to the Life Review to give them an opportunity to talk about their current unhappiness with their relocation. If someone other then the Reviewer—perhaps a child or other relative—instigated the move, Reviewers often feel angry that the choice was made for them despite their wishes. Then, they must deal with their anger as well. Surprisingly, after being given a visit to voice their unhappiness, most newly relocated Reviewers readily begin the Life Review process the following week. Once the Life Review has begun, there are no other alterations for this group as a whole, and the Life Review proceeds as described earlier in the book.

Usually, the newly relocated Reviewers adjust to their new environment during the Life Review process. There is no evidence of a direct, positive connection between adjustment to a new environment and a Life Review, except for the time involved and the presence of a sympathetic ear (the Therapeutic Listener) for social support. However, during that 8-week time frame, Reviewers seem to accept their circumstances. The Life Review does increase their well-being and life satisfaction from the time of their admission, which in turn can influence adjustment. Considering that Reviewers could go either way after relocating (increased despair or increased well-being), the Life Review has proven to be a positive influence for this at-risk group.

Depression Prevention

The Structured Life Review process is also an effective tool for preventing depression. Many older people are at risk for depression because of the multiple losses they endure. In addition to relocation, many experience the loss of a spouse, loss of independence, or loss of health due to a disability or newly diagnosed illness. Regardless of the risk, millions of unhappy older people are struggling to survive by themselves, unaware that they are at risk for developing increased depression. Many people think low feelings are a part of the aging process and accept them without question. They deny depression. They do not pay attention to their own unhappiness because they think they are supposed to feel that way. They do not seek help. They might not have money for treatment or medication and they may attach a stigma to mental health services, believing that mental health services are only for weak people.

Nonetheless, these borderline, at-risk people enjoy doing a Life Review and benefit from it. They consider the Life Review to be a natural storytelling process. Some are used to oral traditions and enjoy them. Thus, when they participate to tell their stories, they also enjoy the therapeutic benefits without even realizing that therapy is happening. Once people start a Life Review, they tend to finish it, participating for the full 8-week time frame, despite the fact that they shun therapy. Involving them in a Life Review may be the best you can do for them that they will accept.

Substance Abuse Recovery

The following account is of a very different Life Review that was essentially a one-shot case study, not yet repeated or tested, but very rewarding. A young woman about 30 years of age came to a nursing clinic located in a high-rise apartment, saying that she had just been discharged from rehabilitation and needed help to be able to make it on her own in her own apartment with no support systems. She was invited to sit down and talk. It was soon discovered that she had been an addict for almost 15 years, though a reluctant one, poorly influenced by the men in her life. She wanted to stay clean because she had a daughter in the foster care system and wanted to get her back to care for by herself.

Our knowledge of drug treatment was practically nonexistent, but we were training students in the building to do Life Reviews and asked if she would like to participate in one of the Reviews. Her answer was yes; she thought of us as a lifeline and we proceeded with her Life Review. Like so many disabled Reviewers, she told a story that included child abuse, running away from home, two bad marriages, and easy access to drugs. Through it all, she had held two well-paying jobs at different times and had been a good mother. She said her husband was angry with her for not wanting to participate in drug parties and had her arrested, then sent her daughter to foster care.

She was bright but meek. The high-rise was in a city and she was from the country and was afraid to take a bus. She needed to get back into life now that she had done away with the old one. She had never used a computer, but was eager to learn. One occupational therapy student took over her care, giving her different bus routes to take each week, ending at the library, where he met her and taught her to use a computer. Today she works as a receptionist for a glass company, uses a computer in her job, and lives independently with her daughter. Drugs are no longer a part of her life.

This Life Review story is told to demonstrate the endless possibilities and uses for a Life Review, regardless of age. Combining the Life Review with an occupational program worked to help this young woman stay away from drugs and get back into a meaningful life.

Dying

One of the most effective ways to help dying people go peacefully while finishing their earthly business is with a Structured Life Review process as presented in this book. Once people have adjusted to the fact that death is inevitable, they are anxious to put their life in order. They do this with wills and bequests, family plans, funeral plans, and arrangements for end-of-life care. Once they have addressed these required tasks, they are often at peace, unless they have "unfinished business." If they do, they need time to talk, and often they want to talk first about their own dying. Those who are dying feel a new urgency to resolve old issues and then to die peacefully. The Life Review gives them some control over events at the end of life when they have lost most of their control over other things. People who are dying are very eager to review the lives that they are leaving behind and to finalize their legacy, regardless of age. Dying is a personal thing between them and the unknown.

> *People who are dying are very eager to review the lives that they are leaving behind and to finalize their legacy.*

Our experience in using the Structured Life Review process with people who are dying has been with those who are in hospice care or who are in the hospital awaiting a bone marrow transplant. People in such situations are quite aware that death may be imminent, and they are eager to take care of things while they are still able to do so. One patient, after revealing childhood sexual abuse by a brother, was anxious to confront her sibling before she died. The confrontation was not a part of the Life Review but something the patient did on her own. The Life Review only brought the issue to the forefront, allowing the patient to think it through. She needed to tell her brother how he had hurt her. Her brother, who had carried guilt for this offense for years and had been estranged from her, apparently also looked forward to the meeting. This reunion provided the opportunity for him to say he was sorry and for her to forgive him. The result was healing and allowed them to have a relationship for a few weeks before her death. The catalyst was the Life Review process and the result was a serene death.

There is only one main adjustment to the Life Review for people who are dying. The Therapeutic Listener needs to tailor the time involved in the Life Review process to the Reviewer's current physical condition. We found that shorter, more frequent visits worked well for the dying, because they tired so easily from talking. Being attentive to the process required more concentration than they could give for 1 hour; thus our visits to this group were about ½ hour in length, twice a week.

Bereavement

The Life Review is a helpful process for bereaved individuals to deal with their grief. The bereaved person often enjoys remembering important times spent with the person who has died. For instance, a woman recalling the death of her sister can relive the joys of playing with dolls when they were little, or talking about enjoying the same activities together as they grew up, such as shopping and first dates. Finally, she can happily recall weddings and marriage and children of her own who played together as the sisters had in the past. Such memories of life events serve to heal the living person as the memories are recalled. By the time that the Review has been completed, the bereaved individuals may have worked through part of the grieving process and are often ready to complete the grieving themselves.

In one particular instance of a Life Review delivered in the home with a man who was dying, the Life Review was arranged for both the husband and wife (Mr. and Mrs. X) together, as an exception. This wife was afraid to leave her dying husband alone with the Therapeutic Listener because she thought he might need something. Consequently, for the Review to take place, it had to be done with the wife by the bedside. The dying man confirmed that he would like to have his wife there. He said they had gone to school together as children and shared many common memories and friends. Mrs. X was counseled to let her husband do most of the talking, even though he became tired when doing so, but that if he invited her to talk, she could then join in. The Life Review process went very well, full of laughter and tears, with Mrs. X behaving as she had been instructed. We were unaware that the Review continued throughout the week, between our visits, as the husband and wife continued to share their memories. They were very involved in the Review together and both enjoyed it tremendously. On the sixth Life Review visit, Mrs. X answered the door with the dismaying news that her husband had died the night before. She seemed composed and talked about the funeral arrangements and the arrival of her children the next day. She also talked about her husband and how much she would miss him. When questioned about her immediate needs, she stated that she had none. She then went on to tell us how important the Life Review had been to them both and how she now felt content about her husband's passing because they had both grieved together about the inevitable end when doing the Life Review.

Several weeks later, in a follow-up visit, we found that she was getting involved with old friends again, lunching out, and coping admirably. She again attributed her good spirits to the Life Review she had done with her husband and thanked us profusely.

Dementia

Using the Life Review process with families who are experiencing dementia requires the most adjustments to the process. Dementia is an umbrella term for all diseases involving cognitive decline, with the most common form being Alzheimer's disease (AD). In the United States, 50% of people over age 85 develop AD. The tragedy of this disease is that there are two victims: the caregiver (the person caring for the individual at home) and the person with the disease. Both benefit greatly from their own Life Review.

Dementia Caregivers

The Life Review reduces stress in caregivers, who are chronically stressed. Their chronic stress often leads to the development of other illnesses. Caregivers are generally just normal laypeople who are shouldering big burdens that cause stress. Therapeutic Listeners should use the same structured process for caregivers that they use with anyone else. Caregiver Life Reviews require only a few alterations, such as fitting into their schedule and visiting them when they can find time to sit and talk for an hour. Because they are usually busy with and focused on the care receiver, they particularly enjoy conversation that focuses attention on themselves. Life Review gives them 1 hour a week to care for their own personal identity rather than that of the individual for whom they provide care.

People with Dementia

The adjustments required for people with dementia are different and multiple because the Life Review process has to be adjusted to allow for their cognitive deficiencies and fading memories. Until recently, it was doubted that people with dementia could actually process a Structured Life Review, but a recent pilot project discovered that they could, and with amazing results. The process was adjusted to allow for their losses as the review went along, resulting in the techniques outlined below.

The Structured Life Review process as described in this Handbook is most effective when used at the start of the disease. When those with AD are in the early stages, they are able to process the structure more easily and have more memories they can recall. Also, at the start they have more cognitive function, which is necessary for reframing and solving troublesome issues of the past. Anyone who works with people with AD knows that many individuals become troubled as the disease advances, leading to wandering and disruptive behavior that can seem aimless but is actually based on an agenda. If the Life Review process can resolve the troubling agenda early on, the Reviewer often is no longer troubled by any particular agenda, resulting in a less troubled disease state.

Although the Life Review process is most effective in the early stages of the disease, it is also effective throughout the disease progression. It is possible to conduct a Life Review with people in more advanced stages as long as they are still able to communicate. In the advanced stages, it becomes necessary to use more props to trigger memories and the work requires greater effort on both of your parts. You should follow the normal process as presented in this Handbook, dealing with one stage of life each week that you visit, following the guidelines set up in the application section (Part II). You should also use the same counseling skills and interviewing techniques that you would use with anyone else who does not have AD.

One allowance you need to make for people with dementia is to move more slowly through the procedure, giving the people with AD more time to process. Because of the disease, they process thought more slowly and deliberately. They are also afraid to make a mistake, making them even more deliberate. Finally, they tire more easily, possibly because they have to concentrate so hard with a shorter attention span.

You have to remember that Life Review is hard work for the person with AD, though they seem to enjoy the attention and the opportunity to think again. They actually are proud to participate and will respond well to more frequent visits for shorter periods of time. The best schedule for people with dementia is probably twice a week for ½ hour, giving them less time to forget between visits than they would if the ½-hour visits were spaced out each week for 16 weeks.

Keeping to the structure of the Life Review is exceedingly important, although difficult, for someone with AD. Depending on how long Reviewers have had the disease, their thinking and organizational skills may not have been used for some time. They are definitely out of practice, but they still do have some remaining abilities. By encouraging those with AD to recall their memories in a structured, more orderly fashion, you begin to help them retain more orderly thinking. Although orderly thinking is not one of the goals of the Life Review, it is a nice side effect that results in improved scores on the Mini-Mental State Exam (MMSE) and may result in a little more self-confidence for the person with AD. Improving and changing brain matter is impossible, but changing the way an AD person processes thought is still possible, making it more orderly.

Cues. Physical and verbal cues sometimes are needed to remind people with AD of events in their past, because the memories of such people are not totally clear. Once reminded, they begin to remember correlating events, and the Life Review process progresses. The best cues are pictures from the past of relatives and friends. Use each picture sparingly and try to elicit conversation about each picture. Do not make the mistake of asking, *"Do you remember?"* For someone with memory impairment, *"Do you remember?"* is a threatening question. Instead say, *"This must be your Uncle Ed whom you were talking about before?"* The Reviewer will either confirm or deny your identification and will tell you more about Uncle Ed if Uncle Ed has meaning for him.

> *For someone with memory impairment, "Do you remember?" is a threatening question.*

Some older people have no pictures of their families or themselves, especially if they were brought up in poverty. Depending on where they lived, it is sometimes possible to find or take pictures of old places and early landmarks that will serve to evoke memories just as well as their own pictures. For example, a community photo of one Reviewer's church reminded the Reviewer of her wedding and of singing in the choir in that particular church. Another Reviewer was absolutely obsessed with having enough to eat and would respond to pictures of food. Show him a fish and the memories would pour forth about fishing with his brothers and the good fish he caught that kept his family eating when they were so poor. Both individuals did a reasonably complete Life Review with the help of generic photographs.

Familiar objects, such as antique washboards or other older implements, can also evoke memories for older people with Alzheimer's disease. Small antique tools, kitchen utensils, old magazines, old postcards, old recordings, or old costumes can all serve to initiate memories. Objects with shapes that can be touched and held make recall easier. Look around the house if you are in a Reviewer's home and note the kind of memorabilia the person has displayed that may lead into memories of the past. Then, use the memorabilia as you would any prop. Family members are often very helpful to Listeners who are trying to learn about a Reviewer's past. The family can and will point out a Reviewer's favorite things.

> *The senses remind Reviewers of the past, with the sense of smell evoking the strongest memories.*

The senses remind Reviewers of the past, with the sense of smell evoking the strongest memories. Thus, the memorabilia you use to instigate recall should include things one can touch, smell, hear, taste, and see. One Reviewer talked about his mother baking bread. He said,

> *For me, the smell of baking bread reminds me of winter days and waiting for the dough to rise by the coal stove where it was warm. Then, on Friday nights especially, having dough cakes and tomato soup for supper. Still a favorite of mine except I can no longer get the dough cakes (bread dough, pan fried in butter and served warm.)*

Other Reviewers may respond to music and old songs more than they will to smell. Therapeutic Listeners need to try various methods of evoking memories until they find a successful method, because different people respond to different triggers and cues.

As the Life Review progresses, memories of events become fainter when they are closer in time, so adulthood memories are not as strong as childhood memories. People with AD have short-term memory loss and remember the distant past more easily than the recent past. Perhaps this is also why people with AD enjoy the Life Review so much. They experience success and have a few weeks of successful remembering when they are talking about their early life. They can recall the past for a limited amount of time, 4 weeks in some cases, depending on how far the dementia has advanced. When they use up their original memories, some Reviewers may need to repeat previously recited memories or conduct the summary portion of the Life Review by constructing a memory book (Life Storybook).

Life Storybook. The Life Storybook is made up of pictures chosen by Alzheimer's Reviewers to represent their lives as they sum up their life experiences. As Reviewers talk about the pictures that they themselves have chosen to represent their lives, the Therapeutic Listener takes notes and chooses a short caption, in the Reviewer's own words, to place under the picture in the book. When the Storybook is done, Reviewer and Listener go over it together, removing any matter that is offensive to Reviewers, and finalize the product. The finished product is simplistic on purpose, so that Reviewers will continue to relate to their own story as their disease progresses.

The Therapeutic Listener should use Visits 6 and 7, which are the summarizing and evaluation stage of the process, to create a Life Storybook. Reviewers with AD do not summarize and evaluate as easily as other Reviewers because of their cognitive losses, but they can summarize and evaluate by going over the past again while creating the Life Storybook. Reviewers tell Therapeutic Listeners exactly what pictures and memories they would like included in their Storybook. Besides assisting in evaluation and being an outcome product of the Life Review, the book serves to remind Reviewers who they are over time as the disease progresses. The Life Storybook becomes a source of comfort and a treasured possession appreciated by Reviewers and family members. Family members often pull the book out to use as a communication tool with Reviewers as they communicate and reminisce about the past together.

While creating the Life Storybook, remember that people with AD sometimes remember events differently than their family members. Their Storybook should reflect their own reality, despite differing realities maintained by the family. For example, one man who had three sons was creating a book. He stated several times that he only had one son and that it was that son's picture that he wanted in his book. He believed the other two sons in his family were fathered by another man and refused to include their pictures. Fortunately, the family was not living nearby. The AD Reviewer was estranged from his sons and the book was made according to the Reviewer's wishes.

Ordinarily, family cooperation is very important to the success of the Life Storybook. Therapeutic Listeners are often dependent on family members to find the pictures and other cues that Listeners need to create a Storybook. Regardless of the amount of help provided by the family, you must remember that this is the Reviewer's book and not a family memoir. Family members may serve as advisors to the content, but not as authors of the book. Although sometimes difficult, you may have to protect the content of the Storybook for the Reviewer who owns it and only include the content that the Reviewer wants.

> *Reviewers enjoy using the Life Storybook to remind themselves of the unique person they once were.*

Life Storybook Confidentiality. There is not a confidentiality issue connected to the Life Storybooks. The books belong to the Life Reviewer, who made them. That is the purpose. Such books may be edited many times throughout the compilation process, usually leaving behind a story that Reviewers would like to keep and share. Sensitive material is not usually included in the book, and as the Reviewer uses the book it often becomes very public information because the Reviewer shows the book to everyone else. The Reviewer is the keeper of the Life Storybook.

Life Storybook Outcomes. Besides enjoyment, the Storybook serves many other useful purposes, as reported by families of people who have made them. One woman with AD who had made a Life Storybook was admitted to the critical care unit of a hospital—a very frightening place for everyone, but especially for the person who has AD. She became very combative and would not respond to the staff, requiring a family member to be present at all times. Eventually, one family member brought in the woman's personal Storybook and found that looking at the book calmed the Reviewer every time she used it. As a result, the hospital staff used the book for the same reasons and gave the Reviewer her book whenever she became agitated. The book continued to comfort her.

The Life Storybook serves as a continuing method of communication for the Reviewer well after the Review is complete. The book also serves as an orienting tool when Reviewers become more confused and forgetful. Reviewers further enjoy using the book to remind themselves of the unique person they once were.

Other Potential Reviewers

Experiences with other groups who would benefit from Life Review are less numerous and often based on single-person case studies. Accepting these constraints, we suggest the possibility of other people who might also benefit from the Structured Life Review process:

- Any elderly person, particularly those who are alone, lonely, or very old
- Residents of senior homes, retirement communities, and recreation centers
- People recovering from a crisis
- Military personnel returning from a combat zone
- Other veterans who experienced stress
- Couples who are candid with each other
- Victims of a holocaust or terrorist situation
- Victims of a violent or traumatic crime
- Recovering substance abusers
- Children or others who have lost a parent or close friend
- Children separated from their families
- People contemplating significant change (e.g., divorce, fired, retirement, moving)
- People who are retiring
- People in settings such as long-term care, hospice care, hospitals, health or social centers, and retirement facilities
- People who are grieving

Actually, most people can benefit from the therapeutic effects of reviewing their lives and their circumstances, reevaluating them, and reaching reconciliation with the past, thereby achieving "Integrity." There is a small group of people, however, who should not participate in a Life Review: those who absolutely refuse to recall the past and those with preliminary psychiatric diagnoses. These two groups of people may need more help than a Therapeutic Listener can give. It is best not to start them on the road to their memories. Rather, refer them to mental health or other professionals.

ANNOTATED
BIBLIOGRAPHY

This chapter contains an annotated bibliography of research and clinical work concerning the Structured Life Review process. The Structured Life Review process has been refined through both research and practice, resulting in the evidence-based process presented in this Handbook.

There are numerous interesting and provocative publications about reminiscing and life review, but they are not necessarily about this particular Life Review methodology. Other authors may have defined Life Review differently, and their procedures may differ from those explained in this Handbook; thus they may well be describing a different process. The methods in the Handbook and the works that follow are based on a Structured Life Review process.

Refereed Publications

Haight, B., Dunn, P., Michel, Y., & Simon, T. (in process). *Life review as an intervention for depression in older adults.* Unpublished manuscript.

> *A manuscript based on the results of using the Life Review with 200 adults for the purpose of reducing minor depression. Results showed significant differences between groups at 6 months (p = .02) (N = 200).*

Haight B., Gibson F., & Michel, Y. (2006). The Northern Ireland Life Review/Life Story Book Project for people with dementia. *Alzheimer's & Dementia: Journal of the Alzheimer's Association, 2*(1), 56–58.

> *Reports on the results of a pilot project in Northern Ireland to test the effects of the Life Review in people with dementia residing in assisted living sites. Significant gains were made on all measures for the group receiving the Life Review: Cornell Depression (p < .01), Communication (p < .005), MMSE (p < .005), Positive Mood State (p < .05) (N = 31).*

Haight, B., Bachman, D., Hendrix, S., Wagner, M., & Meeks, A. (2003). Life review: Treating the dyadic family unit with dementia. *Clinical Psychology & Psychotherapy, 10*(3), 165–174.

> *Preliminary report of a research project testing the efficacy of the Life Review in dyads. Caregivers: Depression (p < .01), Burden (p < .05); Care receivers: Mood (p < .04) (N = 78).*

Dunn, P., Haight, B. K., & Hendrix, S. A. (2002). Power dynamics in the Interpersonal Life Review Dyad. *The Journal of Geriatric Psychiatry, 35*(1), 77–94.

> *Discusses the issue of power and compares the use of power in Life Review with the use of power in therapy.*

Haight, B. K., Barba, B. E., Tesh, A. S., & Courts, N. F. (2002). Thriving: A life span theory. *Journal of Gerontological Nursing, 28*(3), 14–22.

> *Offers a new theory for gerontological nursing using a Life Review as an example for operationalizing the theory.*

Haight, B. K. (2001). Sharing life stories: Acts of intimacy. *Generations, 25*(2), 90–92.

> *Discusses the issues of Intimacy and Life Review.*

Haight, B. K. (2001). Life reviews: Helping Alzheimer's patients reclaim a fading past. *Reflections on Nursing Leadership, V,* 20–22.

> *Presents the Life Review/Life Story Book as a vehicle for helping people with Alzheimer's disease.*

Haight, B. K., & Michel, Y., Hendrix, S. (2000). The extended effects of the life review in nursing home residents. *International Journal of Aging & Human Development, 50*(2), 151–168.

> *Research-based manuscript showing that the positive effects of the Life Review last for at least 2 years in nursing home residents. Depression (p < .05), Hopelessness (p < .01), Life Satisfaction (p < .08) (N = 100).*

Haight, B. K. (1999). An American in Vienna. *Reminiscence, 18,* 12–13.

> *Reports on a keynote address made at a conference in Vienna for the Reminiscing Center in Blackheath, England.*

Haight, B. K., & Hendrix, S. (1998). Suicidal intent/life satisfaction: Comparing life stories. *Suicide and Life-Threatening Behavior, 28*(3), 272–284.

> *A qualitative study comparing the Life Reviews of satisfied women to women who were suicidal (N = 12).*

Haight, B. K., Michel, Y., & Hendrix, S. (1998). Life review. Preventing despair in nursing home residents: Short and long-term effects. *International Journal of Aging and Human Development, 47*(2), 119–143.

Research report on the effects of Life Review at 2 months and 6 months in people residing in nursing homes (N = 250).

Johnson, M., Ball, J., Haight, B., & Hendrix, S. (1998). A life history perspective on parenting. *Narrative Inquiry, 8*(1), 113–149.

A qualitative study taken from Life Reviews that shows the effect of early life events on parenting in later life (N = 30).

Michel, Y., & Haight, B. K. (1996). Using the Solomon four research design to test the life review in a frail elderly population. *Nursing Research, 45*(6), 367–369.

Research report of the use of a particular research design in Life Review research.

Haight, B. K. (1995). Suicide risk in frail elderly people relocated to nursing homes. *Geriatric Nursing, 16*(3), 104–107.

Survey analysis of suicide risk factors in people relocated to nursing homes.

Burnside, I., & Haight, B. K. (1994). Reminiscence and life review: Therapeutic interventions for older people. *Nurse Practitioner, 19*(4), 1–7.

Provides a protocol for the practice of each intervention.

Haight, B. K., & Burnside, I. (1993). Life review and reminiscing: Explaining the differences. *Archives of Psychiatric Nursing, 7*(2), 91–98.

Contrasts the two interventions and highlights the differences.

Sumner, E., & Haight, B. K. (1993). Increasing student/older adult interactions by life review assignment. *American Journal of Pharmaceutical Education, 57,* 117–121.

Describes classes in Life Review for pharmacy students.

Black, G., & Haight, B. K. (1992). Integrality as a theoretical framework for the life review process. *Holistic Nursing Practice, 7*(1), 7–15.

Applies Martha Rogers's framework to the Life Review process.

Burnside, I., & Haight, B. K. (1992). Life review and reminiscing: A concept analysis. *Journal of Advanced Nursing, 17*(6), 855–862.

A concept analysis of two different interventions: Reminiscence and Life Review.

Haight, B. K. (1992). Long-term effects of a structured life review process. *Journal of Gerontology, 47*(5), 312–315.

Homebound older people were retested for the long-term effects of Life Review after 1 year. Scores increased on Life Satisfaction (p < .002) and Well-being (p < .003) (N = 52).

Haight, B. K., & Burnside, I. (1992). Reminiscence and life review: Conducting the process. *Journal of Gerontological Nursing, 18*(2), 39–42.

Compares Reminiscence to Life Review with instructions for conducting each process.

Haight, B. K., & Dias, J. (1992). Examining key variables in selected reminiscing modalities. *International Journal of Psychogeriatrics, 4*(Suppl. 2), 279–290.

Research report on defining the unique characteristics of a structured Life Review process. Results showed that an Individual Structured Evaluative Life Review process (ISELRP) was

most effective when compared with other ways of reminiscing: Depression (p < .01), Life Sat-
isfaction (p < .01), Self-esteem (p < .05), Well-being (p < .01) (N = 240).

Haight, B. K. (1991). Reminiscing: The state of the art as a basis for practice. *International
Journal of Aging and Human Development, 33*(1), 1–32.

First integrated review of the reminiscence literature covering the years 1960–1990.

Haight, B. K. (1989). Life review: A therapeutic modality for home health nurses. *South Carolina
Nurse, 4*(1), 19–20.

Suggests uses of Life Review for home health nurses.

Haight, B. K. (1989). Life review: Part I. A method for pastoral counseling. *The Journal of Religion and Aging, 5*(3), 17–29.

Talks about using Life Review for pastoral counseling.

Haight, B. K. (1989). Life review: Part II. Report of the effectiveness of a structured life review
process. *The Journal of Religion and Aging, 5*(3), 31–41.

*Reports the results of two earlier Life Review research projects with the experimental
group improving on measures of Life Satisfaction: N = 12, p < .005; N = 60, p < .0001.*

Haight, B. K., & Olson, M. (1989). Teaching home health aides the use of life review. *Journal of Nursing Staff Development, 5*(1), 11–16.

Describes a class of home health aides learning about Life Review.

Haight, B. K. (1988). The therapeutic role of the life review in homebound elderly subjects. *Journal of Gerontology, 43*(2), 40–44.

*Describes the use of Life Reviewing in peoples' homes. Group experiencing the treatment
of Life Review improved on measures of Well-being (p < .0003) and Life Satisfaction (p <
.0001) and was unchanged on measures of Depression (N = 60).*

Haight, B. K., & Bahr, R. T. (1984). The therapeutic role of the life review in the elderly. *Aca-
demic Psychology Bulletin, Michigan Psychological Association, 6*(3), 289–299.

*Pilot project testing the effectiveness of Life Review and the use of the LRF on Life Satisfac-
tion (p < .005) (N = 12).*

Books

Haight, B. K., & Gibson, F. (Eds.). (2005). *Burnside's working with older adults: Group work
processes and techniques.* Boston: Jones & Bartlett.

*A revised book about group processes with some content devoted to Reminiscing and Life
Review in varied settings.*

Webster, J. D., & Haight, B. K. (Eds.). (2002). *Critical advances in reminiscence work from theory to
application.* New York: Springer.

*Builds on first book with new opinions and new ways of using Reminiscence and Life Review.
An edited version of known author contributors.*

Haight, B. K., & Webster, J. (Eds.). (1995). *The art and science of reminiscing: Theory, research, methods, and applications.* Washington, DC and London: Taylor & Francis.

   Edited compilation of previously published authors' approaches to Life Review and Reminiscence.

Book Chapters

Gibson, F., Haight, B., & Michel, Y. (2007). Evaluating long-stay settings: A study of a life review and life storybook project. In A. Innes & C. Murphy (Eds.), *Evaluation in dementia care* (pp. 124–143). London: Jessica Kingsley.

   Descriptive report of a long-term care setting in which staff and family members evaluated the use and process of the Life Review in residents with dementia. Based on the Northern Ireland research project.

Haight, B. (2007). The life review: Historical approach. In J. A. Kunz & L. G. Soltys (Eds.), *Valuing and enriching the lives of older adults* (pp. 93–118). New York: Springer.

   Presents a historical view of the use of Reminiscence and Life Review.

Haight, B. K., & Haight, B. S. (2007). Reminiscence. In J. Birren (Ed.), *Encyclopedia of Gerontology* (pp. 418–424). New York: Elsevier Press.

   Compares Life Review, autobiography, and simple reminiscing.

Haight, B. K. (2005). Research in reminiscence and life review. In J. Fawcett (Ed.), *Annual review of research in nursing.* New York: Springer.

   Offers a limited look at the newest research in the field.

Haight, B., & Webster, J. D. (2002). The end of the story. In J. D. Webster & B. K. Haight (Eds.), *Critical advances in reminiscence work: From theory to application* (pp. 314–319). New York: Springer.

   Discusses the confusion in the reminiscing field and provides direction for clarity.

Hendrix, S., & Haight, B. K. (2002). A continued review of reminiscence. In J. D. Webster & B. K. Haight (Eds.), Critical advances in reminiscence work: From theory to application (pp. 3–29). New York: Springer.

   An integrated review of Reminiscence and Life Review covering the years 1995–2000.

Haight, B. (1998). Use of the life review/life story books in families with Alzheimer's disease. In P. Schweitzer (Ed.), *Reminiscence in dementia care* (pp. 85–90). London: Age Exchange.

   Talks about creating a Life Story Book from the Life Review process.

Haight, B. K. (1995). Using life review to prevent depression and suicide. *Getting started: The NMHA director of model program to prevent mental disorders and promote mental health.* Alexandria, VA: National Mental Health Association.

   Description of a Life Review program to enhance mental health.

Haight, B. K., Coleman, P., & Lord, K. (1995). The linchpins of a successful life review: Structure, evaluation, and individuality. In B. K. Haight & J. D. Webster (Eds.), *The art and science of reminiscing: Theory, research, methods, and applications* (pp. 179–192). Washington, DC: Taylor & Francis.

   Discusses application of linchpins to practice of Life Review.

Haight, B. K., & Hendrix, S. (1995). An integrated review of reminiscence. In B. K. Haight & J. D. Webster (Eds.), *The art and science of reminiscing: Theory, research, methods, and applications* (pp. 3–21). Washington, DC: Taylor & Francis.

   An integrated review of the work in Life Review and Reminiscing covering the years 1990–1993.

Haight, B. K. (1993). Reminiscence through the adult years. In R. Kastenbaum (Ed.), *Encyclopedia of adult development* (pp. 401–405). Phoenix, AZ: The Oryx Press.

   Description of the reminiscence field.

Haight, B. K. (1992). The structured life review process: A community approach to the aging client. In G. Jones & B. Meisen (Eds.), *Caregiving in dementia: Research and applications* (pp. 272–292). London: Routledge.

   Depiction of using Life Review at home for people with dementia.

Invited Publications

Haight, B. K. (2000). Research in Japan: Cultural differences. *Dimensions, 7*(4), 4.

   Applying the Life Review to people with dementia in Japan.

Haight, B. K., Nomura, T., & Nomura, A. (2000). Life review as an Alzheimer's intervention: Results of an American-Japanese project. *Dimensions, 7*(4), 4–5, 8.

   Description of a Japanese pilot project.

Haight, B. K. (1997). Life review: Past, present, and future. *South Carolina Gerontology Center Newsletter.* Columbia: University of South Carolina.

   Update on Life Review projects.

Haight, B. K. (1992). The therapeutic use of life review. *South Carolina Gerontology Center Newsletter* (pp. 3–4). Columbia: University of South Carolina.

   Information regarding Life Review projects.

Haight, B. K. (1991). The role of life review in depression and bereavement. *Auctus, Fall/Winter,* 6, 44.

   Discusses the use of Life Review with the bereaved.

Haight, B. K. (1988, August). *The life review as a counseling modality for use by nurses* (Report No. CG 020653). Ann Arbor, MI: Counseling and Personnel Services. (ERIC Document Reproduction Service No. ED292046)

   Explains how to use Life Review as a counseling modality.

Summary

The preceding references serve to demonstrate the work that contributed to the Structured Life Review process to refine it to what it is today. This work is really only a beginning and invites a continued examination by additional researchers as well as testing by practitioners. As an intervention, the Life Review is still in process.

REFERENCES

Barrett-Lennard, G. T. (1998). *Carl Rogers' helping system*. London: Sage.

Bender, M., Baukman, P., & Norris, A. (1999). *The therapeutic purposes of reminiscence*. London: Sage.

Benner, P., & Wrubel, J. (1989). *The primacy of caring*. Reading, MA: Addison-Wesley.

Brink, T. L., Yesavage, J. A., Lum, O., Hiersama, P., Adey, M. B., Rose, T. L. (1982). Screening tests for geriatric depression. *Clinical Gerontologist, 1,* 37–44.

Butler, R. (1963). The life review: An interpretation of reminiscence in the aged. *Psychiatry, 26,* 65–76.

Butler, R. N. (1974). Successful aging and the role of the Life Review. *Journal of the American Geriatrics Society, 22,* 529–535.

Dunn, P., Haight, B. K., & Hendrix, S. A. (2002). Power dynamics in the Interpersonal Life Review Dyad. *The Journal of Geriatric Psychiatry, 35*(1), 77–94.

Erikson, E. (1978). *Adulthood*. New York: Norton.

Erikson, E. (1950). *Childhood and society*. New York: Norton.

Erikson, E. H. (1963). *Childhood and society* (2nd ed.). New York: Norton.

Erikson, E., Erikson, J., & Kivnick, H. (1986). *Vital involvement in old age*. New York: Norton.

Falk, J. (1969). *The organization of remembering the life experience of older people: Its relation to anticipated stress, to subsequent adaptation and to age.* Unpublished doctoral dissertation, University of Chicago.

Folstein, M. F., Folstein, S., & McHugh, P. R. (1975). Mini-mental state: A practical method for grading the cognitive state of patients for the clinician. *Journal of Psychiatric Research, 12*(3), 189–198.

Gibson, F. (2004). *The past in the present.* Baltimore: Health Professions Press.

Gorney, J. (1968). *Experiencing and age: Patterns of reminiscence among the elderly.* Unpublished doctoral dissertation, University of Chicago.

Haight, B. K., & Dias, J. (1992). Examining key variables in selected reminiscing modalities. *International Journal of Psychogeriatrics, 4*(Suppl. 2), 279–290.

Haight, B. K., Michel, Y., & Hendrix, S. (1998). Life review. Preventing despair in nursing home residents: Short and long-term effects. *International Journal of Aging and Human Development, 47*(2), 119–143.

Ivy, A. E. (1971). *Microcounseling: Innovations in interview training.* Springfield, IL: Thomas.

Rogers, C. (1980). *A way of being.* Boston: Houghton-Mifflin.

Rogers, C. R. (1961). *On becoming a person.* Boston: Houghton-Mifflin.

Ross, E. K. (1972). *On death and dying.* New York: Macmillan.

Tolstoy, L. (1960). *The death of Ivan Ilych.* New York: New American Library.

Webster, J. D. (1993). Construction and validation of the reminiscence function scale. *Journal of Gerontology, 48,* 256–262.

Appendix A

CHECKLIST FOR THE LIFE REVIEW PROCESS

❏ Before the first visit with your Reviewer: Assess the location for suitability (noise, glare, light, temperature, privacy, facing chairs).

❏ Before beginning the actual Life Review: Assess and address the needs of the Reviewer (comfort, temperature, vision, hearing, medications, schedule/routine conflicts, glass of water, other personal issues).

Visit 1: Getting Started

❏ Preliminary tasks (glass of water, chairs, comfort, privacy, tape recorder)
❏ Agreement (in writing; get Reviewer to sign)
❏ Permission to tape record (spoken on tape and/or signed by Reviewer); turn on recorder
❏ Begin bonding
❏ Ask about personal issues
❏ Practice good Therapeutic Listening skills
❏ Give pretest(s)
❏ Use other assessment measures
❏ Arrange next visit, date/time
❏ Leave appointment/business card

Visit 2: Childhood

❏ Preliminary tasks (water, chairs, comfort, privacy, tape recorder on)
❏ Erikson's model: Trust vs. Mistrust (early childhood); Autonomy vs. Shame and Doubt (childhood)
❏ Using the Life Review Form: childhood, family, home
❏ Practice good listening skills
❏ Counseling Skill: Acceptance
❏ Interviewing techniques: Attentive Behavior; Repetition; Reframing
❏ Summarize this visit
❏ Arrange next visit date/time (leave an appointment card)

Visit 3: Adolescence

❏ Preliminary tasks (water, chairs, comfort, privacy, tape recorder on)
❏ Clarify previous session
❏ Erikson's model: Initiative vs. Guilt (childhood); Industry vs. Inferiority (young adolescence)
❏ Using the Life Review Form: adolescence, family, home, probing, school, feelings
❏ Counseling Skill: Caring
❏ Interviewing techniques: Responding; Reflecting Feelings

❑ Practice good listening skills
❑ Summarize this visit
❑ Arrange next visit date/time (leave an appointment card)

Visit 4: Young Adulthood

❑ Preliminary tasks (water, chairs, comfort, privacy, tape recorder on)
❑ Clarify last session
❑ Erikson's model: Identity vs. Role Confusion (adolescence); Intimacy vs. Isolation (young adulthood)
❑ Using the Life Review Form: young adulthood, customize, examine decisions
❑ Counseling Skill: Unconditional Positive Regard
❑ Interviewing techniques: Sharing Behavior; Paraphrasing
❑ Practice good listening skills
❑ Summarize this visit
❑ Arrange next visit date/time (leave an appointment card)

Visit 5: Older Adulthood

❑ Preliminary tasks (water, chairs, comfort, privacy, tape recorder on)
❑ Clarify last session
❑ Erikson's model: Generativity vs. Stagnation (older adulthood)
❑ Using the Life Review Form: adulthood, family/work, relationships, interests
❑ Counseling Skill: Empathy
❑ Interviewing techniques: Self-disclosure; Encouragement to Talk
❑ Practice good listening skills
❑ Summarize this visit
❑ Arrange next visit date/time (leave an appointment card)

Visit 6: Summary and Evaluation

❑ Preliminary tasks (water, chairs, comfort, privacy, tape recorder on)
❑ Clarify last session
❑ Erikson's model: Acceptance vs. Denial (maturity)
❑ Using the Life Review Form: start evaluation, use all questions, use repetition
❑ Counseling Skill: Congruence
❑ Interviewing technique: Summarizing
❑ Practice good listening skills
❑ Summarize this visit
❑ Arrange next visit date/time (leave an appointment card)

Visit 7: Integration

- ❑ Preliminary tasks (water, chairs, comfort, privacy, tape recorder on)
- ❑ Clarify last session
- ❑ Erikson's model: Integrity vs. Despair (oldest adulthood)
- ❑ Using the Life Review Form: Complete all questions in the summary
- ❑ Counseling skills and good listening practices: Review and use all
- ❑ Interviewing technique: Integrating
- ❑ Summarize entire Life Review
- ❑ Arrange next visit date/time (leave an appointment card)

Visit 8: Closure and Outcomes

- ❑ Preliminary tasks (water, chairs, comfort, privacy, tape recorder on)
- ❑ Initiate closure
- ❑ Finalize referrals
- ❑ Provide promised health materials
- ❑ Complete all posttests and measures
- ❑ Allow Reviewer to evaluate the process
- ❑ Name of contact person(s)
- ❑ Thank you note; greeting cards

Appendix B

LIFE REVIEW FORM (LRF)

The most important purpose of the Life Review is to ensure that Life Reviewers talk about all the stages of their lives, from early childhood to the present. This Life Review Form consists of suggested questions that guide Reviewers through those stages. The questions that are **bolded** focus particularly on important aspects of the life stages (Erikson's Stages of Man).

The purpose of your first meeting with the Reviewer is to prepare for the Life Review. You should give a copy of this LRF to your Reviewer and point out the various questions. However, you do not start to use the form yourself until the second visit.

Your second meeting with the Reviewer begins the actual Life Review process and addresses early childhood. It is suggested that you start with the very first question on this LRF. Then, follow the Reviewer's lead, remembering to listen closely and to respond to the Reviewer. You do not need to ask all of the questions. Most are mainly prompts and suggestions to aid you in getting the Reviewer started talking and then continuing to recall and dialogue with you. Before each visit, identify several questions that you particularly want to ask the Reviewer during that visit.

Visit 2: Early Childhood

- **What is the very first thing you can remember in your life? Go as far back as you can.**
- What other things do you remember about when you were very young?
- What was life like for you as a child?
- What were your parents like? What were their weaknesses; strengths?
- Did you have any brothers or sisters? Tell me what each was like.
- Did anyone close to you die when you were growing up?
- Did someone important to you go away?
- **Did you feel cared for as a child?**
- Do you remember having any accidents or diseases?
- Do you remember being in a very dangerous situation?
- **Did you play at any adult roles or games? Were you a leader or a follower as a young child?**
- Were you afraid of any adults?
- Was there anything important to you that was lost or destroyed?
- **Did you have childhood friends and playmates? A best friend?**
- Was church a large part of your life?
- **Were you given opportunities to make some decisions for yourself? What independent things did you do for yourself?**

Visits 2 & 3: Family and Home

The family and the home questions cover a large portion of one's possible memories as a child. This section on family/home also helps Reviewers explore their childhood relationships. Family and home questions should be used in Visit 2 (Childhood) and Visit 3 (Adolescence) as the recall and assessment of the Life Reviewer's childhood and adolescence continues.

- **What was life like for you as an older child?**
- **Tell me about your family.**
- How did your parents get along?
- How did other people in your home get along?
- What was the atmosphere like in your home?
- Was there enough food and necessities for your family?
- Were you punished as a child? For what? Who did the main disciplining in your home? Who was the boss?
- Did you feel loved and cared for as a young child?
- **Tell me about projects you started as a child.**
- When you wanted something from your parents (or guardian), how did you go about getting it?
- **Did you ever feel doubt, shame, or guilt as a young person?**
- What kind of person did your parents like the most? The least?
- Who were you closest to in your family?
- Who in your family were you most like? In what way?
- Did you have any unpleasant experiences as a child?
- Tell me about your extended family: aunts, uncles, grandparents, cousins.

Visit 3: Later Childhood–Adolescence

During the third visit, the Listener guides the Reviewer to later childhood and adolescence, making sure the Reviewer has exhausted the memories and stages of early childhood. Remember to insert "feeling questions," such as *"How did you feel about that?"* or *"What did that mean to you?,"* to initiate close evaluation by the Reviewer of both positive and negative events. Note again that these LRF questions are suggestions only and you do not need to use them all.

- **Did you feel well guided growing up?**
- When you think about yourself and your life as a teenager, what is the first thing you can remember about that time?
- **Did you feel good about yourself as a teenager?**
- What other things stand out in your memory about being an adolescent?
- Who were the important people for you? Tell me about them (parents, brothers, sisters, friends, teachers).
- Who were you especially close to? Who did you admire? Who did you most want to be like?
- **Were there cliques or special groups in your day?**
- Did you attend church and youth groups?

- How far did you go in school? Did you enjoy school?
- **Did you have a sense of belonging at school or in groups?**
- Did you work during these years?
- Tell me of any hardships you experienced at this time.
- **Did you participate in sports and/or in school activities?**
- **Did you enjoy school activities? Why?**
- Do you remember feeling left alone, abandoned, or not having enough love or care as a child or adolescent?
- What were the pleasant memories about your adolescence?
- **Did you do well in school studies/academics? Did you work hard at school? Why/why not?**
- All things considered, would you say you were happy or unhappy as a teenager?
- **Do you remember your first attraction to another person?**
- How did you feel about sexual activities and your own sexual identity?

Visit 4: Young Adulthood

Start the fourth visit with: *"Now I'd like to talk to you about your life as an adult, starting when you were in your 20s. What were the most important events in your adult years?"* The Therapeutic Listener should use the adult questions as needed, remembering that your first obligation is to listen and respond.

- **As an adult, did you do what you were supposed to do in life?**
- What was life like for you in your 20s and 30s?
- **Did you think of yourself as responsible?**
- What kind of person were you? What did you enjoy?
- Tell me about your work. Did you enjoy your work? Did you earn an adequate living? Did you work hard during those years? Were you appreciated?
- **Were you happy with your choices?**
- Did you have enough money?
- Did you form significant relationships with other people?
- Did you marry?
  - □ (yes)   What kind of person was your spouse?
  - □ (no)   Why not?
- Do you think marriages get better or worse over time? Were you married more than once?
- **Did you have children? Tell me about them.**
- **What important decisions did you make during this time?**
- On the whole, would you say you had a happy or unhappy marriage?

Visit 5: Older Adulthood

As you proceed to ask about adulthood, remember to follow the lead of your Reviewer and ask only appropriate questions, encouraging Reviewers to talk about their major interests and to *evaluate* major life decisions. Use the interviewing techniques and counseling skills you have studied: be empathic; praise achievements; reframe disappointments; practice good listening.

- Is there anything you would like to add about your marriage?
- **In your entire life, what relationship stands out as most important?**
- **Tell me (more) about your children? Did you enjoy being a parent?**
- Would you call yourself a spiritual person?
- Tell me about your friendships and relationships.
- Was sexual intimacy important to you?
- Did you have hobbies or major interests?
- **Do you think you have helped the next generation?**
- What were some of the main difficulties you encountered during your adult years?
  - □ Did someone close to you die? Go away?
  - □ Were you ever sick? Have an accident?
  - □ Did you move often? Change jobs?
  - □ Did you ever feel alone? Abandoned?
  - □ Did you ever feel needs?
- Have you remembered anything else you'd like to talk about?
- **What piece(s) of wisdom would you like to hand down to the next generation?**

Visit 6: Summary and Evaluation

You need to ask every question in this summary/evaluation portion of the LRF over the next 2 weeks, if possible. Questions for Visits 6 and 7 can be used alternatively as long as they are all asked. These questions cause Reviewers to look at their life as a whole and to evaluate their lives. Evaluation is key to reconciliation and acceptance, and acceptance is key to achieving Integrity.

- **On the whole, what kind of life do you think you've had?**
- If everything were to be the same, would you like to live your life over again?
- If you were going to live your life over again, what would you change? Leave unchanged?
- **We've been talking about your life for quite some time now. Let's discuss your overall feelings and ideas about your life. What would you say the main satisfactions in your life have been? Try for three. Why were they satisfying?**
- Everyone has had disappointments. What have been the main disappointments in your life?
- What was the hardest thing you had to face in your life? Please describe it.
- What was the happiest period of your life? What about it made it the happiest period? Why is your life less happy now?
- What was the unhappiest period of your life? Is your life more happy now? Why?
- **What was the proudest moment in your life?**

Visit 7: Evaluation and Integration

Visit 7 is a continuation of Visit 6. Allowing the Reviewer 2 weeks for the evaluation and integration process ensures that there is enough time to answer all the questions in this section as well as to also begin to consider the future.

- If you could stay the same age all your life, what age would you choose? Why?
- How do you think you've made out in life? Better or worse than what you hoped for?
- **Did you live your life as you had hoped to live it?**
- Let's talk a little about you as you are now. What are the best things about the age you are now?
- What are the worst things about being the age you are now?
- What are the most important things to you in your life today?
- What do you hope will happen to you as you grow older?
- What do you fear will happen to you as you grow older?
- **Are you happy with your life choices and decisions?**
- What do you want for yourself as you look toward the future?
- Have you enjoyed participating in this review of your life?
- Do you have any comments or suggestions?

Visit 8: Closure and Outcomes

Visit 8 is the time set aside for closure and assessing the outcomes of the Life Review in your Reviewer. You finished using the LRF in Visit 7, so you need to refer to Visit 8 in *The Handbook of Structured Life Review* for closure instructions.

Note: The LRF is derived from recent research and two unpublished dissertations:

Gorney, J. (1968). *Experiencing and age: Patterns of reminiscence among the elderly.* Unpublished doctoral dissertation, University of Chicago.

Falk, J. (1969). *The organization of remembering the life experience of older people: Its relation to anticipated stress, to subsequent adaptation and to age.* Unpublished doctoral dissertation, University of Chicago.

Appendix C

SAMPLE AGREEMENT

Life Review Agreement

I _____(Life Reviewer) do hereby consent to participate in an 8-week series of visits for the purpose of participating in a Structured Life Review process. The Therapeutic Listener _____has explained orally to me as described below and I fully understand the following:

A. *Purpose:* The purpose of this Life Review is to review my past life stages from childhood to the present.

B. *Procedures:* I will be visited by the Listener for six to eight 1-hour sessions. The Listener will ask me questions about my life. I will reminisce about only subjects I care to discuss. There may be simple paper-and-pencil tests to determine my situation. The Life Review is a form of reminiscing used therapeutically to help a person reach a better state of well-being. The process is guided by questions that cover childhood, family, home, and adulthood. There is a final evaluation where I will reflect on my life. The questions asked in the Life Review have been shown to me and I approve them.

C. *Risks:* There may be some temporary psychological discomfort when remembering sad times while participating in this project. I may withdraw from this process at any time by requesting to do so.

D. *Costs:* There are no costs to me for participating in this project and I will receive no monetary income.

_____   _____
Signature of Life Reviewer   Signature of Therapeutic Listener

_____   _____
Witness, if needed/available   Date

Appendix D

BASELINE ASSESSMENT OF REVIEWER

This tool should be used to record your observations of the Reviewer during your first and last sessions. Your observations should be both descriptive (qualitative) and numerical (quantitative). You may assign a number from 1 to 10 to each category, with 10 being the best and 1 being the worst, to measure change between Visit 1 and Visit 8.

Reviewer Baseline	Visit 1	Visit 8
Physical limitations:		
Mental limitations		
Cognitive:		
Psychological:		
Social limitations		
Interactions with others:		
Family:		
Friends:		
Outgoing:		
Withdrawn:		
Appearance		
Neat:		
Groomed and cared for:		
Appropriate dress:		
Nutrition		
Cooks:		
Frail:		
Obese:		
Mood		
Appears happy:		
Appears sad:		
Outlook		
Pessimistic:		
Optimistic:		
Financial		
Has enough:		
Needy:		
Help		
Groceries:		
Transportation:		
Housework:		
Yard work:		
Other:		

Appendix E

TEST OF PHYSICAL FUNCTION

BASIC ACTIVITIES

Eating

Bathing

Dressing

Grooming

Continence

INSTRUMENTAL ACTIVITIES

Walking

Driving

Shopping

Cooking

Housework

Managing money

Telephoning

Rate each of the above activities on a scale of 1 to 3: 1 = Independent, 2 = Assistance needed, 3 = Dependent. Make additional comments next to each activity for your own use.

Source: Adapted from various functional skills scales (2007).

TEST OF PSYCHOSOCIAL FUNCTION (MOOD SCALE)

Choose the best answer for how you have felt over the past week:

1. Are you basically satisfied with your life? YES / **NO**
2. Have you dropped many of your activities and interests? **YES** / NO
3. Do you feel that your life is empty? **YES** / NO
4. Do you often get bored? **YES** / NO
5. Are you in good spirits most of the time? YES / **NO**
6. Are you afraid that something bad is going to happen to you? **YES** / NO
7. Do you feel happy most of the time? YES / **NO**
8. Do you often feel helpless? **YES** / NO
9. Do you prefer to stay at home, rather than going out and doing new things? **YES** / NO
10. Do you feel you have more problems with memory than most? **YES** / NO
11. Do you think it is wonderful to be alive now? YES / **NO**
12. Do you feel pretty worthless the way you are now? **YES** / NO
13. Do you feel full of energy? YES / **NO**
14. Do you feel that your situation is hopeless? **YES** / NO
15. Do you think that most people are better off than you are? **YES** / NO

Answers in **bold** indicate depression. Give each answer that is bolded 1 point. For clinical purposes, a score >5 points is suggestive of depression. Scores >10 are almost always depression.

ACKNOWLEDGMENTS

Thanks for the memories.
—BOB HOPE

Thank you to the many research associates, workers, and students who worked on different Life Review projects throughout the past 20 years and who themselves have proven to be stars as Therapeutic Listeners. First we would like to thank Shirley Hendrix, who managed most of the projects, and Kathy Brungard, who managed all of us. Then there is Phil Dunn, another excellent manager who, along with Shirley, became an expert Listener and taught these skills to many other Therapeutic Listeners: Amy Hunt King, Karen Lukacs, Phyliss LaMachia, Kay Swigert, Zola Srour Driggers, Allison Meeks, Jolene Johnson, Debra Brown, Mandy Short, Susan d'Andrade, Linda LaForgia, Sarah Dietsch, Gail Scott, and Vivian Friedman.

Thank you to the few who worked with me before funding happened: Kelly and Lynn Marie and especially my teacher, Sister Rose Therese Bahr.

We need to acknowledge our professional colleagues who worked alongside us as well: Yvonne Michel, statistician; David Bachman, neurologist; Mark Wagner, psychologist; Mario LaVia, immunologist; Ed Sumner, pharmacist; and Charles Kellner, psychiatrist. And our international colleagues: Jeff Webster, Faith Gibson, and Toyoko Nomura.

Lastly we must acknowledge the agencies that gave us the funding to explore the Life Review so fully: Sigma Theta Tau; The American Association of Retired Persons (AARP); the

National Institute of Mental Health (NIMH); the National Alzheimer's Association; the Colleges of Nursing at the Medical University of South Carolina (MUSC) and the University of South Carolina (USC); South Carolina Commission on Aging, Health and Human Services; The Japan Society; and the Centers for Disease Control.

ABOUT THE AUTHORS

Barbara K. Haight, Dr.P.H., is Professor Emeritus at the College of Nursing, Medical University of South Carolina. Now retired, Dr. Haight conducted eight research projects over 25 years developing the Structured Life Review process, and she supervised numerous students and colleagues in the practice of life review. She was the first president of the International Life Review and Reminiscing Society and has conducted hands-on life review projects in the United States, England, Japan, and Northern Ireland. She is co-editor of two books on reminiscing and life review, plus one on group process, and is widely published in the field of life review and gerontology.

Dr. Haight is a fellow emeritus in the Gerontological Society of America, for which she founded and conducted a special interest group on reminiscence. She is also a Fellow in both the American Academy of Nursing and the Florence Nightingale Society.

Barrett S. Haight, J.D., retired as a Colonel from the U.S. Army after serving 23 years in a variety of positions throughout the world. Subsequently, he served as Director of Estate Planning for The Citadel Development Foundation (Charleston, SC) for 17 years. Throughout both periods, he taught undergraduate courses in business and constitutional law and graduate courses in health care law at the Medical University of South Carolina.

COL Haight has authored articles for the *Dickinson Law Review* and the U.S. Army Command and General Staff College. Additionally, he edited *Focus,* the newsletter of The Citadel Development Foundation. In his second retirement, he co-authored an article on reminiscence for the *Encyclopedia of Gerontology* and served as editor for many health care submissions.

۶۵

The authors are presently interested in using the Structured Life Review process to help combat veterans who have returned from war.

INDEX

Page numbers in *italics* indicate tables and boxed material.